# The New Houseplant Survival Manual

# The New Houseplant Survival Manual

## How to keep your houseplants healthy

Jane Bland
and
William Davidson

NEW BURLINGTON BOOKS

A QUARTO BOOK

Published by New Burlington Books
6 Blundell Street
London N7 9BH



ISBN 1-85348-805-4

This book was designed and produced by
Quarto Publishing Limited
The Old Brewery
6 Blundell Street
London N7 9BH

Art Director: Moira Clinch
Art Editor: Julie Francis
Designer: Anne Fisher
Copy Editor: Alison Leach
Senior Editor: Sian Parkhouse
Editorial Director: Mark Dartford
Photographer: Ian Howes
Picture Manager: Giulia Hetherington

Typeset in Great Britain by
Central Southern Typesetters, Eastbourne
Manufactured in Hong Kong by
Regent Publishing Services Ltd
Printed in China by
Leefung-Asco Printers Ltd

# Foreword

My relationship with plants started about the same time as I married, some twenty years ago. Both first house and first tiny garden seemed curiously empty until I discovered the foliage effect. This time could be called my horticultural nursery schooling, but it lasted a great deal longer than two years. My efforts were based on trial and error – in the beginning it was mostly error. I bought all the wrong houseplants – chiefly because I liked the look of them – and killed all but the most robust with kindness. I would now advise someone inexperienced in caring for plants to follow a simple set of rules, use common sense, watch the plants, and listen to what they say. I knew no rules and had seemingly little common sense, but I did watch my plants and I had lots of enthusiasm.

The world of gardening has changed enormously in the last twenty years. It used to be rather sexist. Women were definitely only *seen*, doing a little dead-heading or very gentle weeding, but never *heard*. The age of the great women gardeners, such as Gertrude Jekyll and Vita Sackville-West, had passed and the gardening media was run pedantically by and revolved mainly round men. These writers never seemed to be able to agree with one another and, what is more, they made everything sound so complicated.

As gardening became a major leisure pursuit and conservatories gained wide popularity, the commercial growers developed large-scale plant production: not only with the familiar rubber plants (*Ficus robusta*), spider plants (*Chlorophytum cosmosum*) or wandering Jews (*Tradescantia fluminensis*) but with masses of new houseplants. The public were also becoming more demanding and discerning. The odd bougainvillea or Calamondin orange (*Citrus mitis*) could be seen on sale at garden centres and reminded everyone of their continental holidays. But sadly very few people really understood how to look after their latest horticultural acquisitions. More often than not their beauty and vigour was only short term as their owners killed them with kindness and mismanagement, just as I had done.

The rules are straightforward – just use your common sense. By following them, you can watch your plants fill your homes with beauty and life.

JANE BLAND

# Contents

## A-Z of Houseplants

# How to use this book

This book is laid out to give the maximum amount of information in the clearest possible way. The introduction contains general hints and advice on plant care, which is amplified in the main part of the book. This deals individually with over 70 of the most popular houseplants. Arranged alphabetically, each section contains a picture of the healthy plant, advice on pests and diseases, illustrations to help identify problems, a plant care chart, and an easy care guide, as well as the plant's family or genus name and common names.

Care guide indicates how easy or difficult the plant is to care for.

- difficult
- moderate
- easy

Pests and diseases – advice on how to deal with any pests or diseases which may affect the plant

Family name

Name of plant

Common name(s)

General information about the plant

Picture of healthy plant showing color, shape, and so on

Varieties and purchasing – information on the best varieties available and what to look out for when buying

Names of specific varieties of the plant are abbreviated and given in italics

158 GESNERIACEAE

Saintpaulia

AFRICAN VIOLET

Although these plants are generally difficult to manage, this does not seem to be a deterrent, as worldwide they are among the most popular of all the potted flowering houseplants. The leaves are mostly rounded, hairy and attached to short talks that sprout from soil level, forming a neat rosette that is a background for the flowers when they appear. Flowers of many colours are now available in single and double forms, and a collection of plants growing in ideal conditions will provide a display of flowers throughout the year. Plants can be propagated from individual leaves with stalk attached. These are put into clean peat in a propagating case in a temperature of not less than 21°C (70°F).

**Healthy Plant** The African Violet is one of the most popular flowering houseplants. It is available in a wide variety of colours and flower shapes.

VARIETIES AND PURCHASING

The wide variety of African Violets available today vary in colour and in flower shape and formation. However, a few points should be borne in mind when buying. Select a plant with firm, non-drooping leaves, and, if possible, avoid purchasing from cold premises. Plants with blemishes on the foliage and sign of root or stem rot should always be passed over. Try to choose a plant which is in bud, as this will afford more lasting pleasure than one in full flower.

*S. ionantha* This is the only variety of African Violet in cultivation. All the many examples commercially available are hybrids of *S. ionantha.*

PESTS AND DISEASES

The recent varieties of African Violet tend to be tougher than their predecessors, but care still needs to be taken when caring for the plants. Overwatering and wetting the leaves can cause problems.

**Root rot** Most types of root rot are aggravated by wet soil conditions which prevent oxygen reaching the roots of the plant. Affected roots are brown and lifeless. In the early stages, treat by allowing the plant to dry out and to stay dry for several days. In an advanced state, the whole plant collapses and the leaves go limp. At this stage the plant must be destroyed.

**Botrytis** This fungus disease should also be treated with fungicide. If the attack is severe, destroy the plant.

**Mildew** This should be treated with a suitable fungicide such as propicanizole.

Photograph of a plant with a pest or disease to show exactly what to watch for

Ideal conditions chart gives information on light and position, temperature, watering, feeding, seasonal care, and soil

Temperatures and measurements have been rounded up or down to the nearest convenient figure

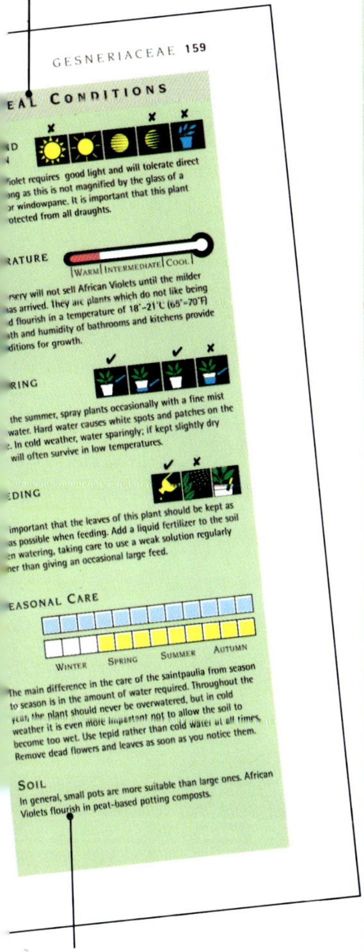
GESNERIACEAE 159

EAL CONDITIONS

...iolet requires good light and will tolerate direct ...ong as this is not magnified by the glass of a ...r windowpane. It is important that this plant ...otected from all draughts.

...RATURE

...rsery will not sell African Violets until the milder ...as arrived. They are plants which do not like being ...d flourish in a temperature of 18°–21°C (65°–70°F) ...th and humidity of bathrooms and kitchens provide ...ditions for growth.

...RING

...the summer, spray plants occasionally with a fine mist ...water. Hard water causes white spots and patches on the ... In cold weather, water sparingly; if kept slightly dry ...will often survive in low temperatures.

...EDING

...important that the leaves of this plant should be kept as ...as possible when feeding. Add a liquid fertilizer to the soil ...en watering, taking care to use a weak solution regularly ...her than giving an occasional large feed.

...EASONAL CARE

WINTER SPRING SUMMER AUTUMN

The main difference in the care of the saintpaulia from season to season is in the amount of water required. Throughout the year, the plant should never be overwatered, but in cold weather it is even more important not to allow the soil to become too wet. Use tepid rather than cold water at all times. Remove dead flowers and leaves as soon as you notice them.

SOIL

In general, small pots are more suitable than large ones. African Violets flourish in peat-based potting composts.

This part of the chart advises on planting and the best soil mixture

**Ideal conditions** This chart shows essential information at a glance. For ease of use, the symbols are explained here in detail. However, the chart also contains captions with detailed advice on treatment and care to help you avoid problems with your plants.

✘ ✔

**Crosses and checks** A check indicates that the plant positively likes, and a cross that it actively dislikes, a treatment or condition.

**Light and position** This symbol indicates bright sunlight. A plant which likes bright sun could stand in a well-lit window, for example.

This symbol shows that the plant likes a bright position, but not direct sunlight, such as a position near, but not directly in front of, a window.

This symbol indicates partial shade. A position in a fairly light room, but away from a window, would suit a plant which likes this condition.

This symbol indicates full shade. Some plants such as ferns may thrive in a very shady position and can brighten dark corners of a room.

**Drafts** Most plants abhor drafts, but a few will tolerate them. Pay particular attention to this symbol.

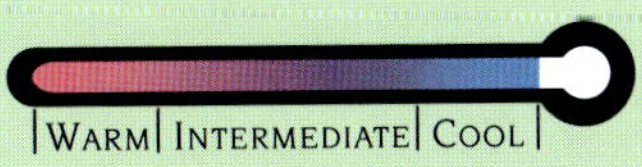


**Temperature** Always keep plants in temperatures they prefer as much as possible. The ideal temperature range is given for each plant. This may be cool (up to 60°F); intermediate or warm (over 65°F).

**Watering** The main methods of watering are applying it directly to the soil (above left), in the container under the plant pot (above right), spraying the plant with a plant spray (above left), and immersing the pot (but not the whole plant) in water (above right).

**Feeding** There are three main ways of feeding houseplants. The three symbols (above) indicate that the plant should be given food in liquid form (left), as a spray on the leaves (center), or as a solid applied to the soil as granules or in stick form (right). It is important to fertilize the plant as recommended. Most plants need food mainly during the growing season, but others require varying amounts of food all year round.

**Seasonal care** This chart shows when plants need watering and feeding. The pale blue color on the watering chart (above) indicates when you should water, and the droplets symbol shows when extra watering is essential. White indicates that no watering is required.

The feeding chart works in a similar way. The yellow area shows when you should feed, the white indicates no feeding. In all cases, the information is amplified in the captions.

# Choosing and Buying Plants

It seems that there are very few retail outlets that do not sell houseplants these days, and although I have been known to buy one at a service station, I would not recommend this. Houseplants need environmental stability; if they are kept outside and exposed to all types of weather, the plants will suffer.

This does not necessarily mean that plants which have been kept indoors will be all right. Those found in a supermarket may well be just as good as those found in a garden center: it all depends on how well they have been looked after.

Obviously, you cannot be expected to monitor the selling environment every time you want to buy a new plant, but you can develop an eye for a healthy plant. Do this simply by looking at them and learning to read the signals they are giving you. Remember that houseplants need a stable temperature. Is the selling area warm? It should not be too near an outside door where the plants will feel the chill air each time it is opened. The majority of these indoor plants really cannot tolerate drafts. The display areas should be slightly damp and, most important, clean.

**Plant buying**
Purchasing a plant requires patience and care. Time, money, and effort can be easily wasted if a plant is bought too hastily. A careful look at the general appearance of the plant will immediately reveal its condition. The leaves should be without blemishes, supple, and healthy in color.

Although light and ventilation are also important to houseplants, the next question to consider is whether they have been properly watered. Confusingly, limp leaves can be a symptom both of overwatering and underwatering. Pick up a pot. If it feels light, it could be a sign that the plant has been seriously underwatered. If the soil has shrunk away from the sides of the pot, replace it and look for another. Now be positive – touch the soil. It should feel damp, but don't worry too much if it feels a bit on the dry side. If the plant looks healthy in all other respects, this hydration problem can be put right as soon as you get home. Overwatering is more serious. Roots that have been allowed to stand in water for any length of time will start to rot. This is difficult to remedy, so it is perhaps better to choose another plant.

Houseplants should appear crisp and green. During this close inspection, look at the growing tips of the plant, underneath the leaves, and at the fresh foliage. If there is any sign of insect life, go somewhere else to buy your plants.

Sadly, houseplants are not cheap any more, and these few guidelines should help you to avoid making costly mistakes. But don't be deceived into thinking that bigger and more expensive is necessarily going to be better. With the exception of annual varieties, such as browallias and really slow growers like members of the palm family, younger, smaller and therefore less expensive plants are often much more adaptable than their more spectacular mature relatives. The reason is that they object less dramatically to changes in their situation, they travel better, and settle down more readily in a new environment. You might want an instant indoor garden, but if cost is an important factor, it is more sensible to buy small plants and watch them mature.

Finally, when taking plants home, always make sure that they are well wrapped in a draft-free container, and never put them in the trunk of the car for the journey. Unwrap the new plants carefully, give them a good watering, and stand them in a cool, shady spot for two or three days so that they can settle down after all the stresses and strains of being moved.

# Watering and Feeding Plants

When planting in groups, make sure that the plants you use have similar watering requirements. Always touch the soil before adding more water; remember it might be quite dry on the surface, but still damp enough underneath.

**Quenching thirst**
The azalea (below) is extremely dehydrated, due to underwatering. In such cases, fill a bucket with water, immerse the pot – keeping the foliage and any flowers clear – and leave until no more bubbles appear on the surface.

Almost all plants have very clearly defined periods when they grow and rest, but these may be difficult for the inexperienced to identify. Learn to look at the plants closely. When they are growing, they look crisp, strong, and green. When resting, the foliage temporarily loses its strength of color, the plant may lose a few, or all of its leaves, and generally looks out of sorts. At this time it will need a great deal less water than normal. Even if it is given, the plant will not absorb it, so watering while resting usually means a scant minimum – just enough to prevent the soil from drying out completely.

Learning how to water plants while they are actively growing can take a little longer to master. Although specific instructions for each plant's watering needs are given, there are several outside factors that dictate the speed with which plants use water.

Water more often if: the temperature is high or the air humidity low; the plant container is made of unglazed clay; the plant is large, but the pot relatively small; the plant has filled its pot with roots; or the plant has large, thin leaves.

Water less often if the temperatures are low, or the weather overcast; the air humidity is high; the plant container is plastic or glazed clay; the plant is relatively small in a large pot; or the plant has succulent leaves or stems.

However, the most important advice is that you must be consistent when watering. If a plant needs water, give it plenty; provide enough to soak through the soil and drain through into the saucer or tray, which should be emptied an hour or so after watering, by which time the plant will have taken up as much as it needs. The soil right through the pot should be thoroughly wetted at each watering. With a very few exceptions, houseplants prefer to be well watered and then allowed to dry out reasonably before more water is given.

It is a good idea to touch the soil. Press it gently with the tip of your finger. If it feels damp, it means that the plant does not need watering. If it feels dry, do not rush for the watering can immediately; probe just a little deeper and you may find that the soil is still quite damp underneath although it is dry on the surface.

Plants like soft rainwater – unless you live in a highly polluted area – at room temperature. They do not mind tap water, as long as it has not been through a water softener. Always let tap water stand for a while so that it can settle and reach room temperature. In hard-water areas, tap water will leave chalky marks on the leaves of your plants.

Humidity is also an important aspect of caring for houseplants. Plants take up the water they are given and use it, together with light and air, to grow. Many plants also need a degree of moisture in the air around them in order to flourish. The air in modern homes tends to be on the dry side, so plants need a humid atmosphere to be created for them. Do this by arranging them in groups wherever possible, as while the air is warm, they will lose a certain amount of moisture making the air around them more humid. Where a plant is being displayed on its own, create a moist atmosphere for it by using two pots, the outer one being much larger than the pot in which the plant is growing. Fill the space between the two pots with moistened peat. The water from the peat will gradually evaporate, creating a moist microclimate around the plant. The peat must be kept damp. Help the plants, too, by misting them regularly with soft rainwater, or by standing them on trays of dampened horticultural aggregate.

Remember the air will be especially dry near radiators and electrical appliances like television sets. Never place plants near or on any electrical appliance, where simple watering will be dangerous and mist-spraying out of the question. Plants simply do not like radiators or heating vents, so keep them well away.

While considering watering, it would be as well to think too about feeding the plants. In the first instance, the plants will gain the nutrients they need from the soil in which they are growing. A newly potted plant will not need any further feeding for between three to six months, but those which have just been bought at a garden center will very probably have been fed at two-weekly intervals for several months, so it is a good idea to establish a feeding regime as soon as possible. There are dozens of different pills, powders, and potions sold as plant food to choose from.

The easiest way is often the best, so for general purposes use a liquid fertilizer, mixed from a powder. Some people might prefer to use a slow-release, or controlled-release granule, or powder. They simplify the job, because feeding is necessary less frequently. The slow-release varieties mean that the nutrients are gradually dissolved over a number of months; the controlled-release varieties are slightly more specific

**Humidity** Many plants require more humidity in the atmosphere than is provided in the average home. If the atmosphere becomes too dry, the plant's rate of water loss increases, which causes it to wilt. You can prevent this by standing the plant on damp pebbles or gravel.

**Reviving a parched plant**
If a plant has not received enough water, the leaves wilt and, if the plant is not watered soon, may drop off.

If a plant is suffering from dehydration, first loosen the top layer of soil. This will allow the water to permeate to the roots.

Then water the plant thoroughly. It is also a good idea, if the plant is very parched, to spray the leaves with tepid water.

Allow some water to stand in the saucer or tray, but not for more than an hour or so. Let a plant drain after watering.

as they allow the nutrients to enter the soil moisture according to its temperature. As the temperature of the soil increases, the plant becomes active. When this happens, the nutrients are there for the plant to use.

Most plant feeding is done during the spring and summer while the plants are growing, but there are exceptions to this rule. Plants freshly potted in a soil-based mixture will not need extra feed for four to six months as these mixtures have a built-in nutrient value. If a peat-based soil has been used which contains fewer nutrients, the plant will need feeding sooner rather than later, particularly if it is a fast grower. When plants have reached their final pot size and are therefore annually top-dressed in the early spring, feeding would need to start mid to late spring.

In addition to feeding through their roots, plants also absorb nutrients through their leaves. Foliar feeds are a fairly instant way of providing plants with essential nutrients as the leaves absorb moisture more readily.

Whatever method is used, remember that plants kept in pots – other than those that are newly potted – need to be fed at regular intervals while they are in active growth. Obviously, the intervals will alter according to the type of fertilizer used. Directions are always included in the manufacturer's recommendations.

**Types of food**
Liquid and powdered fertilizers (above) can be applied with the regular watering of the plant. Pellet fertilizers (left) do away with the necessity of accurate measuring and mixing. When the plant is watered, the pellet releases the correct dosage of feed. Fertilizer sticks (above left) are even less time-consuming.

# Light and Position

Obviously, the amount of light plants receive is extremely important as they use it to grow. Although they have quite specific needs, plants are, within reason, quite tolerant of a variety of light levels. For the most part, it is the harmful effect that spells of strong direct sunlight have on the majority of plants that matters. Green foliage plants will generally do much better in poor light than their variegated relatives. Flowering plants usually need a daily dose of strong sunshine to make them flower. It is relatively easy in a sunroom or conservatory to make sure the right amount of light as they are completely glazed. Indoors, it is more difficult – even in a room that gets a lot of sun, the degree of light is reduced progressively farther away from the glass.

As there are different degrees of light intensity and plants grow best when they are in a particular position, each plant is given individual treatment in the text, using symbols to show its requirements. However, this may not be enough.

**Strong Direct Light** Many permanent flowering plants need this to ripen their wood. In rooms keep the plants close to, but not touching, a sunny window. In sunrooms and conservatories position the plants near the roof space where they will absorb as much of the direct light as possible. Although sunlight is preferable, do not worry if the weather is overcast – the "solar" effect will still be working.

**Good Light with Some Sun** These plants will need the light from an east- or west-facing window. Remember morning light is not as strong as evening light. Either way, these plants need a couple of hours of sunlight every day, but no strong midday sun.

**Light Shade** This is easier to achieve. It will be found underneath sun-loving plants or at a tree-shaded window.

**Shade** These plants need to be as far away from the source of light as possible. You can put them a fair distance from the source of light, where they will thrive in quite subdued light.

Do not worry too much about poor light levels during the winter as most plants will rest then. Their growth will slow down or stop altogether for a while. Although they still need to be in the light, their need for good light conditions is minimal.

# Soil and Potting Mixtures

The sort of soil a plant requires is dictated by the type of drainage it needs. Peat-based mixtures and peat retain their moisture, are light, clean and easy to handle, but have few nutrients; peat itself has no nutrient value at all. Soil-based mixtures contain some peat, but the majority is made up of sterilized soil. They are much coarser in texture so they drain more freely, and their nutrient content is relatively high. Sometimes other ingredients are added to these mixtures either to increase their drainage capacity – washed river sand or horticultural grit – or to provide moisture-retention – perlite.

Don't try and cut costs by using soil from the yard; buy a sterile commercial variety in which the unwanted microorganisms have been killed.

Inevitably, plants will need repotting. Previously healthy plants might suddenly lose their strength of color, or a few leaves. Check for signs of insect infestation, then turn the plant out of its pot. If it needs repotting, there will be a healthy mass of roots covering the soil, with the majority in the lowest third of the root ball. Take care, as a plant that does not need re-potting will have far fewer roots on show, and the soil will break up easily. It is usually best to re-pot into pots one size larger. Although it would save time if the final pot size were used immediately, unfortunately the soil in the larger pot would turn "sour" well before the plant has the chance to fill it with roots. Normally re-potting is done in spring or late winter, just as the plant starts back into growth, but there are no absolute rules here. Any plant in active growth should be potted on whenever it needs it.

Repotting plants is not difficult. Water them a couple of hours beforehand and make sure that all the fresh soils are moistened. Having put some fresh soil in the new container, hold the existing pot upside down and tap the base so that the plant and its soil drop out into the palm of your hand. Then place the plant centrally in its new pot, and gently but firmly fill the space around the root ball with more fresh soil, making sure that the surface of the root ball is about 1 inch below the rim of the pot. After potting, give the mixture a good watering. No further water should be needed for about ten days. This will encourage the roots to grow while actively searching for moisture in the new soil.

When repotting a big plant, you may need to ask another person to help you. Larger plants may have reached their final pot size, in which case they must be top-dressed. Do this by removing as much of the surface soil as possible (a small stick or pencil is good for this job) without damaging the roots too much and replacing it with fresh soil.

**Soil and potting**
By gently tipping the root ball out of its pot into the palm of your hand, you wil be able to tell if a plant needs re-potting. Once you have the plant in its new pot, pack firm, fresh, moist soil around the root ball.

# Pests and Diseases

In a perfect world, houseplants would never be troubled by pests and diseases, but unfortunately most are. These are usually a rather nasty sounding double act, as it is secretions from the pests themselves that encourage fungal attack.

**Prevention is Better Than Cure**

Greenhouse pests will usually feed on the fresh green parts of the plant. They also like the type of protection provided by dead leaves and other litter lying around the plants. So keep the plant area scrupulously clean. Deadhead every day and remove any dying, affected, or fallen foliage immediately. These simple instructions will also help to prevent the risk of fungal disease.

Greenhouse pests like the air to be hot and dry, just like it is in centrally heated houses. So maintain a humid atmosphere around the plants by misting daily or by standing them in trays of moist aggregate, and give them adequate ventilation.

Greenhouse pests multiply at a phenomenal rate. As soon as you see just one, take action – never put this job off until tomorrow. Don't be squeamish; pick off all the visible adults and squeeze them between a finger and thumb. Whitefly and greenfly can be washed away with a diluted spray of soapy water. Where mealy bugs have started nesting, remove the nests with a cloth soaked in denatured alcohol. Scale insects can be brushed away with an old toothbrush. Honeydew and sooty mold are both easily remedied with a soapy spray. Finally, never underestimate the value of a fine spray of soft rainwater, or of wiping the leaves and stems with a moistened cloth or sponge – both will get rid of dying foliage and flowers, which are often the point of entry for disease, as well as a good hiding place for pests.

All these are easy, direct forms of attack, which will help to keep things under control. (Remember, that with the exception of the mealy-bug eggs, the adults are controlled, not their offspring.) However, if none of the safe remedies work, you may have to try something stronger.

Chemical sprays will certainly do the job – provided that the manufacturer's instructions are followed exactly; but they are not user-friendly – they smell bad, can kill off other beneficial insects, and may cause you harm if not used with care. The most harmless are soft soap and pyrethrum. Resmethrin and permethrin are very similar to pyrethrum; derris is another alternative. Dimethoate and malathion are very effective against greenhouse pests, but should only be used as a last resort. Propicanizole, a chemical fungicide, must be regarded in the same way.

**Safety First**

- Before using any chemical, always read the manufacturer's directions and follow them to the letter. Too strong a solution won't help – it will damage both the plants and the environment.
- Do not mix chemicals, unless the manufacturer's instructions specifically recommend this.
- Approved chemicals for gardens and greenhouses do not require the use of protective clothing, but it is sensible to wear rubber gloves. Any exposed skin that becomes contaminated with any chemical solution should be washed immediately and thoroughly.
- Do not breathe in the spray drift. Those with breathing difficulties may be adversely affected by it.
- Keep children and pets away from the treated plants until the leaves have dried.
- Store chemicals in a cool, dark place, well out of reach of children and pets. Keep the chemicals in their original containers with their tops firmly closed.
- Wash all spraying equipment thoroughly after use. Use separate sprayers for pest-spraying, fungicide-spraying, and mist-spraying.

**Biological Controls**

Quite simply, these are bugs that eat bugs. The big difference between greenhouse pests and their predators is the fact that the latter do only good. Generally you won't even notice that they are there, and they won't fly out of the windows. Of course, their survival depends upon the presence of a particular pest, so by introducing a successful "biological" control, you will never get rid of that pest; the predator will just keep it under control, preventing the pest from doing any real damage. These "green" soldiers are just a telephone call away; they are sent by mail accompanied by plenty of helpful instructions. They are available through gardening magazines or your local garden center or nursery.

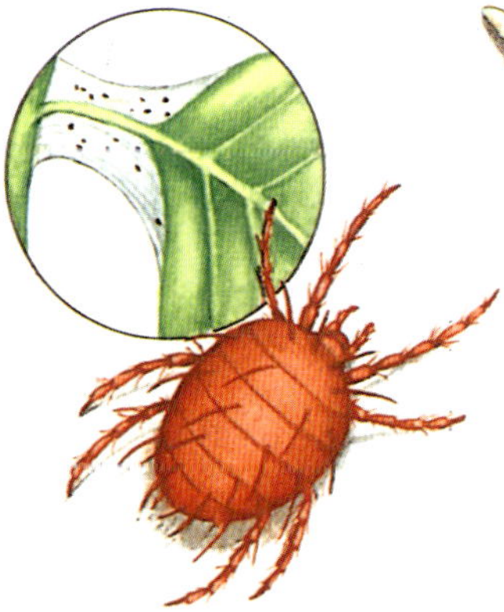

**Red spider mite** Adult insects are reddish-brown, but the young are flesh colored, and it is vital to eradicate both if the plant is to live. An infestation of spider mites is shown on the leaf of a *Chamaedorea elegans* (top). The insects make tiny webs on the undersides of the leaves, which may then fade and turn yellow. Inspect the plant frequently, with a magnifying glass if necessary, as mites must be dealt with at an early stage.

- Spray with derris.
- Introduce predatory mite *Phytoseiulis persimilis.*
- Throw away badly affected plants.

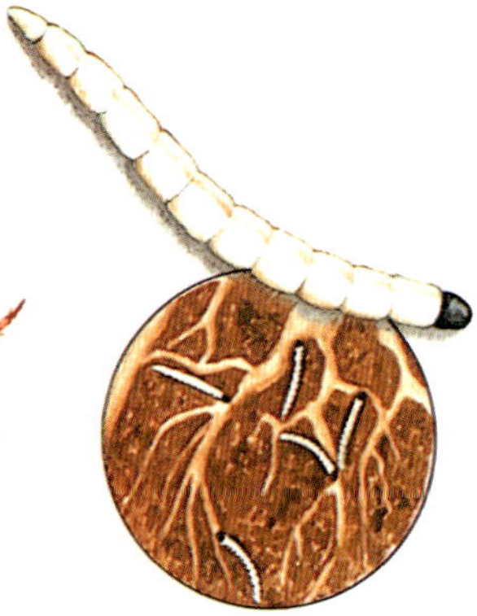

**Sciarid fly** These insects, also known as fungus gnats, are encouraged by wet, dank conditions, such as when the plant is overwatered and the atmosphere is not warm enough to dry out the soil. In themselves they are more unsightly than harmful, but they lay eggs in the soil, and the maggots which hatch will sometimes attack the roots of a plant. This undermines the health of the plant, causing it to droop like the *Calathea makoyana* shown here (top).

- Spray malathion over pot surfaces when adults are flying.
- Soak soil with malathion.

**Symphalids** These rarely occur in houseplants, but are extremely destructive when they do. Symphalids resemble small, cream-colored centipedes. They gnaw into large roots and completely devour small ones. A plant such as the dieffenbachia (top) may suffer badly, but most potting mixtures are composed to prevent such problems. To find out whether symphalids are present in the soil, stir some into water; the insects should rise to the top.

- Soak the potting mixture with malathion.

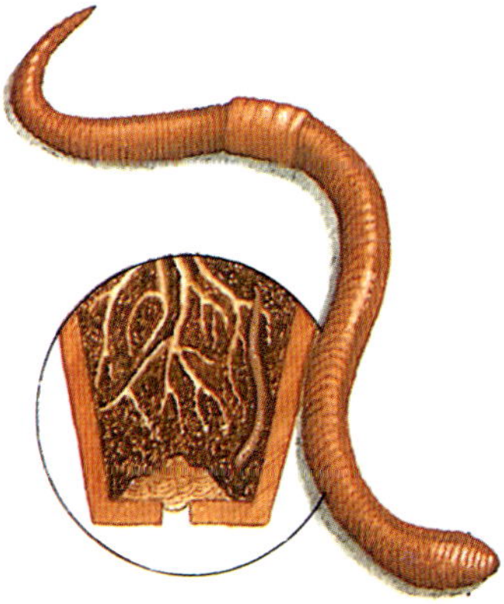

**Earthworms** A plant which is taken outside during warm weather may be troubled by the presence of an earthworm which has made its way into the soil. The problem here is that the worm will throw off casts as it moves through the soil, which can interfere with the drainage of water. This may cause the leaves of the plant to wilt or curl and become discolored. The *Dracaena deremensis* (top) shows signs of this problem.

- Remove the plant from the pot and shake off the potting mixture from the rootball. Clear the drainage holes of the pot and repot the plant in fresh soil.

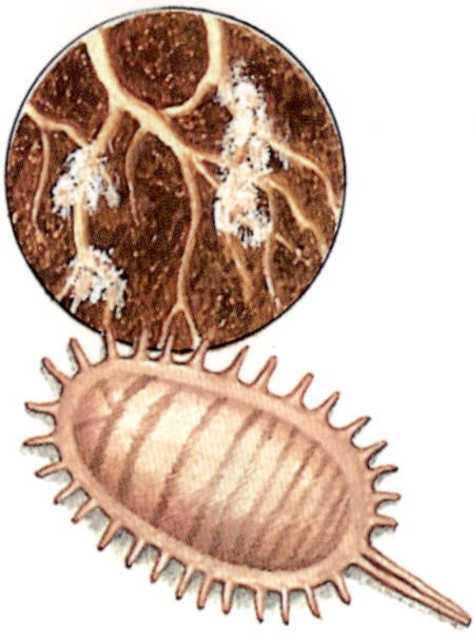

**Root mealy bug** These small, pale insects, often covered with a fuzzy white coating, infest the roots of plants, particularly cacti and succulents. As they suck sap from the roots, the plant itself becomes stunted in the new growth and cannot continue a healthy development.

- Soak the potting mixture thoroughly with malathion every two weeks. Repeat at least twice.
- If a small plant is affected, wash away the potting mixture with tepid water and cut out badly damaged roots. Soak the roots in malathion and repot in clean soil.

**Aphids** Also known as greenfly, these pests attack the soft tissue of plants, sucking the sap and depositing sticky honeydew. The stems and leaves of the plant are weakened and distorted. Aphids can carry viruses and cause susceptibility to sooty mold, and may be black, gray, or yellow as well as green. Prompt and repeated treatment is needed.

- Spray the plant very thoroughly with a soap spray, pyrethum, resemethrin, or permethrin, and repeat the spraying regularly.
- Soak the soil by using any of the above in solution.

**Whitefly** The larvae live on the undersides of the leaves, looking like greenish scales. They suck sap from the plant and secrete honeydew. The first sign of whitefly may be yellowing leaves, which quickly drop when badly infested. A more certain indication is that the little flies rise up in a cloud when the plant is disturbed.
It is difficult to get rid of the larvae completely, so treatment may be prolonged.

- Spray the leaves thoroughly, particularly the undersides, with malathion, repeating the spraying at three-day intervals.

**Scale insect** Because these creatures are immobile, usually a yellow or brown color, they are sometimes camouflaged on plants with woody stems, but are easier to detect among green foliage, for instance, on a fern (top). The insects are protected by a waxy coating, and once in place, they suck the sap from the plant, causing it to wither.

- Scrape off insects, then wash the whole plant with soapy water.
- Spray stems and foliage thoroughly with dimethoate.

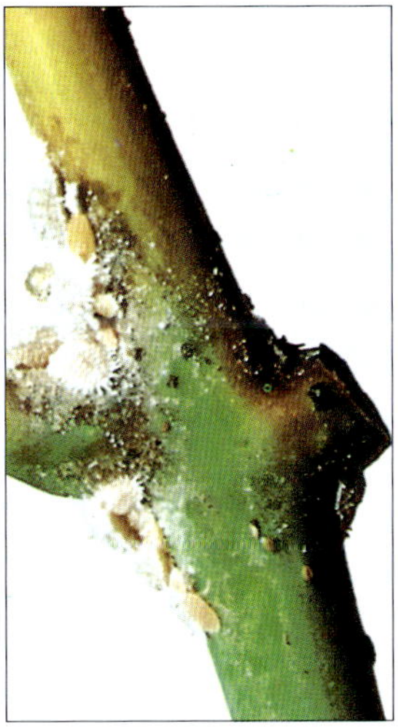

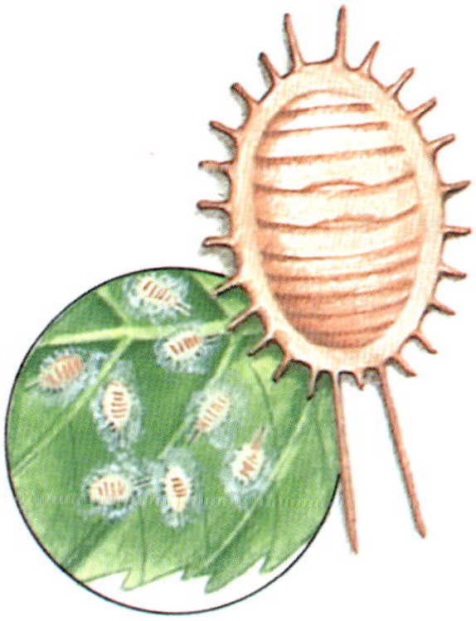

**Mealy bug** A visitation from mealy bugs is usually quite easy to see. The young are wrapped in a cottony coating. They may build up into a thick cluster on the stem, as on the bougainvillea (top), or under the leaves. A light infestation can be dealt with quickly and easily, but if the problem is allowed to continue untreated, the plant will wilt, and the leaves will turn yellow and fall.

- If there are few bugs, pick off those most noticeable and wipe away nests with cotton pads soaked in denatured alcohol.
- Spray the plant with malathion or dimethoate.

**Thrips** Although thrips are also known as thunderflies, they usually move by jumping, rather than by flying. They suck the sap of soft foliage and also attack flowers. Foliage and flowers will become streaked and spotted. Excretion from the flies turns black on the plant, speckling the leaves. The insects are less harmful than some, but the effect is extremely disfiguring to the plant and stunts growth. Deal with thrips promptly at the first sign of attack.

- Spray the plant with malathion or dimethoate.
- Remove seriously damaged foliage and place diazinon granules in the soil.

**Mildew** This is evident as a powdery white deposit on the leaves, which can also spread to stems and flowers. It is a fungal disease which particularly attacks plants with soft growth. Although not harmful, it is not very attractive and certainly does the plant no good. Fortunately, it is not a common complaint in houseplants. When it occurs, as on the begonia (top), it is clearly visible.

- Cut away badly affected leaves and spray the plant with propicanizole.

**Botrytis** This is another fungal disease, clearly distinguishable from mildew because of the fluffy, gray mold which forms on the plants. Again, plants with soft leaves such as the aglaonema (top) are the most likely to be affected, but botrytis is quite common in all houseplants. It is usually a sign that the plant is being kept in the wrong conditions – too cold and damp, and also being overwatered.

- Cut away leaves with mold on them. In addition, remove any sodden, moldy soil and reduce watering or misting.
- Spray the plant with propicanizole.

# Plant Doctor

## Leaf Clinic

**Symptom** Leaves lack usual color and look dull
**Cause** Too much light? Infested with red spider mite? Plant undernourished? Plant dirty?
**Cure** Move plant to shadier position; check under leaves for the fine white webs of red spider, cut away affected parts of plant, spray with insecticide, make sure air around the plant remains humid – mist spray regularly or stand plant in a tray of damp horticultural aggregate. Check the feeding regimes – unless they are newly potted, all house plants need regular feeding when in active growth; spray plant with soft rainwater.

**Symptom** Yellowing of upper leaves
**Cause** Is the plant a lime hater?
**Cure** Repot in ericaceous soil; always use soft rainwater when watering these plants.

**Symptom** Plant develops spots, in mottled patches on leaves
**Cause** Droplets of water left to scorch on leaves? Pests in the soil? Pests on plant?
**Cure** Water plants at a time when they are not in direct sunlight; check the plant and its soil for pests, treat accordingly; re-pot if necessary. Watch out for virus; if the stems become stunted and/or deformed, throw the plant away.

**Symptom** Lower leaves dry up and drop off
**Cause** Excessive heat? Insufficient light? Underwatering?
**Cure** Check environmental conditions, move plant if necessary; provide more water only if you are sure that the temperature and light levels are correct.

**Symptom** Variegated leaves become totally green
**Cause** Insufficient light?
**Cure** Move plant to a lighter position.

**Symptom** Lower leaves yellow and fall off
**Cause** This could be completely natural; all plants lose some leaves from time to time. Overwatering? Plant in a draft?
**Cure** Check the moisture content of the soil; if it is saturated, remove it from its drip tray and let the soil dry out before watering again.

**Symptom** Leaves curl up and drop off
**Cause** Underwatering? Exposure to cold drafts? Too cold?
**Cure** Check the moisture content of the soil; provide more water on a regular basis. If the soil has contracted away from the sides of the pot, submerge the pot in a bucket of water; wait until the earth is saturated before removing. Check environmental requirements.

**Symptom** Wilting leaves
**Cause** Under- or overwatering? Too hot? Pot bound?
**Cure** Check the plants watering requirements, act accordingly. Move the plant to a cooler position. Check the root ball by taking the plant out of its pot; a plant that needs repotting will have a spiral of roots all around the outside of the root ball – re-pot in fresh soil.

**Symptom** Sudden leaf fall
**Cause** Environmental change; moving the plant from the garden center to your home. Pot bound?
**Cure** All new plants should be given special care for the first few days in a new environment; keep them out of direct sun in warm, humid conditions. Check whether the plant needs re-potting.

**Symptom** Brown tips or edges on leaves
**Cause** Lack of humidity? Scorch?
**Cure** Mist plant regularly with soft rainwater; do not water when the plant is in direct sunlight.

# Stem Clinic

**Symptom** Rotting stem
**Cause** Environmental needs incorrect? Overwatering?
**Cure** Check temperatures, especially nighttime minimums; plants watered late in the day may still be damp when the temperature drops – this will cause stem rot. Check watering requirements.

**Symptom** Black base to stem
**Cause** Overwatering?
**Cure** Plant unlikely to recover.

# Flower Clinic

**Symptom** Flowers fading quickly
**Cause** Temperatures too high? Underwatering? Air too dry? Insufficient light?
**Cure** Check temperature requirements; is the soil too dry? If so, increase the amounts of water you are providing; increase humidity levels by misting daily with soft rainwater, or by standing plant in a tray of damp horticultural aggregate. Move the plant into a lighter position.

**Symptom** Plant fails to flower
**Cause** Too little light? Air too dry? Overfeeding? Insect infestation? Plant pot bound or in a container that is too large?
**Cure** Check all the environmental requirements of the plant; make a close inspection for any insect life and act accordingly. Re-pot the plant if necessary, but remember that some plants need to be in a relatively small pot.

**Symptom** Flower buds fall prematurely
**Cause** Underwatering? Too little light? Temperature too high? Insufficient feed? Insect infestation? Change of position while plant is in bud?
**Cure** Check all the plant's environmental needs; check the plant for insects and act accordingly. Plants in bud can react very dramatically to sudden changes in their environment; try not to move them at this time. If it is absolutely necessary – perhaps the plant is newly purchased – make sure it is well-wrapped during transportation and cared for correctly in its new surroundings.

# Plant Clinic

**Symptom** A white coating on leaves and stems
**Cause** Powdery mildew
**Cure** Avoid wetting the leaves while watering; improve ventilation; treat with an appropriate fungicide.

**Symptom** Slow growth
**Cause** Insufficient feed? Plant is pot bound? Overwatering? Pest infestation? It could be that your plant is resting; if so, don't worry.
**Cure** Check that you are feeding the plant regularly. Turn the plant out of its pot, if you see the root system spiraling around the perimeter of the root ball, it needs re-potting. Remember, only provide water when the plant really needs it; check the whole plant for any signs of pests and act accordingly.

**Symptom** Small leaves and spindly growth
**Cause** Insufficient feed, red spider infestation
**Cure** While in active growth, potted plants need to be fed at regular intervals. Check under the leaves for signs of red spider infestation; if you find any at all, cut away the affected parts and spray with an appropriate insecticide without delay.

**Symptom** Plant surfaces become mottled with a black substance
**Cause** Sooty mold
**Cure** Sooty mold grows on honeydew. Check for pest infestation; clean the plant with a dilute soap solution.

**Symptom** Plant surfaces become sticky
**Cause** Honeydew
**Cure** Honeydew is a direct effect of insect infestation. Check the plant for pests; remove honeydew by spraying the plant with a dilute soap solution.

**Symptom** Fluffy gray mold on any parts of the plant
**Cause** Botrytis
**Cure** Botrytis is a fungus that thrives in cool damp conditions; soft-leaved plants are particularly prone. Destroy all affected parts and scrape away any affected soil. Spray plant with an appropriate fungicide; reduce watering; improve ventilation.

# A-Z
## of Houseplants

# Abutilon hybrids

## Flowering Maple or Parlor Maple

If you have a cool, draft-free spot and want a plant that looks like a small tree, an abutilon could easily fit the bill. These plants have quite hairy, medium green and often variegated, five-fingered leaves. Grown purely for its foliage, it would grace any indoor garden, but unlike many other houseplants, this one is not shy about flowering. Abutilon hybrids come in a variety of colors from yellow to deep red, with many variations in between. They can be single-colored, in two colors, or two shades of a single color. The bell-shaped flowers are about 2 inches long, and they appear all through the summer and fall.

Abutilons are not too difficult to grow from seed, but a heated propagator is necessary, as the seeds require a constant temperature of 65°F to germinate. A much easier way to multiply your stock is to take cuttings during the summer. Simply take "tip" cuttings, about 3 inches long, dip them in a hormone rooting powder, and plant in a mixture of equal parts potting soil and sand. Keep the cutting in a moist atmosphere by covering the rim of the flowerpot with a plastic bag and place it out of direct sunlight. Cuttings should root within three or four weeks.

A word of warning, though – given a free rein and the right environment, abutilon hybrids will quickly grow to 10 feet or more. If necessary, you will have to keep it under control by pruning. Don't worry, even if you have to cut out half the growth in the spring so that it fits the space available, it will quickly produce side shoots and provide you with a bushier plant.

### Varieties and Purchasing

*Abutilon × hybridum* This is the name given to a group of hybrids of mixed parentage, so there should be plenty to choose from at good garden centers. Mainly grown for their attractive flowers, many abutilons also have highly decorative leaves.

Try to find *A. × hybridum* 'Savitzii'; its foliage is almost white with a minimal pale green coloring.

*A.* 'Cannington Red' has striking rose-red flowers and golden variegated foliage.

## Pests and Diseases

**Whitefly** This can be quite a problem, but their grayish, wedge-shaped form makes the flies easy to spot. Once established, they congregate in their hundreds on the undersides of leaves and on developing foliage and flower buds. Act quickly with a safe spray – remember you will have to use this spray frequently to prevent a potentially damaging expanding population.

**Red spider mites** These pests do their worst on the undersides of leaves. Although they are difficult to see, their webs are not. Perhaps the first and most obvious sign that they are at work will be the sticky honeydew they secrete. Spray the plant with a soapy solution to wash away the honeydew and use derris to eliminate the mites. For slightly more permanent control, use one of the available pesticide sprays, such as malathion. Always follow the manufacturer's directions when spraying with this sort of deterrent.

**Cyclamen mites** These tiny sap-sucking insects lay their eggs in such quantities that they look like a layer of dust. Leaves and flower stems become twisted and brittle and are eventually covered in small scabs. Control with an insecticide.

**Aphids** The flies are easy enough to see, but for each one you spot, there are likely to be another ten hidden away somewhere. Act quickly, remove all the adult flies you can find, and spray the plant with a diluted soap solution.

**Healthy Plant**
Choose a bushy plant, with plenty of laterals, or side shoots, as the flowers appear between the leaf stalk and the stem. If possible select one that is actually in flower, or one that has plenty of buds. As abutilons are exceptionally prone to attack from red spider mite and greenfly, always give any plant you are about to buy a quick check.

## Ideal Conditions

### Light and Position

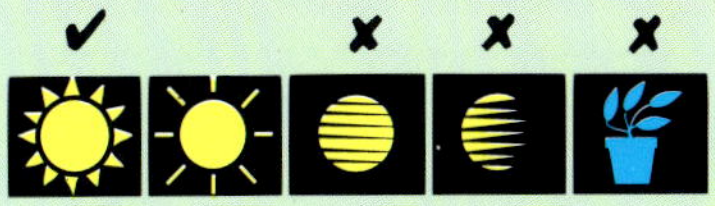

Give an abutilon a position where it is going to receive as much direct sunlight as possible. Large plants can become top heavy, so make sure their containers are sturdy enough to prevent them from toppling over.

### Temperature Range

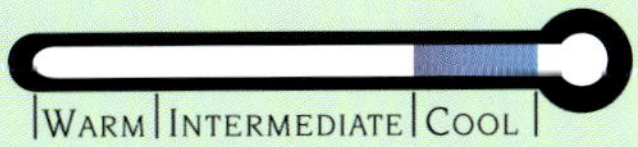


A minimum of 50°F will suit these plants perfectly, but they can be kept at a lower temperature during the winter if preferred. Those plants kept cool during the winter will need very little water and they might lose their leaves for the dormancy period.

### Watering

The plant is easy to water by any method and likes a lot of water in the growing period. In the rest period, water more moderately, allowing the top layer of soil to dry out between waterings.

### Feeding

Give the plants liquid fertilizer once every two weeks through spring and summer.

### Seasonal Care

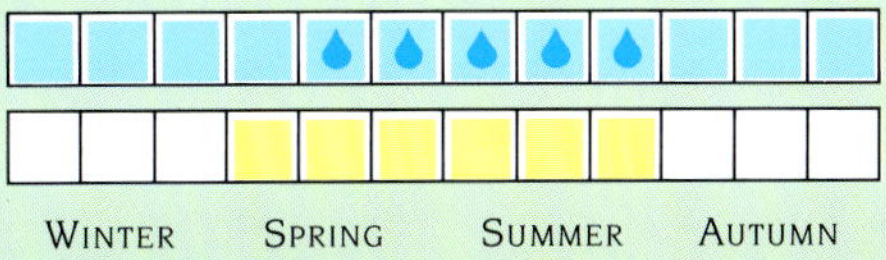


Dead head regularly through the summer, as this will encourage more flowers. These plants may become messy; when this happens, they need cutting back in early spring. Remove thin shoots that crowd the center and reduce other stems by a third.

### Soil

Abutilons do well in a soil-based mixture; repot annually until the final pot size is reached, then top-dress with fresh mixture annually.

# Acalypha hispida

## Varieties and Purchasing

*A. hispida* This shrub can grow to 6 feet. The flowers are petal-less, with bright red, drooping, tassel-like spikes which appear in late summer and fall.

*A. wilkesiana* This variety is grown chiefly for its lovely foliage. The leaves are a coppery green, mottled and streaked with copper, red, and purple.

**Healthy Plant**
The *Acalypha hispida*'s chief charm lies in its long red bracts. During the growth period, the plant requires heavy feeding; this takes place primarily in summer, though, given the right conditions, the plant will produce a few bracts throughout the year. Keep it in a good light, but away from full sun, at a temperature of around 65°F.

This woody tropical shrub, originating from Southeast Asia, can reach a maximum height of around 6 feet when grown as a pot plant. It has big, coarse green leaves 8–10 inches in length, depending on how well the plant is cared for, but they are really grown for their drooping, bright red 10–12-inch bracts that appear in profusion during the summer. However, well-cared-for plants, grown in good light in a reasonable temperature, will oblige with at least a few bracts throughout the year. To improve the appearance of the plant, bracts should be removed the moment they have lost their sparkle.

New plants can be made by taking cuttings in warm, moist conditions in the spring. Top cuttings with about four leaves attached should be dipped in a rooting hormone and potted singly in small pots filled with moistened peat. Maintain an even temperature of 65–70°F and keep in a propagating unit until rooted. These are hungry plants that must not be allowed to remain pot-bound for too long, so they should be removed from their pots occasionally so that the roots can be inspected. When potting becomes necessary, a soil-based potting mixture should be used.

## Pests and Diseases

**Red spider mite** This is the chief pest which attacks the acalypha. Initially, the signs are dull green leaves with tiny spots.

## Ideal Conditions

### Light and Position

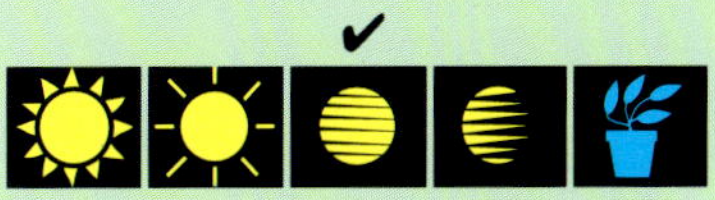

The acalypha likes a bright position, but not one which is continually exposed to bright sun. On the other hand, it cannot tolerate too much shade. Keep it away from a hot radiator, as the dry heat will encourage red spider mites, and out of drafts.

### Temperature Range

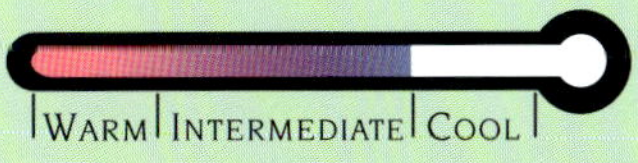


A fairly warm temperature range is required, no lower than 59°F and up to 70°F. Cuttings and young plants require the higher temperatures in the range.

### Watering

The plant will flourish if the soil is kept quite moist at all times, which means extra water in summer when the soil dries out more quickly. The acalypha dislikes standing in water, so water from the top through the soil and discard the excess. A high level of humidity is also required which can be achieved by standing the pot on a tray of damp pebbles and occasionally spraying the foliage.

### Feeding

This is a voracious plant during the active summer months and it will require plenty of food, but as it rests in the winter, it needs no food at all until signs of growth reappear.

### Seasonal Care

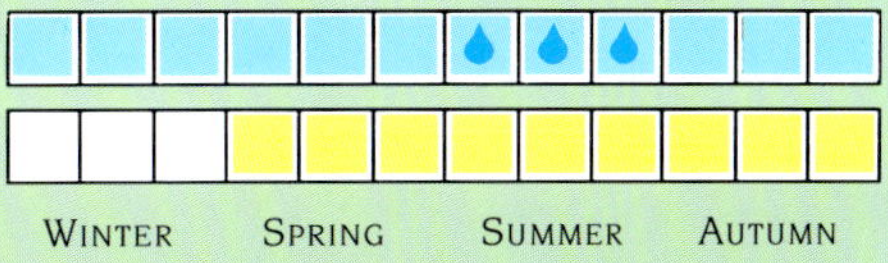


The acalypha is difficult to grow unless the right conditions of warmth and humidity can be maintained. However, there are steps which can be taken to ensure a moist atmosphere and if the plant flourishes it can be propagated from top cuttings taken in the spring.

### Soil

Cuttings do well in small pots filled with fresh peat. When repotting becomes necessary, use a soil-based mixture which can sustain the plant during the growth periods. Remember that moisture is vital to the plant, in the soil and in a humid surrounding atmosphere.

# Achimenes hybrids

## Cupid's Bower, Magic Flower, Nut Orchid, or Hot-Water Plant

This group of plants has quite a few rather attractive common names, but the most familiar is probably hot-water plant. Why use such an unromantic name when there are alternatives? It refers to rather an unusual method of kick-starting the plant into growth. Achimenes plants grow from tubers. Dip these into hot water at the start of the season, put them into a suitable growing soil, and they will start to grow.

However you decide to grow them, you will find achimines easy-going, capable of producing a spectacular flowering display every year. The trumpet-shaped flowers can be blue, purple or pink, or shades of these colors. Some of the hybrids are upright, usually growing to about 12 inches, while others trail and look good in hanging containers. The little potted plants can be grouped together and simply plunged into a large shallow container filled with moist peat or a horticultural aggregate. This way, the plants can be removed and replaced as they begin to lose their vitality, so it is easy to have a long-lasting display.

A collection of achimenes can be increased either by taking cuttings or by dividing the tubers. Take the cuttings during the spring and place them in individual pots containing moistened potting soil. They should root very quickly if kept warm, damp, and out of the sun. Divide the tubers by removing some of the scaly rhizomes when the plants are repotted in early spring. Plant the scales in trays of peat where they will begin to "shoot." Once this has happened, pot the new plants in single pots of potting mixture.

### Varieties and Purchasing

Don't worry too much if the achimenes on display seem to have lost a few of their flowers, as each individual flower only lasts a couple of days. The actual flowering period is extensive so there should be plenty more to come.

There are more than 50 varieties of achimenes hybrids to choose from, so there is plenty of variety. Buy them during the spring and summer from your local garden center or nursery. If you become interested in these undemanding little plants, you might like to ask a specialist grower if they have 'Prima Donna' or 'Pendant Purple,' both super varieties.

## Pests and Diseases

**Aphids** These easy-going little plants are very occasionally troubled by greenfly. They will be attracted to the fleshy new growth at the growing tips of the plant. React immediately by removing the flies with cotton pads soaked in a soap solution, then spray the whole plant with a similar solution or a safe spray. Remember, this biologically safe way of dealing with pests will only eliminate the adult flies, so you have to spray again in two or three days to control their offspring. Try to encourage friendly insects like ladybugs to live among your plants, as they will eat the greenfly absolutely free of charge.

**Healthy Plant**
Look for plants that have plenty of fresh, dark green, velvety leaves. The smaller varieties should be quite bushy; those grown for hanging containers may have stems up to 18 inches long.

## Ideal Conditions

### Light and Position

During their growing season achimenes plants need good light, but no midday sunlight as this will damage their lovely foliage. If small brown spots appear on the leaves, this is almost bound to be the result of scorching.

### Temperature Range

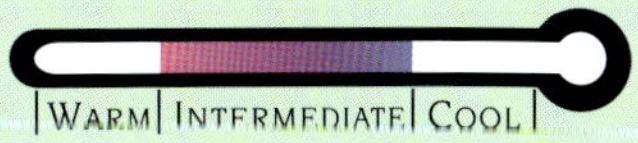


Providing the right minimum temperature for achimenes is not too much of a problem as their main performance takes place during the summer months when the mean temperatures are relatively high. Keep an eye on the thermometer in the early spring when you are starting the tubers into growth – they are very slow to sprout if the temperature drops below 50°F and they might lose their leaves for the dormancy period.

### Watering

As soon as the tuber starts to sprout, provide the plant with enough water to make the potting mixture really moist and keep it that way. Obviously, once it starts to flower, the potting mixture will dry out much more quickly, so the plant must be watered more often, but never allow it to stand in water. When the flowering period is over, gradually reduce the amount of water. During achimenes' winter rest allow the compost to dry out completely.

### Feeding

Use liquid high-potash fertilizer in normal recommended doses in late summer and early autumn.

### Seasonal Care

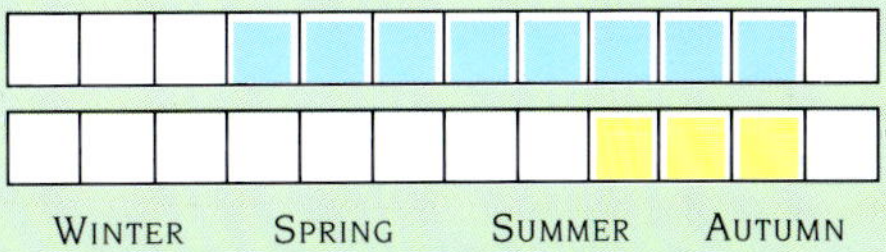


During the tubers' winter rest all they need is to be kept completely dry and frost-free. In the early spring, add water to the compost to kick-start the tubers into growth.

### Soil

Once the tubers have started sprouting in early spring, take them out of their pots carefully and shake off the old soil that surrounds them gently. Place the tubers ½ in below the surface of fresh house plant soil – don't pack the mixture down too tightly as this will cause water-logging.

# Aechmea

## Urn Plant

### Varieties and Purchasing

The greenhouse culture for aechmeas is highly specialized, and it can take as long as five years to bring them to the flowering stage. Because the plants occupy space in the greenhouse for so long, they are quite expensive to buy. Smaller, cheaper plants which are not in flower can be found but are less attractive. Choose a plant which has bracts showing above the urn shape formed by the leaves, but not one which is so advanced that it is flowering from the bract. The tough, leathery leaves are not easily damaged, so it should not be a problem to find a good-looking specimen.

*A. rhodocyanea* This variety, also known as *A. fasciata*, is produced in large quantity by growers and is the most suitable for growing at home. It is extremely decorative, having gray-green foliage and, as its principal attraction, a fist-sized bract in a true, clear pink which is dotted with tiny flowers of an intense blue. The great benefit of this plant is that the bract remains colorful for a full six months from the time of purchase. When the plant has flowered, the main rosette from which the bract emerged dies off naturally, and smaller plants develop at the base of the main stem. These baby plants can eventually be removed and potted individually, but it may be several years before a plant propagated in this way will flower. An attractive way of displaying an aechmea is to wrap the roots in damp sphagnum moss and wire it to a natural or chiseled hollow in a piece of bark.

*A. fulgens discolor* This is a much smaller plant than *A. rhodocyanea*, with a more open rosette and leaves with a dull green upper surface, but red underneath. The scarlet bract is also more open, but if it is put in a group of plants, it produces an interesting contrast of color, shape, and texture. The flowers are purple and spread along the stem.

Originating from tropical South America, this is not only one of the most exotic flowering houseplants, but also one of the most durable. Its foliage is very coarse and edged with quite vicious spines, and its coloring varies from light gray to dark red. The recurving and overlapping leaves form into a natural watertight urn shape, which gives the plant its common name of Urn Plant. In the plant's natural jungle habitat, this urn fills with rainwater or heavy dew which, together with insects, twigs, and other debris, can provide nutrients and water for the plant for many months in the event of drought.

## Pests and Diseases

In keeping with the general tolerance and easy care of this tough and durable plant, you will find that it is rarely visited by pests.

**Mealy bug** This may attack older bracts. Gently remove the bugs with a small toothbrush dipped in denatured alcohol.

Perhaps the most spectacular time in the life of the aechmea is when, after a number of years, it produces its fascinating bracts. These may vary in shape, becoming studded with tiny flowers that are mostly intense blue. Additionally, this plant is epiphytic, which means that it grows on trees, by becoming lodged between branches, or around rotting stumps for example.

Although the commercial grower propagates aechmeas from seed in optimum conditions, this is not advisable for amateurs. It is much better to remove offsets from the base of mature plants that have flowered and to pot them individually in a very loose mixture of peat and perlite.

**Healthy Plant**
The curving leaves should be tough, grayish-green, and the bract a clear pink with no sign of browning. A fully grown leaf may be 12 inches in length. The cup-like center from which the flower stalk rises should never be allowed to dry out.

## Ideal Conditions

### Light and Position

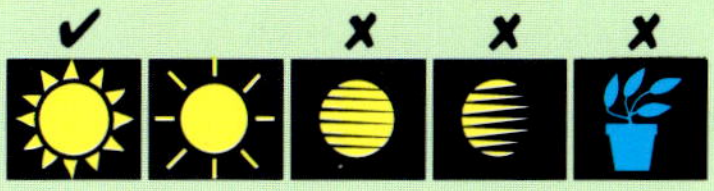


The Urn Plant is a bromeliad, and these usually object to a dark location. In good, strong light with partial sun, it will be found that the leaf coloring is bright and attractive. Although the plants are tough, do not place them in drafts or near heating appliances.

### Temperature Range

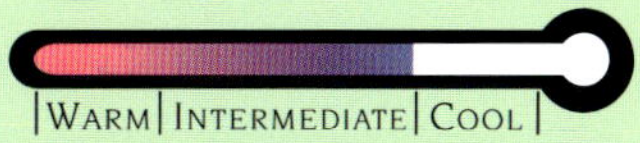


The plant is not especially fussy about temperature, and a moderate to warm range of 59–70°F suits it very well. A slight change at either end of this scale will be tolerated, but do not subject the plant to extremes of hot or cold.

### Watering

Leave about 1 inch of water in the central rosette, changing it every three weeks. Keep the soil just moist. It has no special requirements for humidity, but the watering will tend to encourage a moist, rather than dry, atmosphere.

### Feeding

It is not essential to feed this plant, but occasional liquid fertilizer, via the funnel or urn, added to the water will do it no harm. If something seems wrong, do not resort to extra feeding. Check the temperature and look for pests.

### Seasonal Care

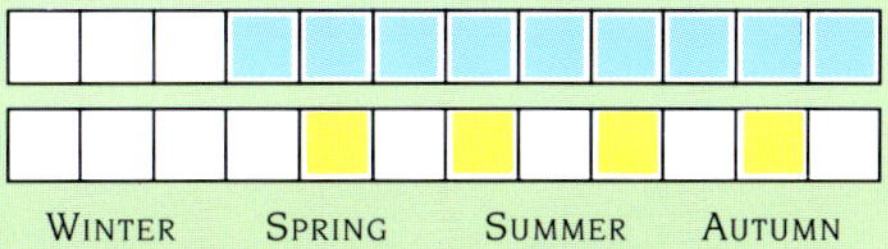


Despite its exotically tropical appearance, the Urn Plant is quite easy to care for, requiring only regular, but not excessive, attention to watering. As the plant develops, the old flower bract can be cut away, and in time the parent rosette can also be discarded. New rosettes are put into small pots and may be repotted before flowering. The plants are usually trouble-free.

### Soil

It is vital to provide free drainage through the soil, so use an open mixture. Equal parts of a peat-based mixture and peat, worked together with a little fresh sphagnum moss, will be ideal. Pot on only every other year.

# Aglaonema

## Chinese Evergreen, Silvered Spear, and Painted Drop-Tongue

Most aglaonema plants are compact and low-growing, with congested leaves borne on short stalks that are produced at soil level. A. *pseudobracteatum* has a more branching habit and is much less common, and therefore more difficult to find. An important quality of most aglaonemas is their ability to grow where there is very poor light.

New plants can be propagated at any time by splitting large clumps into smaller sections and potting them independently.

**Healthy Plant**

*A. crispum* 'Silver Queen' (below, left) is an excellent plant for indoor use. It gains its name from the silvery markings of its foliage. Its leaves are usually between 5 and 6 inches long. The plant looks extremely attractive. Although it does require warm conditions, it will tolerate a very shady position.

### Varieties and Purchasing

When buying, avoid plants with brown leaf margins, as this shows that the plant has been raised in poor conditions and kept in too cold a temperature. It is best to select a young plant with firm leaves.

*A. modestum* This is the true Chinese Evergreen, but it is a rather dull plant.

*A. crispum* 'Silver Queen' This has a blotched silver and green foliage.

*A. treubii* This has cream and green mottled leaves.

**Healthy Plant**

*A. treubii* (below, right) has mottled cream and green markings on its leaves. Although it is perhaps not so exciting to look at as *A. crispum* 'Silver Queen,' it is still relatively popular with houseplant enthusiasts.

## Pests and Diseases

**Mealy bug** The congested leaves and stalks of the aglaonema provide ideal conditions for mealy bug. Rather than spraying with insecticide as normal, it is better to mix the insecticide (malathion) in a watering can and apply through a large-holed nozzle.

**Root mealy bug** These small pests can only be found by removing the plant from its pot. Apply insecticide. Malathion is recommended.

**Botrytis** This fungus is directly related to low temperatures and poor ventilation. Move the plant, having removed badly affected leaves.

**Leaf spot** For leaf spot disease, spray the plant with an appropriate fungicide.

**Cold conditions** The leaves of this plant have been damaged through cold – make sure you keep your aglaonema at the correct temperature. The warmer they are, the better they grow.

## Ideal Conditions

### Light and Position

The aglaonema will tolerate poor light with no ill effects, but must not be exposed to direct sunlight as this may scorch the leaves. It is seen to best effect when grouped with other more colorful plants.

### Temperature Range

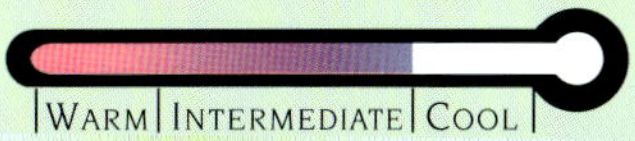


This plant must not be placed in cold conditions. A warm room anywhere between 59–70°F is suitable, but an aglaonema will grow more vigorously if the temperature is even higher than this. Any slight chill may cause leaf discoloration.

### Watering

Aglaonemas should be watered regularly so that the potting mixture stays moist. Only the very surface should dry out between waterings. In the winter months the plants will require slightly less water. If the roots become too wet the leaves will begin to wilt. Humidity can be increased by placing trays of moist pebbles under the pots.

### Feeding

Established plants should be given a liquid fertilizer each time they are watered if they are to flourish well. Again, less food is necessary during the dormant winter period. The fertilizer should be administered in a fairly weak solution.

### Seasonal Care

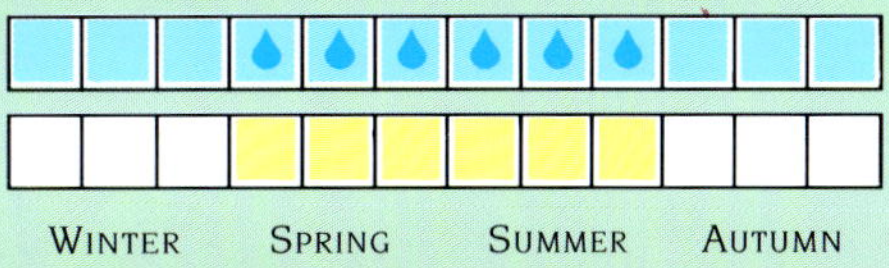


If kept in suitable conditions, aglaonemas tend to stay healthy. Aglaonemas should be kept away from windows and drafts throughout the winter months, and whenever the weather is very cold.

### Soil

A peaty mixture is needed for aglaonemas, and repotting should be avoided in winter if possible. The pots that are used should not be too large, as these plants grow best when their roots are confined in quite small containers.

# Allamanda cathartica

## GOLDEN TRUMPET VINE

Anyone who has seen this lovely climber in flower will agree that its common name describes it perfectly. Although it is called a climber, it is more likely to sprawl or lean, which makes it a good plant to grow on a trellis or a pillar.

Coming from Central America, allamanda's main demand will be for warmth during the winter months, when the temperature should not be allowed to drop below 61°F. During this low-temperature period, allamandas should be given their annual prune.

Provide more allamandas by taking 3–4-inch long tip cuttings of fresh growth during the early spring. Plant these in moistened potting soil and make sure the air around the plant remains moist by keeping them in a propagating case, or by covering the rim of the pot with a plastic bag. Keep the cuttings warm – around 70°F should be fine – and keep them in bright light but out of direct sunlight. New growth will start to appear as soon as the roots have started growing; then remove the cuttings from their moist atmosphere, water them enough to keep the soil moist, and allow them to grow on.

**Healthy Plant**
The healthy sheen on the glossy, bright green leaves is unmistakable. The flowers appear in clusters at the end of leaf stalks through the summer and well into the fall, which is when you will see them for sale. They are usually trained around hoops, but despite the fact that their stems are tough, they are very flexible so are easy to unwind.

### VARIETIES AND PURCHASING

They can be bought at good garden centers and occasionally at florists, but you may have to visit a specialist grower for some.

*Allamanda cathartica* 'Grandiflora' This is the variety you are most likely to find.

*A. nerifolia* This is slightly more unusual; it has the same large, clear yellow flowers, but is more of a shrub than a climber.

## Pests and Diseases

**Mealy bug** (right) These plants are usually quite resilient, but they are sometimes attacked by mealy bug. The adult bugs look like tiny pink wood lice; they lay their eggs protected within white wooly nests. Take immediate action by wiping away adults and young with a cloth moistened with denatured alcohol. You may wish to resort to a chemical spray of some kind – malathion is very effective, but remember you will have to spray more than once as it only controls the adults.

**Yellow leaf** From time to time, allamandas may lose a considerable number of leaves; they simply turn yellow and die. This is quite normal, though unsightly; pruning the naked stems by half will encourage new leaf buds to break.

**Collar rot** Mature allamandas have stout, quite woody stems, whereas the stems of young plants are fleshy and soft. Collar rot is a fungus that attacks soft fleshy stems in damp conditions, like those present on the surface of a healthy potting soil. The plant will inevitably die as the base of the stem rots away. Help to prevent this by scattering horticultural grit on the surface of the soil around the stem of young allamandas.

**Honeydew** This sticky coating is a secretion from sap-sucking insects. Check the plant for infestation and wash the leaves with a diluted solution of soapy water.

**Scale insect** Remove with an old toothbrush and wash the whole plant with soapy water, repeating one week later.

## Ideal Conditions

### Light and Position

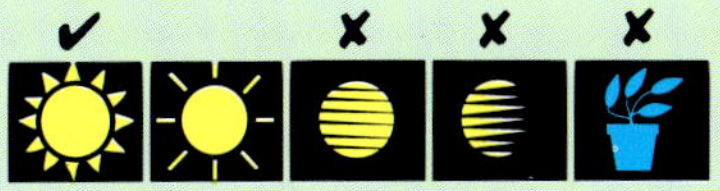

Allamandas love strong direct sunlight, for two or three hours a day in summer whenever possible. If the allamanda is grown in a sunroom, encourage the plant to grow up into the roof space; it will love it there and provide the plants below with some natural shade.

### Temperature Range

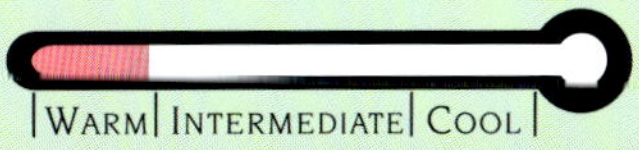


Winter minimums around the 61°F mark are vital to the well-being of allamandas.

### Watering

Provide allamandas with moderate amounts of water during the spring and summer, allowing the top ½ in of compost to dry out between waterings. In winter only give enough water to prevent the soil from drying out completely. They like to be grown in a moist atmosphere, so mist the plant regularly with soft rainwater. If this presents a problem, stand the plant in a tray containing a dampened horticultural aggregate. The moisture from this will gradually evaporate as the temperature rises, providing just the sort of humidity that an allamanda thrives on.

### Feeding

Feed allamandas with a liquid fertilizer once every two weeks during the growing season.

### Seasonal Care

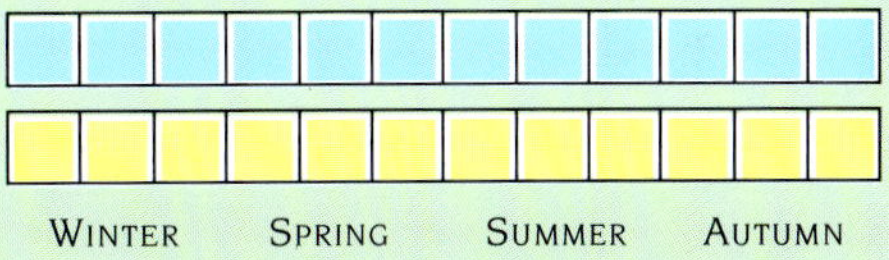


During the growing season allamandas can make a huge amount of growth. They will need an annual prune in early spring, not just to keep them under control but because pruning also encourages new growth to break out along the stems, and it is the new growth that carries flowers. Pruning will kick-start the plant into growth, so start giving it extra water as soon as the pruning has been completed.

### Soil

Allamandas prefer a soil-based mixture, which provides them with good drainage. They will grow best in a large planter or a border. Repot annually. When the maximum pot size has been reached, top-dress annually.

# Aphelandra

## Saffron Spike or Zebra Plant

Having grayish green foliage with silver markings, the aphelandra is one of the more attractive foliage plants. Its appearance is further enhanced when colorful yellow bracts are produced at the top of each growing stem. The small, yellow, tubular flowers are fairly insignificant, but the bracts remain colorful for many months, making the aphelandra a spectacular, long-lasting plant. There are now two worthwhile varieties of the original plant, which comes from Mexico. A. *squarrosa Brockfeld* is the more robust plant, while A. *squarrosa* Dania is smaller but flowers more prolifically.

New plants are propagated by removing the top section of the stem with two opposite pairs of leaves attached, or by removing a pair of lower leaves with about an inch of stem above and below where the leaf stalk is attached. Use moistened peat and sand mixture, make sure the temperature is not less than 70°F, and keep in a propagator or sealed within a plastic bag.

**Healthy Plant**
Avoid buying plants which have a yellow look to their foliage (left). The bracts tend to attract greenfly and the leaves scale insects, so both should be checked.

### Varieties and Purchasing

*A. squarrosa Dania* This is the most readily available type of Zebra Plant. It is also the variety best suited to normal room conditions as it needs less care and growing space than some of the other kinds of aphelandra. It is quite difficult to make *A. squarrosa Dania* flower, but the dark green leaves have very pretty silvery markings.

*A. squarrosa Louisae* (see illustration right) The leaves of this plant are 8-12 inches long, and it has broad, conspicuous orange-yellow flower bracts. When buying this variety (which is also known as Saffron Spike), make sure that the flowers are not too far advanced. The flowers themselves should not be visible along the edge of the bract.

*A. squarrosa Brockfeld* This is a compact plant with dark green leaves.

*A. chamissoniana* The variety has close-set leaves which are 4–5 inches long. Its flower bracts are yellow, narrow, and pointed.

## Pests and Diseases

Despite its tough appearance, the aphelandra is vulnerable to a number of pests and should be examined regularly.

**Scale insect** These look like miniature limpets and are skin-colored when young, and dark brown or yellow when mature. They attach themselves to the undersides of the plant's leaves and to its stem. Excreta falling on lower leaves encourages sooty mold fungus. This blocks the pores of the leaves and considerably weakens the plant. Scale insects can be removed by wiping the leaves with a firm sponge or small brush dipped in a soapy solution. Alternatively, the plant can be sprayed with dimethoate. Take care with these chemicals – always follow the manufacturer's instructions exactly.

**Aphids** These are frequently found on the bracts of the aphelandra. They can be removed fairly easily with one of the standard insecticides.

**Sciarid fly** Often known as fungus gnats. They tend to occur when the potting mixture becomes excessively wet and sour, depositing their larvae in the soil. Most of them are not harmful, but some may damage the roots of the plant. Drench the soil with a liquid insecticide such as malathion.

**Springtails** These pests are so-called because they jump around on the top of the soil. They are white, wingless insects, usually harmless but occasionally gnawing at the stems of young plants. They can be removed in the same way as fungus gnats.

**Red spider mite** This is not a common problem, but red spiders will attack aphelandras that are growing in very hot and dry locations. Spray the undersides of the leaves with insecticide.

**Black leg** This is a fungus that attacks cuttings at rooting stage. Throw affected plants away.

## Ideal Conditions

### Light and Position

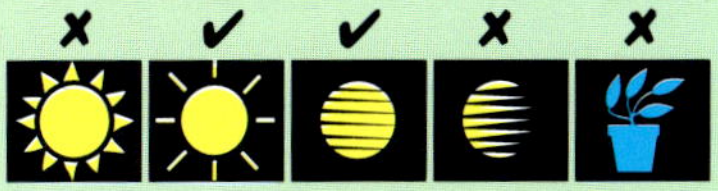

The aphelandra is an exception among flowering plants in that it does not require full light in order to flourish successfully. Good light is needed, but not full sun. The plant should be given plenty of room in which to spread its leaves.

### Temperature Range

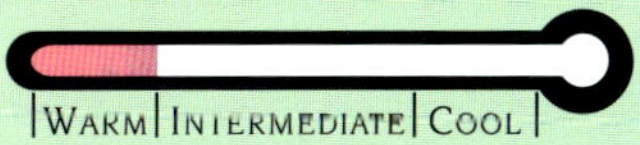


Warm temperatures of 65-70°F are essential; this is a plant which is particularly vulnerable to a cool environment.

### Watering

The aphelandra must be watered regularly, although over-watering may encourage botrytis and should be avoided. If the plant is allowed to dry out, the leaves will rapidly fall. Less water can be given for a few weeks after flowering to allow a period of rest. A humid atmosphere is also appreciated. The pot can be packed with moist peat or left to stand on a tray of pebbles if the room is normally dry.

### Feeding

This plant produces a mass of roots and is a heavy feeder. Liquid fertilizer should be supplied through the soil, and it is possible to double the recommended strength of the feed without harming the plant.

### Seasonal Care

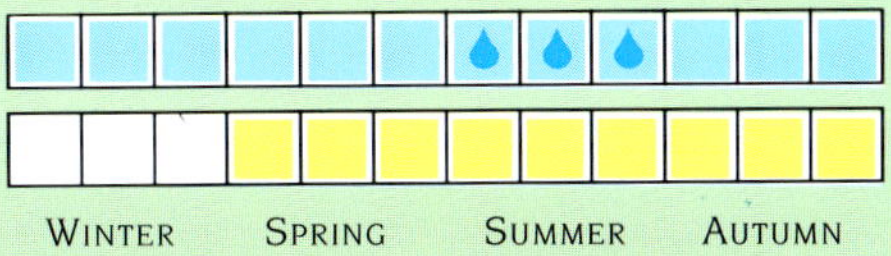


The only real variation in the treatment of this plant is after flowering, when it can be kept at the cooler range of its preferred temperatures and given less food and water while it rests. It is not a plant which can survive neglect, but provided its basic needs are satisfied, it is not as difficult to keep as is sometimes imagined.

### Soil

Pot on an aphelandra soon after purchasing, using a soil-based potting mixture. The plant must be firmly potted and at a later stage can be potted on at any time of year other than the coldest winter months.

# Aspidistra lurida

## Cast Iron Plant

In the business of houseplants, new varieties come along from time to time, eventually making the grade and being retained, but the aspidistra is a plant that, although popular in Victorian times, has made its mark through being able to withstand practically any adverse environmental condition. It is very easy to care for, but slow to mature.

New plants are made by dividing established clumps and potting them individually. Either single pieces or clusters of leaves can be potted, with the latter producing better plants more quickly.

### Varieties and Purchasing

Choose a plant of full appearance with lots of stems and an elegant arching shape. Do not buy plants with split or speckled leaves or leaves that have been cut back.

*A. lurida* (or *A. eliator*) This is the only species in cultivation and is known as the Cast Iron Plant because it will survive in tough conditions.

*A. l. 'Variegata'* Very like the parent plant, this has white or cream stripes on some of the leaves.

**Healthy Plant**
Seen at their best, as lone specimens in an attractive china pot, aspidistras provide a fine display of dark green or green and white striped arching leaves. The aspidistra can flower unexpectedly in late winter or early spring, but this event is by no means frequent – say once every 7 years.

## Pests and Diseases

These plants rarely suffer from pests, which normally find the leathery leaves too tough to penetrate.

**Damaged leaves** Over-feeding may be the cause of split and damaged leaves. Feed only when in active growth, and if your leaves show signs of splitting, reduce the number of feeds by half. Speckled or damaged leaves often indicate that the plant has not been watered correctly.

**Red spider mite** These will cause the leaves to turn brown and will produce white webs on the undersides. Spray with an appropriate insecticide. Most leaf problems are caused by too much sunlight or overfeeding.

**Browning** This indicates that the leaf has been scorched. It may be too close to a heat source or in a position where it receives too much direct sunlight. Cut away unsightly leaves and move plant if necessary.

**Mealy bug** These may occasionally attack this plant. If white wooly patches appear, remove them one at a time with a piece of cotton dipped in denatured alcohol or spray with an insecticide such as malathion.

## Ideal Conditions

### Light and Position

Aspidistras will grow in very little light, but will do best in a moderate light – in a window with not much sun, for example. The striped variety will need more light, but neither type of plant should be placed in direct sunlight as this will soon scorch the leaves.

### Temperature Range

These plants will usually thrive in a wide range of temperatures – between 55–70°F – and they can therefore be kept almost anywhere in the house. They will even survive below this range, provided that they are kept free from frost.

### Watering

Water these plants moderately throughout the year, allowing the top two-thirds of the soil to dry out before watering again. Water less in the winter months.

### Feeding

These plants do not require much feeding. Apply liquid fertilizer once every two weeks in the growing period, but stop feeding for the rest of the season if the leaves start to split.

### Seasonal Care

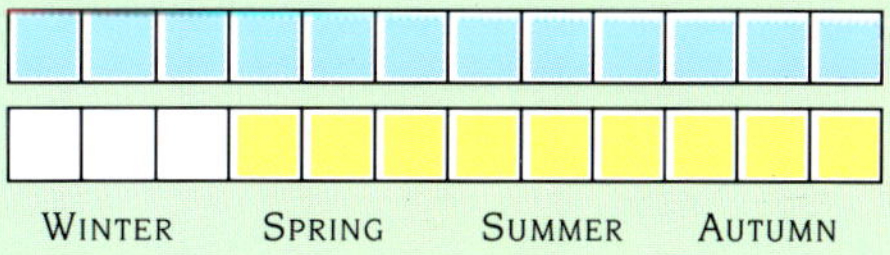


One of the main advantages of the aspidistra is that it requires much less care than most other houseplants. Water it a little more frequently in the growing period and feed it occasionally. The plant will need less water in winter. New plants can be grown by splitting off clumps of stems in the spring when the pot is overcrowded. Each section of the rhizome will need at least two leaves. Do not feed the new plants until the following spring.

### Soil

Use a soil-based mixture. Aspidistras rarely need repotting and can be top-dressed once they reach the best size for the pot for several years. Very old plants are best left in their original pots. Remove new shoots and some roots if necessary.

# Azalea indica

## FLORISTS' AZALEA

There is nothing that can compare with A. *indica* as a specimen plant in full flower. The oval-shaped leaves are small, coarse, and evergreen; the flowers, which grow at the ends of branches, may be either single or double, with their color ranging from pristine white to dull red. There are also splendid multicolored varieties. Most of the better plants start their life in Belgium, from where they are shipped all over the world. In temperate climates, azaleas flourish as garden shrubs, but they do well in pots either outdoors or inside the house.

**Healthy Plant**

One of the most beautiful of the winter flowering plants, many azaleas flower naturally in spring, but are often forced into bloom for the Christmas season. They are very slow-growing plants, which is one reason why they are often expensive to purchase. Situated indoors in individual pots, azaleas always look attractive with their rich clusters of pastel or deeply hued colors displayed against deep green foliage.

### VARIETIES AND PURCHASING

If carefully tended, the azalea can be one of the most rewarding of all the flowering houseplants. Because they are one of the few plants which flower in winter, they are usually seen in abundance in florists' shops from late fall onward. Selecting a healthy specimen is important if the plant is to survive. A healthy plant will be clean and bright in appearance. Some of its flowers should be open, but there should also be an abundance of buds. Tempting as it may be, avoid plants which have opened entirely. On the other hand, avoid those with small, underdeveloped buds, or no buds at all. When lifted, the pot should feel heavy and wet, which is how it should remain for the rest of the plant's life.

*A. indica* This is a common azalea and the one which is most easily available. It includes many variations of color and is usually chosen for this quality and its general decorative appearance. *A. indica* needs a humid environment and should be sprayed with lime-free water every day.

*A. obtusum* This plant is known as the Japanese Kurume. It is not as easy to force into bloom as *A. indica* and is thus not available to buy until its natural flowering period in late winter. *A. obtusum* has small flowers that nestle among the leaves of the plant. It makes a fine potted plant with its clear, pink flowers. It can be planted outdoors following indoor flowering, whereas *A. Indica* must be carefully guarded from frost.

## Pests and Diseases

Azaleas are prone to few pests and diseases, which makes them easier to care for than other plants. There are, however, signs of ill-health which should be heeded. If the leaves dry and fall, the environment is too hot and dry. Spray the plant with lime-free water and move it to a cooler place. Buds which fail to open mean the plant is either in a draft or waterlogged. Move to a new location and water less frequently.

**Dehydration** Azaleas need copious amounts of water all the year round. When they do not receive enough, their leaves and flowers will wilt. The best way to water an azalea is to submerge the pot in a bucket of soft, tepid water. Let it rest there until all the bubbles have stopped coming out of the soil. Now set the plant aside to drain.

**Aphids** These may collect on the soft new leaves of your azalea; they are easy to see and control with a soapy water spray. Remember that these sprays will only eliminate the adults, so you will have to spray again three or four days later. Prevention is better than cure, so check your plants regularly for signs of infestation.

## Ideal Conditions

### Light and Position

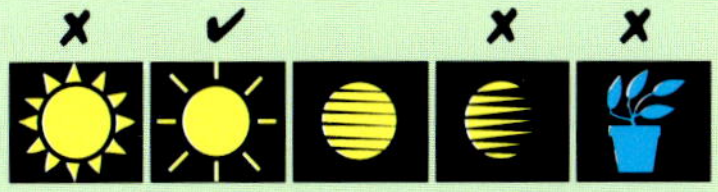

Azaleas can be grown both indoors and out, and in both cases need a light location out of direct sun. If there is danger of frost, azaleas must be brought indoors. So they will survive from one year to the next, azaleas should be put outside during the summer months.

### Temperature Range

Azaleas prefer cool temperatures of between 50–59°F which will mean that the plants should continue to flower abundantly. When moved indoors, the temperature in the room should not be allowed to rise above 50°F, or the plants will dry out.

### Watering

When in flower, azaleas need copious amounts of lime-free water which should be given every two days. Never let a plant dry out; check it at least twice a week. If dry, plunge into a bucket of tepid water until beads of moisture appear on the top soil.

### Feeding

A weak liquid fertilizer given at regular intervals will help maintain lush, green foliage, but avoid heavy applications. When in flower, add fertilizer to the water every two weeks.

### Seasonal Care

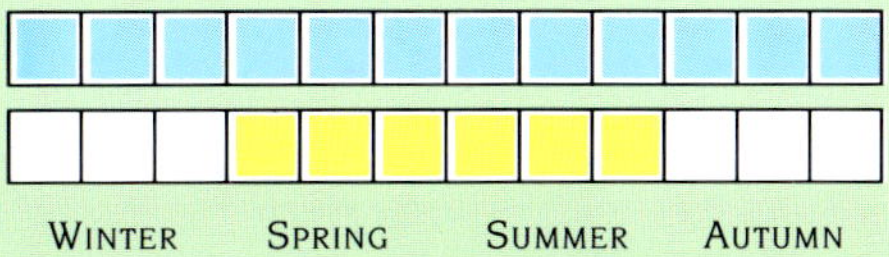


Much greater than the danger of pests and diseases is that of neglect, especially neglecting to water the plants adequately. At all stages of development, whether indoors or out, the roots of the azalea must be kept wet. In late spring, the plants can be moved outside. Plunge the pots to their rims in a bed of wet peat in a shady location. Bring the plants indoors before the first frost. Avoid pruning, as this will result in fewer flowers the following year.

### Soil

Potting should be done in the spring with a commercially prepared azalea soil. Press the mixture firmly around the rootball, water it well, and place the plant in a shady location.

# Begonia

Among the most exotic of all foliage plants, B. *rex* can have many color combinations on the upper sides of its leaves, while the undersides are mainly reddish brown. Although mature plants can produce a few clusters of single pink flowers, these are not their main attraction, as the *rex* type begonias are simply foliage plants. The leaves remain healthy for a reasonable time after they have been cut from the plant, making them useful material for inclusion in more colorful flower arrangements.

New plants can be raised from leaf cuttings, for which there are two methods of preparation. The first and simplest way is to remove a firm and unblemished leaf and cut the veins on its back in several places with a sharp knife or razor blade. The leaf should then be placed, plain side down, on a bed of moist peat and sand in a shallow box or pan, with a few small pebbles on the leaf to hold it in position. The new plants will grow out of the knife cuttings. The other method is to cut up the mature leaf into sections about the size of a large postage stamp and place these about an inch apart on a similar bed of peat and sand. From then on, the temperature must not fall below 70°F, and the atmosphere should be moist but not heavily saturated.

There is a large variety of begonias which creep or climb, and almost all of them have decorative foliage and long-lasting, colorful flowers. Many can grow to a

**Healthy Plant**
Two attractive examples of *B. rex*. The plant is kept for the beauty of its colorful leaves, and for these to show to best advantage, it should have a compact shape. The effect is undermined by straggling stems and untidy, formless growth.

**Foliage begonias**
There is so much variety in leaf color within this plant family – red to delicate pink, dark and light green through to subtle silvery grays – that you can make a super display using just a few plants to provide extra color and texture, or with flowering varieties which will complement the various hues.

## Varieties and Purchasing

When buying a begonia of any type – whether foliage, those with woody, trailing stems known as the cane types, or a flowering variety – always look for a clean, unblemished plant, making sure there are no signs of pests.

*B. rex* The varieties of these attractive foliage types are too numerous to mention. Visit a retailer with a good selection and choose the most pleasing. If the plant is quite large and crammed in a small pot, be sure to re-pot it as soon as possible or the plant will deteriorate through lack of nutrition from the soil.

*B. glaucophylla* This is one of the cane type begonias, a plant of natural trailing habit, with light green leaves. In late winter and early spring, it produces clusters of orange flowers.

*B. haageana* Another cane variety, this plant has brownish leaves with a hairy texture and pale pink flowers. The plants are easy to manage, becoming very bushy and reaching a height of up to 6 feet in time. The flowers appear almost continuously.

*B. 'President Carnot'* This is probably the best of the cane type begonias. It has brownish-green leaves and during many months produces large clusters of pink flowers. Properly cared for, it can reach 6–8 feet.

*B. hiemalis Reiger* This is a flowering begonia with soft and brittle growth which is easily damaged. Inspect the leaves to make sure there is no sign of botrytis and choose a plant with plenty of buds and only a few flowers fully open, so that the best is still to come.

*B. tuberhybrid* These can be bought as pot plants or as tubers to be potted. Select firm tubers which are clean and healthy. If choosing a growing plant, look for one with a few buds about to open so the color of the flowers can be determined. A mixture of unnamed varieties can be bought quite cheaply in tuber form. The list of varieties of the tuberhybrid begonias is extremely lengthy, and new specimens are being added all the time. To take up serious cultivation of these plants, take advice from a specialist grower and go to see the plants at their best in a good, comprehensive flower show.

**Healthy Plant**

*B. hiemalis Reiger* (left) is an exotic, colorful variety which, given good care, will flower consistently during its life. The heavy green leaves give a rich contrast to the luxurious red flowers.

**Healthy Plant**

Flowering cane type begonias (below) are beautiful plants, with their rich leaves and clustering, delicate flowers. The begonias need regular feeding and sufficient water, or they may suffer from starvation.

height of 6–8 feet, while others are shrubby or trailing plants.

Given proper care, there are few plants that can produce flowers quite as spectacular as the tuberous begonias when they are grown as potted plants. The best of these are invariably grown from tubers, and good-quality named varieties can be very expensive. Tubers are started into growth in early spring in boxes filled with moist peat, at a temperature around 65°F. When clusters on the shoots and a few leaves have formed, the young plants are transferred to 5-inch pots filled with a peaty mixture in which they may be grown for the season, or more vigorous plants can be advanced when they are well rooted to pots of 7 inches in diameter.

There is a completely new strain of begonia that goes variously under the names of *Reiger* or *Schwabenland*. As the names suggest, it originated in Europe. Initially, they were mostly red with single flowers, but now they are available in many colors with both single and double flowers. The foliage is glossy green and very dense, so that there are many branching stems, all of which bear flower clusters providing a rare wealth of color. They are ideal room plants that can flower throughout the year, though fewer flowers are produced in winter.

New plants are raised from cuttings. These should be from the top of the stem with two or three leaves attached and all the flowers removed. A mixture of peat and sand and a temperature of around 70°F are needed.

## Pests and Diseases

Because of their thick sappy stems, watch out for fungal attack. Keep a check on their temperature and ventilation requirements.

**Overwatering** Too much water coupled with low temperatures will cause leaves to wilt and turn brown.

**Botrytis** This is a fungus that attacks plants kept in cool, damp conditions. Remove and destroy affected leaves and move the plant to a warmer spot; if necessary, treat with a fungicide.

**Discoloration of leaves** Check your feeding regimes if leaf tips become yellow or brown and flowers become prematurely discolored. Begonias are robust growers and in season need regular feeding and watering.

**Milew** This white "bloom" caused by badly ventilated conditions. Although it is unattractive, it is not too damaging; in bad cases, remove and destroy affected parts of the plant and improve ventilation.

## Ideal Conditions

### Light and Position

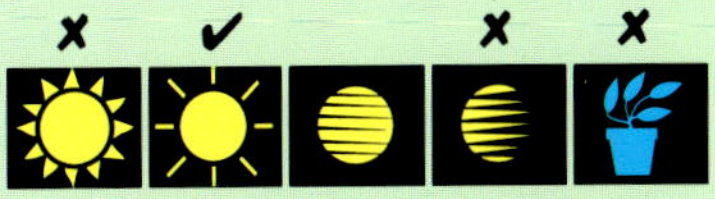

Fibrous-rooted and rhizomatous begonias, grown primarily for their foliage, require bright light but not direct sunlight. Tuberous begonias need bright, indirect light all the year round.

### Temperature Range

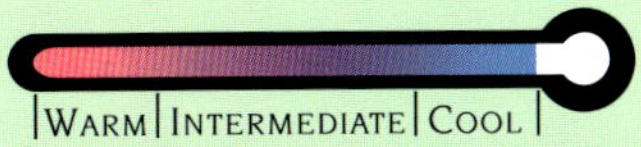


Fibrous-rooted, rhizomatous, and tuberous begonias all do well in normal room temperatures of around 60°F. In winter, dormant tuberous types should be kept at 55°F. In normal conditions, cane types should be kept at 55–70°F; *B. hiemalis reiger* around 59°F; *B. rex* 59–70°F, and *B. tuberhybrid* 55–60°F.

### Watering

Begonias do not like dry air. The plants can be stood in their pots on moist pebbles, or, if hanging, saucers of water can be suspended beneath. During active growth, water moderately allowing the top 1 inch of soil to dry out. Reduce watering as growth slows down. If in doubt with begonias, water less rather than more.

### Feeding

For actively growing plants, apply a standard liquid fertilizer every two weeks. Cane types should be liquid fed, erring on the side of too much. *B. hiemalis*, *B. rex*, and *B. tuberhybrid* should all be fed a weak mixture with each watering.

### Seasonal Care

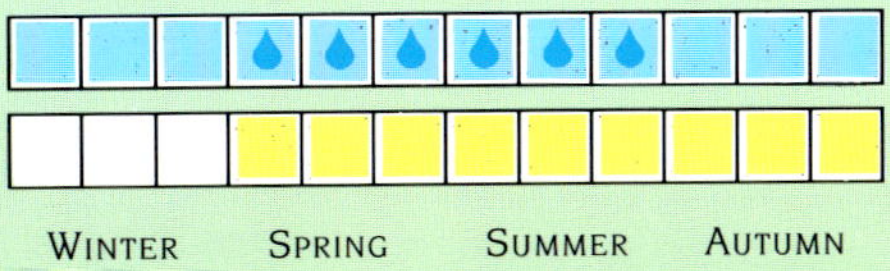


In winter, *B. rex* requires limited watering. Cane types require year-round attention, with dying petals and leaves removed to avoid fungus. Avoid overwatering *B. hiemalis reiger*. After flowering in late summer, *B. tuberhybrid* should have the foliage removed and the corm stored in a frost-free place in dry peat until early spring.

### Soil

For *B. rex*, use peaty mixtures and keep the plants in pots large enough for new growth. *B. hiemalis reiger* does best in mixtures without soil; avoid repotting into pots too large. With cane types, use a soil-based mixture.

# Beloperone guttata

SHRIMP PLANT

This self-contained little plant comes from Mexico. It is grown not for its foliage and flowers, but for the attractive reddish-brown bracts. Given good light, these shrimp-like bracts will produce an abundant display almost all the year round.

New plants are propagated from firm top cuttings about 4 inches long, with all bracts removed. They are put in a peat and sand mixture in temperatures of around 70°F, and like begonias, B. *guttata* requires moist, but not saturated, conditions.

## Varieties and Purchasing

*B. guttata* is an easily grown little plant that is widely available during the summer, when the flowering bracts will be seen at their best. Other than the commonly found Shrimp Plant, there are two slightly more unusual varieties, one with yellow bracts and the other with red ones. Check that the plant you buy is robust and bushy; although naturally quite lean and delicate, it should not be leggy. The bracts should be strongly colored; any fading or thinning indicates poor plant care, and such plants should be avoided.

**Healthy Plant**
The common name Shrimp Plant refers to the unusual bracts, dark red at the base and shading gradually to light green at the tips. These are produced during most of the year, and in summer they contain small white tubular flowers. The Shrimp Plant does thin out as it grows in height, but should not be bought in this condition, as a new plant which has been well cared for will appear quite bushy. The Shrimp Plant is not very demanding as long as it is given good light and adequate water during its summer growing period.

## Pests and Diseases

**Underfeeding** Limp leaves with browning tips indicate that more feed is necessary.

**Aphids** These greenfly are found on the softer top leaves of the plant. Their activity weakens the plant, and in addition they secrete a sticky substance called honeydew which is unsightly and unpleasant. The flies should be easily disposed of by spraying the plant with malathion.

**Whitefly** This common and persistent pest attacks the undersides of leaves to suck sap from the plant. They multiply quickly, and treatment must be repeated to be effective. Spray the plant with a safe soap spray at least four times, with four-day intervals between each spraying. If whitefly persist, treat with Malathion.

**Red spider mite** These flourish in warm, dry conditions. They must be treated at an early stage, but they are difficult to see with the naked eye. Look out for mottled, drooping leaves which indicate the presence of mites on the plant. Isolate the plant to prevent the problem from spreading, and spray the undersides of the leaves with malathion. Unfortunately, if the mites have really taken hold and formed small webs, it is too late to treat the plant with any insecticide, and it is better to remove and burn the badly affected areas or, indeed, the whole plant if necessary.

**Mealy bug** These little insects are like woodlice with a white, floury coating. On a Shrimp Plant, the bugs are easily visible and accessible and can be removed with a sponge soaked in denatured alcohol. Direct contact with this kills the bugs immediately. A malathion spray may be effective in killing the adult insects, but wiping should also remove the protected young, freeing the plant completely.

**Black leg** This is a fungus which may attack cuttings of this plant if they are allowed to get too wet before roots have formed. The only sensible remedy is to remove and burn the affected cuttings and treat the surrounding soil with streptomycin.

## Ideal Conditions

### Light and Position

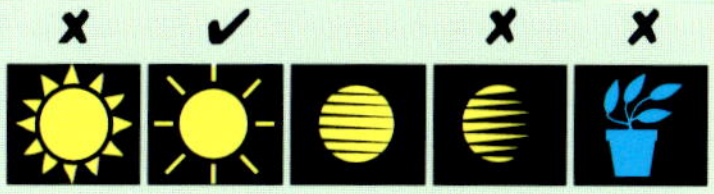

The Shrimp Plant needs plenty of light to maintain the color of its bracts and encourage flowering but, in common with many plants, it must be protected from direct, hot sunlight. It will not tolerate continual shade or a cold, drafty position.

### Temperature Range

The plant is fairly tolerant with regard to temperature, enjoying a range between 55–70°F. Extreme conditions of heat or cold are not usually good for any houseplant, and the Shrimp Plant is no exception. It will prefer the cooler end of the temperature range during winter.

### Watering

Water can be added to the soil from the top of the pot. This is a plant which likes moist conditions, but not saturation. If the soil is allowed to become too dry, on the other hand, the leaves will quickly droop, so watering should be frequent in summer.

### Feeding

Frequent, regular fertilizing is essential for a well-established plant. If the plant develops yellowing, curled foliage, it is probably suffering from chlorosis (iron deficiency) and should be treated by watering the soil with a special iron solution.

### Seasonal Care

Active plants require ample watering during summer months and may need almost as much during the winter, since the soil must not be allowed to dry out. The Shrimp Plant has a tendency to become rather spindly, which can be countered by pinching out the growing tips of a young plant to encourage bushiness. When the plant needs pruning, this can be done following the main summer flowering, or in the spring when it moves into a more active period of growth..

### Soil

It may be necessary to repot a strong, young plant twice in its first year, and in general, frequent repotting is essential. Use a soil-based potting mixture and pot the plant firmly. For propagating top cuttings, use a peat and sand mixture.

# Bougainvillea

PAPER FLOWER OR PAPER VINE

In their natural tropical environment, the brilliant flowers of the bougainvillea can outshine almost everything in sight. Its strong stems have vicious barbs and carry thin and insignificant foliage, but the defects of the plant are more than compensated for when it flowers throughout the summer. It would be misleading to suggest that the bougainvillea is the ideal houseplant. It can be most frustrating as it is very reluctant to produce flowers in a situation that offers only limited light. However, they can be grown successfully in a sunroom or bay window.

New plants are raised from cuttings taken in spring, using 3-inch sections of stem with a heel of older wood attached. A minimum temperature of 70°F is essential if the cuttings are to survive.

## VARIETIES AND PURCHASING

*B. glabra* This is the species most easily obtained in nurseries and florists. It has purple bracts which appear in summer and fall. There are several variegated sorts, including *B.g.* 'Harrisii,' which has leaves streaked with cream, and *B.g.* 'Sanderana Variegata,' which has cream-bordered leaves.

*B. buttiana* This is the original parent of several hybrid bougainvilleas which are now very popular as it is easy to train them into shrub form. They are happy in most indoor locations and are therefore very suitable as houseplants.

**Healthy Plant**

(left) The decorative papery bracts of the bougainvillea make it a most attractive plant. If the plants receive plenty of light, they can make a very effective display, especially if trained to wind around a tall framework. Choose clean plants with some open flowers and clusters of flowers about to open.

## Pests and Diseases

Bougainvilleas are fairly tough plants and do not suffer a great deal from pests. However, it is as well to watch out for the following:

**Aphids** These can quite often be found on the tips of new growth. They suck the plant's sap, making the leaves turn yellow, and in extreme cases causing distortion. They also secrete a sticky substance called honeydew, upon which an ugly sooty mold may grow. Aphids also carry incurable viruses. They can be controlled by regular spraying with a soap solution.

**Mealy bug** This often attacks older plants in the greenhouse, but is less frequent in the house, unless it is brought in on the plant. The open leaves of the plant make detection of mealy bug an easy matter. The adults are a powdery-white and resemble woodlice. The young are wrapped in a protective waxy coat and tend to be attached to the more inaccessible parts of the plant where the branches intertwine.

## Ideal Conditions

### Light and Position

Maximum light is vital to the bougainvillea, so place it in a sunny window, right against the windowpane. There is a chance that it will be scorched by the sun, so keep an eye on the leaves, though scorching is a minor risk.

### Temperature Range

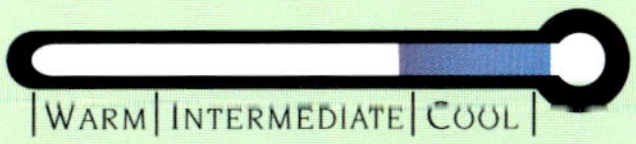


Temperature is not crucial during the plant's period of active growth, but should probably remain at 55°F or above if possible. While the bougainvillea is dormant in the winter, a cooler temperature of 50°F is preferred. Although it requires plenty of light and enjoys the sun, it will not be the better for being allowed to bake.

### Watering

Water the plant from the top of the pot, but do not leave it standing in a full saucer. The soil should be moist while the plant is in active growth, but it will not require water during the winter until new growth begins to appear.

### Feeding

Suitable feed for the bougainvillea is fertilizer containing a high proportion of potash. Again, this is not necessary during the winter dormancy, but is vital in spring to encourage new growth. Use a liquid fertilizer when the plant is watered.

### Seasonal Care

Whereas many plants need less food and water in the winter, the bougainvillea can go for two or three months without any nourishment and then requires further attention when new growth starts in early spring. If the plant becomes straggly, it can be gently pruned in the fall, but flowering is better if growth is wound around established stems and tied back.

### Soil

Use soil-based potting mixtures. Bougainvilleas can be potted on in spring once new growth has begun. A pot of 8-inch diameter is ample, and when the plant has reached this stage, sustain it by fertilizing.

# Browallia speciosa

## Sapphire Flower or Bush Violet

Browallias are short-lived annuals, but as these little plants provide a spectacular flowering display and are simple to grow, it is easy to forgive their shortcomings. In shades of blues and purples, their flowers have open faces at the ends of narrow tubes. They appear singly and only last a short while, but they appear in such profusion that the plant is constantly covered.

Mature browallias, already in flower, can be bought, but they are not difficult to grow from seed. Start the seeds in March or April for fall flowers, or later to produce winter/spring displays. Sow the seed thinly in small pots of damp seed mixture. Place the pots in a propagator or secure inside plastic bags and make sure of an even temperature around 59°F. When the seedlings are about ½ inch tall, remove them from the propagator or plastic bag, water enough to moisten the soil (this is best done with a fine spray while the seedlings are small), and allow them to grow about another 2 inches before transplanting in individual 3-inch pots containing a soil-based potting mixture. Once the roots have filled the pot, move them again, into 5-inch pots.

For a hanging basket or massed display, six or eight plants can be used to fill a larger pot.

**Healthy Plant**

A mature plant from a garden center should be well rounded and bushy. The bright green leaves are naturally slightly drooping and are carried on very short stalks. A healthy plant should have plenty of flowers, and there should be evidence of many more to come. Always check these purchased plants for harmful insects. Greenfly is common on browallias, collecting on the growing tips, so select a plant that is quite clean.

### Varieties and Purchasing

These little plants can be bought almost anywhere. Take care with those bought from non-horticultural outlets; they may well have been subjected to poor standards of watering and sudden variations in temperature which is likely to cause buds and flowers to drop.

*Browallia speciosa* 'Major' is worth trying. With violet-blue flowers, it will grow to 2 feet.

*B.* 'Silver Bells' This carries white flowers.

## Pests and Diseases

**Aphids** Like many greenhouse annuals, browallias are particularly prone to attack from greenfly, which cluster around buds and shoot tips. Act quickly, these sap-sucking insects multiply at a phenomenal rate; where you can see one, there are bound to be more. Wipe off those you can see with a cloth soaked in a diluted soap solution and then spray the whole plant.

There are effective biological predators for greenfly – a parasitic wasp, *aphidus*, and a predatory gnat called *aphidoletes*. The gnat eats almost any sort of greenfly, while the wasp prefers some species more than others, but acts more quickly. As with any form of biological control, never resort to a chemical back-up, since this will wipe out the predator, too.

**Danger signs**
This Browallia has suffered some form of fungal attack. The diseased or dying leaves should be removed and destroyed. Plant diseases thrive in cool, damp conditions, so check the plant's environmental needs and act accordingly.

## Ideal Conditions

### Light and Position

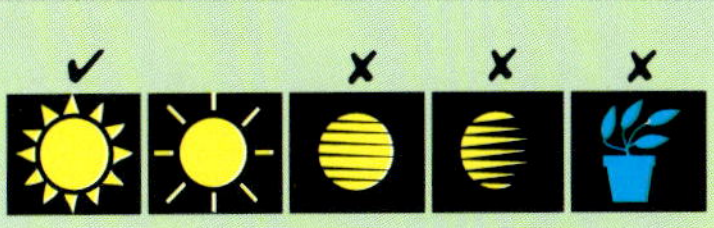

Once mature, browallias need strong light, two or three hours of direct sunlight a day whenever possible. Seedlings will need to be kept out of direct sunlight, but they do need good light.

### Temperature Range

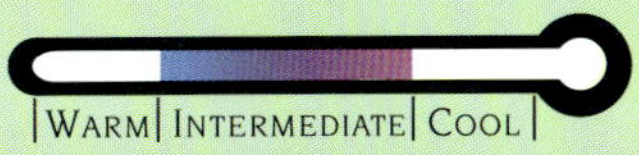


Anything much higher than 61–63°F while flowering will make the buds drop, which will in turn shorten the flowering period. While raising seedlings, maintain a minimum temperature of 50°F.

### Watering

Water browallias freely while flowering, providing as much as is necessary to moisten the soil thoroughly at each watering but allowing the top ½ in of potting mixture to dry out before watering again. At other times allow the top ¾ in to dry out between waterings. Remember that while browallias are growing freely in good strong light, the compost will dry out very quickly during warm weather, so they may need plenty of watering attention. Although these little plants thrive in normal humidity levels, hot dry air may cause bud drop. Help to prevent this by standing the pots on trays of horticultural aggregate, or by regular spraying with soft rainwater.

### Feeding

Once the plants have started flowering, provide normal doses of liquid fertilizer at two-weekly intervals.

### Seasonal Care

Pinch out growing tips from time to time to encourage bushier plants. Provide good winter light when growing on winter seedlings. Dispose of plants after flowering.

### Soil

If grown from seed, the plants will need to be started in seed soil and then moved to a soil-based potting mixture as they mature. Mature plants purchased from a garden center will not need repotting at all.

# Brunfelsia pauciflora

## YESTERDAY, TODAY, AND TOMORROW PLANT

Brunfelsia pauciflora (syn. Calycina) acquired its common name because its sweetly scented flowers last three days. On the first day they are deep blue, by the second they will have faded to a pale violet, and by the third they will be almost white. Each flower is flat and open, about 2 inches wide. Well looked after, the plant should always have a couple of flowers, but the main show is during the spring and summer.

It is easy to propagate this little shrub by taking 3–5-inch tip cuttings. Dip the cutting in rooting hormone and plant in a 3-inch pot of dampened peat and perlite or sand. Place in a propagator and maintain an even temperature of 68°F. As soon as new growth starts appearing, remove the cutting from the propagator and grow on, watering enough to keep the soil moist and providing a liquid fertilizer once every two weeks. When the roots have filled the pot, move the growing plant into a pot one size larger, using a soil-based potting mixture.

### VARIETIES AND PURCHASING

Until recently, brunfelsia plants were only available through specialist nurseries, which made these plants rather expensive. Public demand has made them more freely available through good garden centers; even if they are not on show, it should be possible to order one at almost any time of year.

Increasing popularity has encouraged growers to produce hybrids, some of which have none of the original scent, so look for *Brunfelsia pauciflora* or *B. pauciflora* 'Macrantha' to be assured of perfume.

**Healthy Plant**
Potted brunfelsias grow into stout bushy shrubs, finally about 2 feet tall. The evergreen leaves are 3–6 inches long and have a glossy, leathery appearance.

## Pests and Diseases

Sadly, brunfelsia are prone to both scale insects and mealy bugs. Both insects are sap-suckers and will seriously weaken and finally kill the plant if left untreated.

**Mealy bug** Adult mealy bugs wander freely over the plant, increasing their number by laying clutches of eggs protected within wooly nests. Wipe both nests and adults away with a cloth moistened with denatured alcohol, or a diluted soap solution, immediately.

**Aphids** (top) These sap suckers must be controlled with soapy sprays or an appropriate insecticide.

**Sooty mold** is a direct result of pest attack. Clean the leaves with a soapy solution.

**Scale insects** Their presence is also easy to spot. Look for brown raised scales on the undersides of the leaves; the insects themselves are protected underneath the scale, so they need rubbing off as soon as you see them. Having done this, wash the whole plant with soapy water, repeating the process one week later. Bad infestations may need treatment with dimethoate. Very often, honeydew and sooty mold are side effects of scale-insect infestation. The sticky honeydew is a secretion from the insect itself, sooty mold a result of the honeydew. The recommended soapy wash will remove both.

**Scorched leaf** Although Brunfelsia needs direct light to flower, water will scorch the leaves.

## Ideal Conditions

### Light and Position

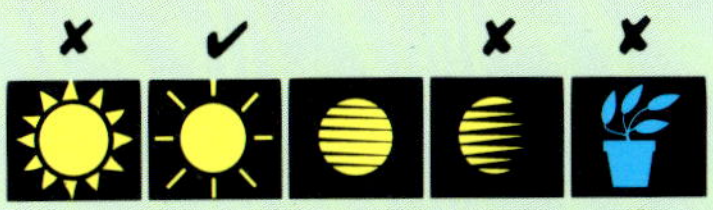

Brunfelsias need light shade during the summer, the sort they will get if they are placed beneath another taller plant. During the winter months they need stronger light, if possible two or three hours of sunlight a day.

### Temperature Range

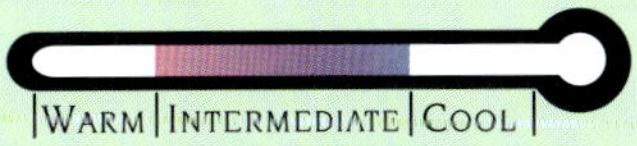


A minimum winter temperature of 50°F is perfect for these plants while they are resting. Given a slight boost to 59°F in the early spring, the plant will start to produce new growth in preparation for the summer flowering display.

### Watering

Water freely during the spring and summer when the plants are actively growing. Give as much water as is necessary to keep the soil thoroughly moist at all times. During their resting period they need the bare minimum of water, so provide only enough to prevent the soil from drying out completely.

Brunfelsias will really thrive if the air around them is kept moist, so give them a daily spray with soft rainwater. Alternatively, stand their pots on trays of moist aggregate.

### Feeding

Plants kept at temperatures higher than the recommended winter minimums will need a liquid fertilizer once every two weeks throughout the year. Those plants kept cool during the winter will not need feeding at this time.

### Seasonal Care

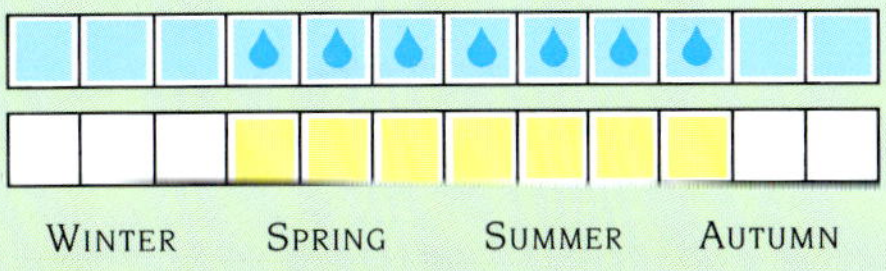


To encourage the plants to produce new flowering wood and to keep them within their allotted space, they will need a really good prune in early spring. Using sharp secateurs, remove as much as half of the previous season's growth.

### Soil

Brunfelsias like to be firmly planted in a soil-based soil. Provide extra drainage in the form of broken shards at the base of the pot. Repot annually at pruning time until the final pot size is reached, thereafter top-dress.

# Bulbs and corms

Many houseplants come into this category. Conveniently they fall into two distinct cultural groups: hardy plants, which in reality can withstand frost but are raised indoors temporarily, purely for their short-lived flowering displays after which they are usually planted outside; and far more permanent indoor plants, which are always kept indoors during cold weather and which, looked after correctly, will live and bloom indefinitely.

All these plants grow from a fleshy organ – the bulb or corm – from which roots are produced and in which food and water are stored.

The hardy bulbs and corms are bought dry and potted up in the fall, and many will have been specially prepared for early flowering. By using these as well as unprepared bulbs and corms, indoor flowering displays can be prolonged. The flowering of individual bulbs only lasts for two or three weeks.

### Potting Hardy Bulbs and Corms

These temporary visitors must be potted as soon as they are bought. Otherwise they will probably begin to sprout, which will prevent them from producing a

## Hardy Bulbs Varieties and Purchasing

*Crocus* These heralds of spring are familiar to everybody. They are not difficult to grow in pots, brought indoors only to flower and fill the late gray days of winter with a breath of what is to come.

The potted corms must be kept cold until flower buds begin to show. When flowering is finished, they can be planted out in open ground.

Choose the big-flowered varieties from the enormous selection available, and plant only one type of crocus in each pot, as different color hybrids may flower at different times.

*Narcissi* Daffodils must be the easiest hardy bulbs to bring into flower indoors. Remember to use a peat- or soil-based mixture and not bulb fiber if you want to plant them outside afterward. Just follow the general instructions for flowering bulbs. Try to choose some of the lovely miniatures or the exquisitely scented varieties.

**Healthy Plant**

If you plant them in the fall and keep them cool and dark for 8–10 weeks, you can beat the weather and have these lovely spring flowers indoors weeks before they appear outside.

good flowering display. Peat, or soil-based potting mixture, or specially prepared bulb fiber can be used. The latter is clean and easy to handle. As it is extremely porous and therefore very suitable for watertight containers, it is good for the bulbs. However, do not use bulb fiber if you intend to plant your bulbs outdoors after flowering.

Before planting, water the soil or fiber, making sure that it is thoroughly moist. Place the bulbs or corms close together but not touching, half-buried with their necks well above the surface. Store them in a dark, unheated place, such as a garden shed or a cupboard under the stairs. If you have nowhere suitable, stand them in a shady position outside and cover them with damp peat.

### After Care

By subjecting the potted bulbs or corms to these cold dark conditions, they are obviously deprived of warmth and light. This encourages the bulbs or corms to make roots, but little or no top-growth. Check them from time to time to see that the soil is still damp, but generally speaking they will need little or no care for eight to ten weeks.

When the bulbs or corms have produced leaves 2–3 inches tall, bring them into the light and maintain a temperature around 45°F until the leaves have made another 3–4 inches of growth.

With the exception of crocus, which must remain as cool as possible until the buds open, the bulbs can be brought into the warmth – maximum temperature 65°F – once the leaves are 4–5 inches tall.

### Potting Permanent Indoor Bulbs

These remain in their pots of soil-based potting mixture throughout the year. Although they have a resting phase when the potting mixture is kept relatively dry, they are never allowed to dry out altogether. Plant the bulbs singly in pots that are about 1½ inches wider than the bulb. Set the bulb in the pot so that one-third of it is above the surface of the soil, which should be packed firmly around the bulb and kept evenly moist.

## Ideal Conditions

### Light and Position

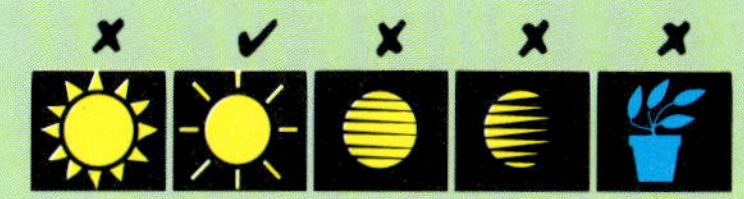

Keep crocus in bright light but out of direct sun.

### Temperature Range

A maximum of 61°F – cooler if possible.

### Watering

Provide enough to keep the soil moist but allow the top 1 inch to dry out between waterings.

### Feeding

Provide liquid fertilizer once every three weeks during spring and summer.

### Special Care

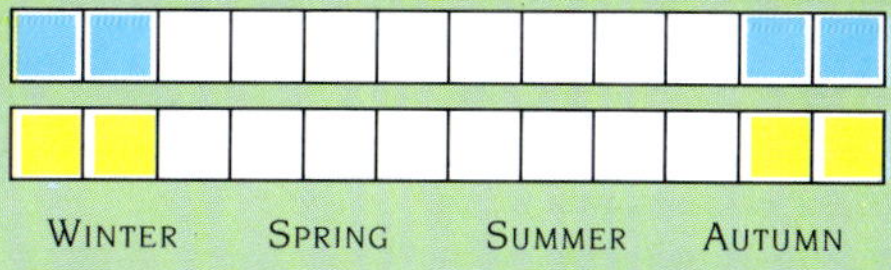


May need staking.

**Healthy Plant**
For a lovely show like this, you must keep crocus corms as cool as possible right until the last minute. Only bring them indoors when the buds are opening.

## Permanent Indoor Bulbs
## Varieties and Purchasing

*Crinum* These large bulbs have long necks. With bulbs of this size, sometimes more than 6 inches in diameter, the flowering display is pretty spectacular. The strap-shaped leaves last for a year, only dying when there are fresh new leaves ready to replace them. The trumpet-shaped flowers are borne at the tops of 2–3 foot long stalks. They are held in groups of between five and eight, each bright pink flower being 3–5 inches long. They are extremely impressive, and the flowering period lasts for about a month.

Crinums are available prepacked at good garden centers, or they can be bought from one of the many bulb specialists. Try to find *C. bulbispermum* or *C.* 'Powellii.'

*Hippeastrum* This is another extremely popular permanent indoor bulb, often incorrectly referred to as amaryllis, which is quite a different plant, although it belongs to the same family. They differ from crinums as they have a truly dormant season when all the leaves die. The specially prepared bulb you buy will be in this dormant state; follow the instructions, give it a little tender loving care, and it will flower. The trick is to make them flower the following year, too.

The bulbs are sold in pots of soil for the Christmas season. They are also available loose in garden centers or already in bud.

Such is their popularity that plant breeders have produced so many hybrids that they are now sold by color and not by their definitive name.

## Ideal Conditions

### Light and Position

**Crinums** need three to four hours of direct sunlight every day.

### Temperature Range

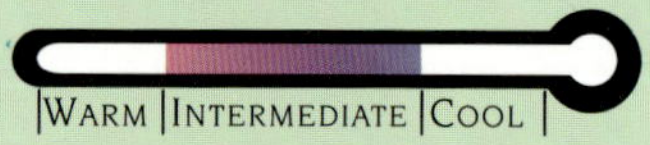


**Crinums** do well at normal room temperatures, but need an annual winter rest at about 50°F.

### Watering

**Crinums** Provide plenty of water during the summer months, but never allow the pot to stand in water. During their winter rest they only need enough water to prevent the mixture from drying out completely.

### Feeding

**Crinums** Provide liquid fertilizer once every three weeks during spring and summer.

### Seasonal Care

**Crinums** Allow a cool winter rest at 50°F. Trim off yellowing portions of leaves; remove entire leaves only when they become messy. Crinums only need re-potting once every three or four years.

### Soil

Use a soil-based mixture for these bulbs, and add plenty of clean shards to the base of the pot for extra drainage.

**Healthy Plant**
Buy the large Hippeastrum bulb in its dormant state, pot it in a soil-based potting mixture, and watch it grow.

**Healthy Plant**
The flowers produced by the huge crinum bulb are quite magnificent (far left). They are trumpet-shaped and carried on 2-3 foot stalks. The flowering display lasts about a month.

## Ideal Conditions

### Light and Position

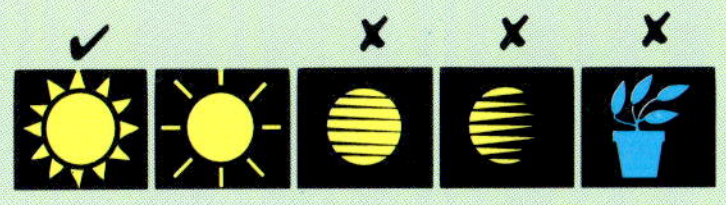

Hippeastrums need bright light with some direct sun during their growing season. Provide them with too little light and the bulbs will produce too much leaf, thus forfeiting next year's flowers. Place them in continuous bright light from the time the flowers fade until the middle of the fall.

### Temperature Range

Stable room temperatures will quickly bring a hippeastrum into flower; too much heat will shorten the life of the flower.

### Watering

Newly potted, the soil should be kept barely moist. When new growth appears, start providing more water, allowing the top half of the potting mixture to dry out between waterings. Once in full growth, provide enough water to keep the potting mixture thoroughly moist at all times. As growth slows down, gradually reduce the amounts of water, until mid-autumn when watering should be stopped completely.

### Feeding

Use a liquid fertilizer once a week from the time the flowers have finished until mid-summer. After this, use a tomato fertilizer once a week. Stop feeding in mid-autumn.

### Seasonal Care

Prepare the bulbs for dormancy by removing all the dried foliage. Leave the bulbs in their pots and store them in a dry place where the temperature does not drop below 50°F. Hippeastrums do not need re-potting regularly. At the first signs of growth, take them out of their pots, remove a little of the soil from above and between the roots, and replace in the same pot, working fresh soil into the spaces made.

### Soil

Use a soil-based potting mixture for these bulbs, and add plenty of clean shards to the base of the pot for extra drainage.

# Cacti and succulents

For most people, the fascination with cacti begins at an early age. This is no doubt why more of them are sold during school vacations than at any other time of the year. Surprisingly, sales of these plants exceed those of any other kind of potted plant, with much of their popularity due to their interesting shapes; and the fact that they are easy to grow and never very large means that a considerable collection can be kept in a relatively small area.

There are two distinct groups of cacti – the desert cacti that come mainly from the desert regions of the American continent, and the forest cacti, all of which have smooth foliage, except for the Rat's Tail Cactus, *Aporocactus flagelliformis*.

**Healthy Plant**
*Trichocereus* or White Torch Cactus (right) is a fast, strong grower. Under the right conditions, it can reach 3 feet. The flowers are large, nocturnal, and white.

**Healthy Plant**
*Echinocereus*, the Hedgehog Cactus (left). There are about 35 species of this cactus, grown for their colorful flowers and attractive spines. All echinocereuses are ribbed, the ribs varying in size and shape according to species.

## Varieties and Purchasing

With succulents, always look for fresh plants that are free of blemishes and pests. Large plants are frequently sold in smallish pots; in such a case, re-pot the plant as soon as you get it home. Cacti are particularly prone to pests – especially mealy bug – so always go to a reliable dealer and check the plant carefully before buying it. Dry brown marks on foliage are not harmful, but do not buy plants with wet brown areas at the base of their stems. Also check cacti carefully for stability. They are sometimes sold with very little root or incipient basal rot, both of which show up through a little gentle movement.

*Astrophytum* This is a globular desert cactus. There are two main varieties – *A. capricorne*, or Goat's Head, and *A. myriostigma*, Bishop's Hood. This keeps its globular shape for about two years, after which it becomes cylindrical. From three years on, it flowers, each flower lasting a day or so.

*Epiphyllum* The two varieties generally available – *E.* 'Ackermanni' and *E.* 'Cooperi' – are both hybrids crossed with other jungle cacti. 'Ackermanni' produces flowers liberally through the year; 'Cooperi' is a plant which flowers at night.

*Lithops* These pebble-like succulents are given the common name Living Stones because of their appearance. Their shape is ideally suited to desert conditions. One of the chief characteristics of many succulents is their rosette shape, which acts as a water-conserving aid in nature.

*Echinocereus* The Hedgehog Cactus is a very popular houseplant because of its attractive flowers and spines.

*E. pectinatus* is slow-growing, taking more than five years before it reaches maturity.

*Hamatocactus setispinus* is a colorful single-stemmed desert cactus. It gets its common name, Strawberry Cactus, from the fruit it bears after flowering.

**Healthy Plant**
The *Notocactus leninghausii* (above) is recognizable through its mass of dense yellow spines, which tend to lie flat on the top of the plant facing the sun.

**Healthy Plant**
*Euphorbia pseudocactus* (above) is a succulent that looks very much like a true cactus. It has spines along its ridges and can grow up to 5 feet tall.

**Healthy Plant**
This opuntia (right) shows all the characteristics of its family, with its prominent ribs, long columnar stem, and closely packed areoles. These are made up of small bristles, so take care in handling.

A few of the desert cacti are extremely difficult to care for, but in the main, they are very tolerant plants that will survive however badly they are treated. Unfortunately, the common belief is that cacti should be given minimal attention in order to get the best from them. Provided the temperature is reasonable during the winter months, spartan treatment will not do very much harm, but during the rest of the year all the plants will respond very much better if they are given a little extra attention.

Propagation of new plants is not difficult either, which must also contribute to their popularity. To produce new plants in quantity, the best propagation method is to raise them from seed. Ideally, the seed should be fresh and sown as soon as it becomes available. Shallow seed boxes filled with a well-drained mixture will give them a good start. Keeping the seeds in a temperature in the region of 65°F will be

**Healthy Plant**
*Echeveria glauca* (left) and *Echeveria setosa* (below) are both good plants for beginners as they require little attention. They are among the easiest cacti to propagate, too, as cuttings root extremely easily. Take these in late spring or early summer. You might like to try growing these cacti from seed – it's not difficult.

enough to germinate them, and they should have the lightest position available, with airy rather than stuffy conditions.

### Succulents

Very varied, the succulents embrace a multitude of differing forms and have among them plants with the most subtle coloring. The echeverias in particular offer a wide range of metallic colors, and make a fascinating collection of plants by themselves. Ranging in size from the tiny sedums to the giant aloes, succulents are excellent plants for the beginner. They will adapt to a wide range of conditions and even seem to thrive on periods of neglect, the main problems with succulents nearly always being due to overwatering.

Not all, but most, succulents can be propagated with little difficulty. The stems as well as individual leaves of many can be removed and allowed to dry before being inserted in a sandy mixture in reasonable warmth. Wet soil conditions at any time can be damaging for succulents, but during the rooting stage of cuttings it can be positively disastrous.

**Healthy Plant**
*Echeveria gibbiflora* (above) This little succulent can grow to 2 feet. Its spoon-shaped leaves form a rosette at the top of a short stem. These leaves are extremely delicate, so take care when watering as even the tiniest drops of water may scorch them or, in extreme cases, cause rot.

## Pests and Diseases

Both succulents and cacti are prone to various pests and diseases; cacti are more susceptible than succulents. In the former case, there is an added problem; frequently cacti fail through too much attention. The most common example is giving the soil too much water while the plant is dormant and unable to take up the moisture.

**Mealy bug** This affects both succulents and cacti. In the former, it can be controlled by spraying with insecticide, though always check suitability first. Cacti often need the individual bugs dabbed with a thin paintbrush moistened with denatured alcohol. Alternatively, plants can be drenched with malathion.

**Root mealy bug** This is almost always present on older succulents and forest cacti. Thoroughly drench the soil with malathion.

**Scale insect** On cacti, these resemble tiny shells tightly clamped to the skin of the plant. Treat with insecticide.

**Red spider mite** Always treat this pest as soon as possible with insecticide. By the time its characteristic webs appear, it is very difficult to eradicate.

**Botrytis** Wet rotting patches around the base of the stem and, to a lesser extent, higher up the plant indicate this fatal fungus disease. If possible, cut out the infected area and treat with a fungicide. Otherwise, remove undamaged sections and use as cuttings for fresh plants.

## Ideal Conditions

### Light and Position

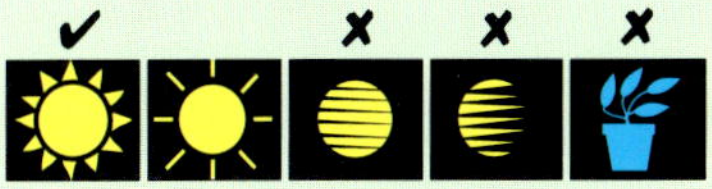

A sunny windowsill is ideal for most succulents, with the exceptions of the haworthias and gasterias, which like quite a shady position. Desert cacti need as much sun as possible. Forest cacti like light, but need to be shaded from the sun.

### Temperature Range

Unlike most other houseplants, succulents thrive if the temperature varies between day and night. They do well at a modest average temperature of between 55–65°F. In general, desert cacti like the same basic temperature range, though they should be kept at the lower temperature in winter. It is a fallacy that cacti like excess heat; desert nights are often cold. Forest cacti thrive between 55–59°F.

### Watering

Water succulents well from spring to fall, letting them dry out between each watering In winter, reduce to the absolute minimum. Desert and forest cacti should not be watered at all from late fall to early spring. Then, water as succulents.

### Feeding

Feed well-established succulents with weak liquid fertilizer every week, if necessary, but not in winter. Feeding is not essential for cacti, though a little will not hurt the plants.

### Seasonal Care

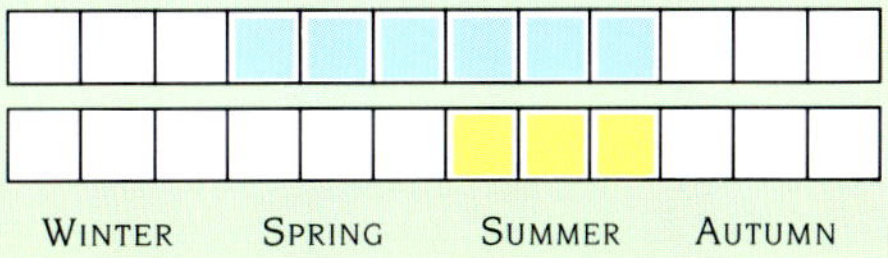


Succulents need fresh air, especially in summer. Trim back overgrown non-flowering plants in the fall and flowering ones after they have flowered. Use a shallow pot, not a deep one, and repot only when essential. Desert cacti, too, require fresh air. Repot young plants annually into slightly larger pots to give roots space to spread. Forest cacti need misting in summer. Repot annually after flowering, with the exception of epiphyllums which flower better if kept in quite small pots.

### Soil

Commercially prepared cactus soil is certainly best for these plants. Both types of cacti grow well in the same basic mixture, though some varieties need more specialized ones.

# Calathea makoyana

CATHEDRAL WINDOWS

**Healthy Plant**
(left and below) It is easier here to talk of an unhealthy plant – being kept in too much light will cause the leaves and stalks to brown, the surface of the leaves gradually becoming covered in large beige-colored, papery patches. Both the leaf and stalk will die. Leaves with brown tips and margins mean that the plant has been subjected to dry air or hard water. If the lowest leaves are turning yellow, it could mean that the plant has been kept too cold. Obviously, it would be unwise to buy a plant with any of these characteristics.

## VARIETIES AND PURCHASING

Being purely foliage plants, these beauties are on sale all the year round. Always buy from a good garden center where the greenhouse conditions are carefully controlled.

*C. insignis* Also worth looking for. It has multicolored foliage, the leaves being chocolate brown on one side and olive green on the other.

Here is a houseplant that will give pleasure all the year round as it is not grown for its flowers, but for its beautiful foliage. The leaves are oval and handsomely marked with large and small blotches, and dark green lines, all on a silvery green background. The patches on the upper surface of the leaf are darker green than those underneath, which are often almost maroon. All these lovely leaves are held on stalks, which are up to 12 inches long. They also appear to turn slightly so that both sides of the leaf can be seen at the same time.

Calatheas are quite a challenge to grow well as they need very particular light conditions, high humidity levels, high temperatures, and fairly specific watering requirements. However, they will then grow to quite a size.

Once they have become established, propagation is easy. All the leaves rise from a main root stock, and as the plant matures, a clump of roots will form. When the clump gets overcrowded, it simply needs dividing, and early spring is a good time to do this. Divide the stock gently so that some roots remain on each portion. Plant each section in a 3-inch pot filled with moistened potting mixture, cover the rim of the pot with a plastic bag, and keep the new plants in medium light. Remove the bag when roots have formed.

## Pests and Diseases

**Red spider mite** This can be a problem with calatheas. Remember, all houseplant pests dislike a humid atmosphere, so regular mist-spraying with soft rainwater is a way of preventing the pest before it becomes a problem.

Red spider mites are minute red or pink sap-suckers. Although they are hard to see with the naked eye, their fine webs are not. They weave them on the undersides of leaves and between the leaf stalk and stem. If any leaves turn yellow, look for other signs of this insect. If the plant has become affected, cut away the damaged parts and spray the whole plant with derris.

**Environmental problems** All calatheas need a relatively warm, stable, and humid environment to thrive. The foliage is easily damaged by too much light or dry air. Keep your calatheas out of direct sunlight and mist them daily. Rainwater is best for this task as it leaves no unsightly lime deposits.

**Underwatering** A soil that feels dry to touch probably needs water. Add plenty – enough to soak the soil thoroughly. Empty the drip tray an hour after watering.

## Ideal Conditions

### Light and Position

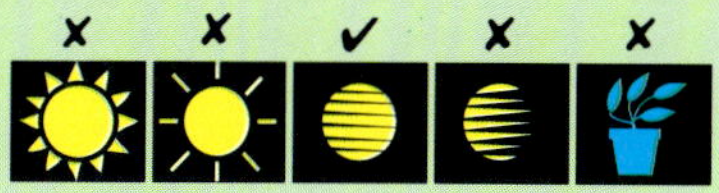


Calatheas prefer to be in a position where they receive medium light, a tree-shaded window for example, or perhaps underneath other taller plants where they will be in dappled shade.

### Temperature Range

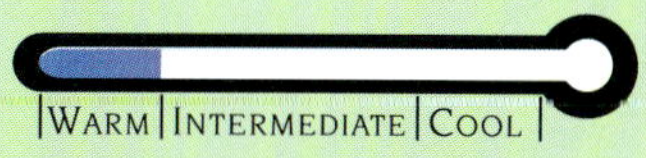


A minimum temperature all the year round of 61°F is ideal. Try not to let the temperature rise above 70°F during the summer.

### Watering

During the spring and summer give calatheas plenty of water, enough to keep the soil thoroughly moist at all times, but remember never to let the plants stand in trays of water. During the winter provide enough water to keep the compost moist, allowing the top ½ in to dry out before watering again.

Calatheas also need high humidity so spray them daily. Whether watering or spraying, calathea plants will do a great deal better if soft rainwater is used.

### Feeding

During the spring and summer provide a liquid fertilizer once every two weeks.

### Seasonal Care

Keep the temperatures even at all times. Never allow the plant to become waterlogged.

### Soil

Repot once every other year using a peat-based potting mixture.

# Chlorophytum comosum

SPIDER PLANT, ST. BERNARD'S LILY, OR RIBBON PLANT

The green and cream grassy foliage of the Spider Plant is extremely popular. This must be because it is extremely easy to grow, and the fact that new plants are so easy to raise from the natural plantlets that are produced on long stalks as the plants mature. When they have grown to a reasonable size, the plantlets begin to form roots at their base even though they are only suspended in the atmosphere. After these roots have developed, the plantlets can be removed from the parent and simply pushed into small pots filled with houseplant potting mixture. It is better to peg the small plantlets down in the potting soil while they are still attached to the parent plant and to cut them away when they have obviously rooted.

## Varieties and Purchasing

Spider Plants are usually sold in small pots, and they are cheap, cheerful, and easy to grow. Selecting a plant is a question of looking for the cleanest and most fresh-looking plant on display. It is sensible to check among the central leaves for pests, such as aphids, which have a particular fondness for the Spider Plant.

*C. comosum Variegatum* is the only variety worth keeping. It is sometimes given the common name St. Bernard's Lily, as well as the Spider Plant.

**Healthy Plant**
A Spider Plant grows well on its own, but also enjoys the company of many other plants and can be an attractive addition to a mixed display.

## Pests and Diseases

**Aphids** These are the main pests which bother the Spider Plant. Leaves that are attacked bear pit marks produced by the probing creatures (see below). Inspect the central leaves regularly, pick off the adults immediately, and spray with a soapy solution. If the trouble persists, use pyrethrum, permethrim, or resemethrim.

**Symphalids** Commonly called springtails, on account of their dancing motions on the surface of the soil when the plant is watered, symphalids are not harmful to the plant. They are often present on plants when the soil is musty and very wet. They can be killed if necessary by drenching the soil with malathion.

**Underwatering** Inadequate watering or insufficient nourishment may cause browning.

**Mealy bug** Spider Plants can suffer from these common little white pests. They are destructive and can cause the plant to wilt, shed leaves, and eventually die if left untreated. The bugs are easy to recognize as tiny pale lumps with a wooly casing, sitting on the leaves (see above). Spraying with water is an effective treatment. A better remedy is to sponge the leaves with denatured alcohol. Alternatively, spray with malathion.

**Sciarid fly** These pests, better known as fungus gnats, are found in the soil if it is very wet. Again, they are not at all harmful, though they may be irritating and unsightly. If you wish to get rid of them, this is easily done by soaking malathion into the soil.

## Ideal Conditions

### Light and Position

Good light is required if these plants are to retain their coloring and not become thin and wispy, but very strong light can damage the leaves. Protect the plants, too, from cold drafts, especially if they are placed on a windowsill.

### Temperature Range

These plants thrive at normal room temperatures in the range 50–65°F. They will not do well if the temperature is allowed to drop below 45°F.

### Watering

The Spider Plant is easy to water by any method and likes a lot of water in the growing period. In the rest period, water more moderately, allowing the top layer of soil to dry out between waterings.

### Feeding

Feed every two weeks throughout the year with a good liquid fertilizer, especially once the plant has started to produce plantlets. Without feeding, the tops of the leaves will quickly turn brown, marring the appearance of the plant and retarding its growth.

### Seasonal Care

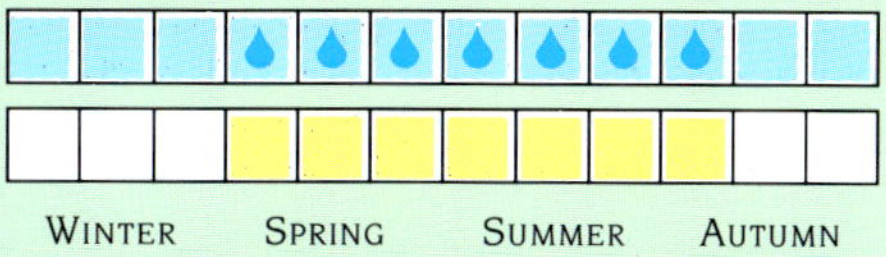


In general this is an easy plant to care for, but remember to water it less in the rest period and to protect it from direct sunlight and sudden drops in temperature. New plants can be grown at any time in one of two ways. Either cut off the plantlets when their leaves are 2–3 inches long, place them in a jar of water until the roots are 1 inch long, and then pot them. Alternatively, put the plantlets into soil and leave them attached to the mother plant until they take root.

### Soil

Use a soil-based mixture for potting and make sure there is enough space around the plant for the growth of its thick fleshy roots. Place the root ball about 1 inch below the rim of the pot. Repot in a larger pot whenever the roots force the soil to the rim.

# Citrus mitis

CALAMONDIN ORANGE

The citrus is one of the most fascinating of all the many houseplants that may be grown in a pot indoors, or in the conservatory. Not only does it bear flowers and fruit at the same time, but also the fruit, which can be produced in abundance, is quite edible and makes delicious marmalade.

**Healthy Plant**
The Calamondin Orange is an expensive plant and should be chosen with care. The mature plant is quite compact and has an abundance of glossy, unblemished leaves and will grow in a bushy and pleasing shape, whether straight and tall or slightly branching. Its heavily scented white flowers usually appear in late summer, and a percentage of them become small green fruits that, given careful culture, will eventually develop into miniature oranges. These are exotic and unusual, and will make an exciting change if you already have a number of flowering plants.

### VARIETIES AND PURCHASING

*C. mitis* This compact and decorative variety is the only one which fruits reliably indoors and retains a good shape.

## Pests and Diseases

**Aphids** These small insects are also known as greenfly, but may in fact be gray, black, or yellow as well as green. They suck the sap of the plant, preferring new growth such as small top shoots and flower buds. The plant gradually becomes stunted, with distortion of stems, leaves, and flowers. In addition, the aphids deposit a sticky honeydew on the plant which causes it further damage and makes it very susceptible to sooty mold. Thorough and repeated spraying with malathion will get rid of aphids.

**Mealy bug** This pest may be a nuisance to older plants, but fortunately it is easily spotted and treated.

**Scale insect** This could be the worst problem for a citrus mitis. The young flesh-colored insects and dark brown adults attach themselves to the stems of the plant and the undersides of the leaves. Scrape off scales as soon as they are visible; then wash the plant well with soapy water and repeat in a week. A large plant may benefit from a thorough spraying with dimethoate.

**Red spider mite** If the signs of infestation of red spider mites occur in the plant, prompt action must be taken. A steady stream of lukewarm water run over the foliage may dislodge the mites and their webs, as may a thorough spraying with derris. However, if the problem is widespread, treatment with insecticide is unlikely to be effective and the insects will move to other plants if left. In this case, there is nothing to be done but to remove and burn the infected areas, or burn the entire plant.

**Sooty mold** This is a mold which lives on the excreta of the above pests. It is not harmful, but is very unsightly. Sponge off mold with a soapy solution.

## Ideal Conditions

### Light and Position

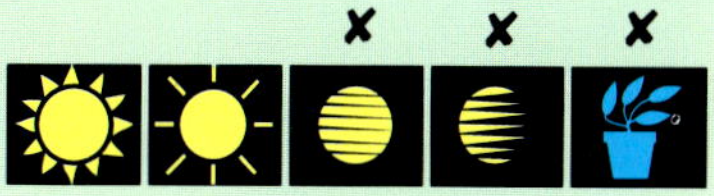

Direct sunlight is essential to this plant, and it will benefit from a period outdoors in the summer months. Place it in a sunny, sheltered corner, preferably on a stone base, and remember to keep up the necessary watering and feeding. Indoors or out, it will not stand drafts or too much shade.

### Temperature Range

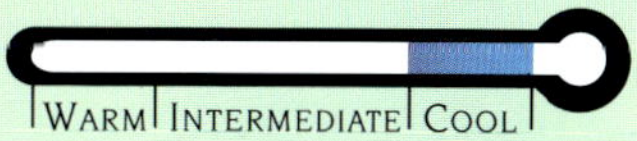


The Calamondin Orange prefers cool temperatures and will survive comfortably in temperatures of 50–59°F. However, if it becomes too cold, this may contribute to browning of leaf tips which can spread across the whole leaf, and this is aggravated if the plant is overwatered.

### Watering

This plant requires ample watering, especially in summer and if it is outdoors. Less water is required in winter, but the soil must never be allowed to dry out completely. If the plant is watered too lavishly in cold conditions, this may cause discoloration of leaves and root failure.

### Feeding

It is recommended that the Calamondin Orange is fed at each watering, but it will require less food in winter. Soil deficiency will result in yellowing leaves, rectified by watering with a solution containing iron, as directed by the manufacturer.

### Seasonal Care

The plant requires plenty of water all year round, though rather less in winter than in summer. The plant may be placed outdoors in late spring and can remain there until the nights become too chilly. Regular feeding during spring and summer will be beneficial, and the plant does require food through the winter, although less than needed in the growing season.

### Soil

Pot the plant in a soil-based mixture, preferably in a clay pot with shards placed at the bottom before the soil is put in. The soil should be free-draining, and a properly fed plant should not need frequent repotting unless the growth is extremely vigorous.

# Clerodendrum thomsoniae

## Bleeding Heart Vine or Glory Bower

This is another lovely evergreen climber. Being a native of tropical West Africa, it needs warmth and humidity to grow well. Given those conditions, it will twine vigorously to 10 feet or more, but it can easily be kept to a neat 3 or 4 feet, provided the tips are pinched out regularly during its growing season. In these circumstances, the plants do very well anchored to thin stakes inserted in the soil. Alternatively, it will make a wonderful trailer if planted in a large hanging basket.

Propagate clerodendrums by taking 4–6 inch tip cuttings in the spring. Dip these in a rooting hormone and plant in a mixture of moistened peat and perlite in 3-inch pots. Create a humid atmosphere for the cuttings by covering the rim of the pot with a plastic bag and keeping the temperature at an even 70°F. Once the cuttings show signs of growth, remove the plastic bag and provide the young plants with moderate amounts of water, enough to keep the soil moist. Because the plants are in a peat mixture with no nutrients, they must also be given liquid fertilizer once every two weeks. After four months, pot new clerodendrums on, using a soil-based potting mixture.

## Pests and Diseases

Clerodendrums are prone to scale insect and red spider mite; both these pests dislike a humid atmosphere so regular spraying will help deflect attack.

**Scale insect** Look for signs of infestation under the leaves, where the scale insect lives quite protected under its waxy scale. The scales are easy to see. Wipe them off immediately with a brush and wash the whole plant with soapy water. Repeat this process in a week. Bad infestations may need treatment with dimethoate.

**Red spider mite** This is less easy to see as it is minute, but the webs they weave under the leaves are easily recognizable. The leaves turn yellow, curl up, and finally drop off completely. New growth may become stunted and flower buds blackened. There will also be sticky honeydew on the plant, which is a secretion from the red spider. Act immediately, cutting away any damaged parts of the plant, and spraying with derris. Biological control for red spider mite comes in the form of *Phytoseiulus persimilis*. These bright red mites feed on all stages of the red spider mite and are best introduced in the spring and summer once you have noticed the offending insects on the plants.

**Healthy Plant**
The heart-shaped, rather dull, medium green leaves look rather coarse. The flowers that are produced on wiry flower stalks at the stem ends during spring, summer, and fall are both startling and unusual. Each one consists of a 1-inch long cream, or greenish cream, bell-shaped calyx, the scarlet, star-shaped blooms peeping through a split in its tip.

## Varieties and Purchasing

The flowering period dictates the times of year when clerodendrums are widely available, as without flowers the plant looks rather unattractive.

Two varieties are available: *C. thomsoniae* and *C. ugandense*; the latter flowers in spring and has bright blue and violet flowers with prominent blue stamens.

## Ideal Conditions

### Light and Position

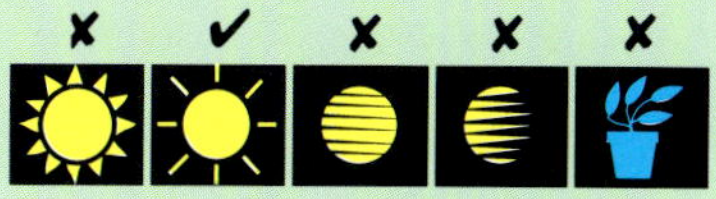

If a clerodendrum is to grow tall, it should be planted in a large tub or planter and provided with some means of support. It needs to be in a position where it will receive good light but some protection from strong midday sun.

### Temperature Range

A minimum of 55°F will allow the plant a winter rest. During the remainder of the year, a minimum of 61°F will encourage growth and bud formation.

### Watering

Give clerodendrums plenty of water during the time they are actively growing, enough to make the soil really moist at each watering. Allow the top ½ inch of soil to dry out before providing more. Encourage high humidity levels by standing the pots in trays of damp aggregate and by mist-spraying daily with soft rainwater.

### Feeding

Clerodendrums are fast growers and the nutrients in their soil will be quickly used up, so weekly liquid feeds are necessary for these plants while they are in active growth.

### Seasonal Care

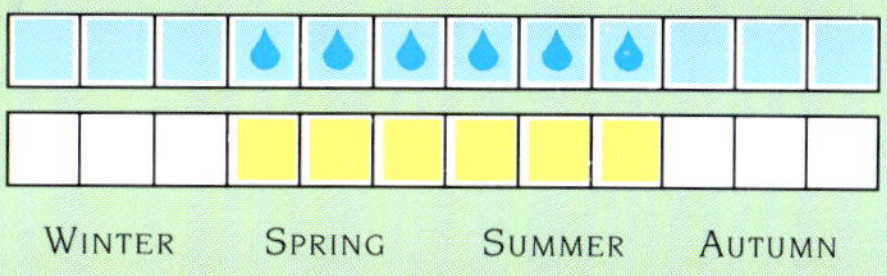


All clerodendrums need a fairly dramatic annual prune, not just to keep them in shape, but also to encourage bushy plants. In spring cut back at least half of the previous season's growth. In addition, prune about 3 inches from their stems immediately after flowering.

### Soil

Clerodendrums should be repotted once a year after the annual spring prune. Using a soil-based potting mixture, carefully remove as much of the old soil as possible before replanting it in a larger pot or replacing it in its permanent container.

# Codiaeum

## CROTON OR JOSEPH'S COAT

One common name of the codiaeum refers to Joseph's coat of many colors, for the plant's leaves are also many-colored – yellow, orange, red, and green. Mottled and general mixtures of these colors make the Croton the most brilliant of all the foliage plants that are grown indoors. Indigenous to Ceylon, codiaeums are temperamental and require a degree of skill if they are to survive in room conditions.

Almost all these plants are raised from cuttings about 4 inches long taken from the top section of main stems. The cuttings should be put in a peat and sand mixture, and kept humid in a temperature of not less than 70°F.

**Healthy Plant**

Although there are several varieties freely available, they are mostly sold unnamed. When names are given, they can be confused or wrong. Some to look out for are *Aeubifolium*, *Bruxellence*, *Craigii*, and *Reidii*.

### VARIETIES AND PURCHASING

Whichever of the numerous varieties you choose, inspect it carefully for browning or dull leaves which may be a sign of root rot or an invasion of red spider mite. The following are popular among the many codiaeums:

*C. reidii* This has broad leaves, mottled in rich pink and orange and with proper care may grow to 6 feet.

*C.* 'Eugene Drapps' This plant has predominantly yellow foliage and is the best variety with this coloring.

*C. holufiana* This is a variety which is easy to manage and is one of the most commonly available.

*C. reidii*

*C.* 'Eugene Drapps'

*C. holufiana*

## Pests and Diseases

**Red spider mite** These share the codiaeums' preference for warmth and are likely to be found (see illustration, right). They are difficult to detect on the bright foliage. Spray the plants with malathion once a month as a precaution. If the mites get a firm hold, the plant must be destroyed.

**Scale insect** This is a less common pest, but it may attack older plants. Spraying with malathion should get rid of it.

**Damaged leaves** Codiaeums like warm temperatures and some humidity, but excessive moisture in a cold position discolors and shrivels the leaf (below).

**Botrytis** This is a disease which is not usually found in sturdy plants, but may attack soft, damp foliage. Check temperature and light requirements and space the plants out. Remove the damaged leaves. If necessary, spray with propicanizole.

## Ideal Conditions

### Light and Position

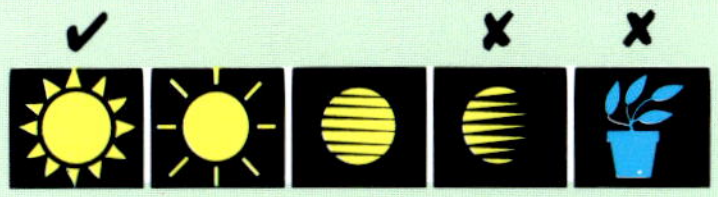


The codiaeum requires good light and plenty of sun to retain the beauty of its multi-colored leaves, but take care that it is not scorched or parched during a hot summer. In poor light, the leaves will revert to green and the plant cannot flourish as it should.

### Temperature Range

Warm, moist conditions are essential to this plant and the minimum temperature at which it is kept should be 59°F but it will benefit from more warmth and may prefer a temperature nearer 70°F. These are the conditions which would prevail in its native country of Sri Lanka.

### Watering

The codiaeum requires plenty of water in summer and regular watering during mild weather and the winter months. Water should be supplied to the soil from the top of the pot and the plant may prefer that the water is tepid. Do not spray the leaves of a codiaeum.

### Feeding

Established plants are rather greedy, requiring nourishment with every watering, except possibly during the winter months. The food may be introduced through the soil as a liquid, but never try to use a foliar feed.

### Seasonal Care

The plant requires a good deal of attention throughout the year and will need more water the better its health and growing conditions. In winter it will require slightly less water, but over-watering at any time may encourage disease which will damage the leaves, especially in older plants. Periodic cleaning of the foliage will improve the appearance of the plant.

### Soil

Soil-based mixture must be used and the plant should be potted with reasonable firmness. Regular repotting is advisable, annually in summer, until the plant is in a 10 in pot. Continue careful attention and regular feeding.

# Columnea

## GOLDFISH PLANT

The strange common name of the columnea must surely relate to the open flower, which could be compared to the open mouth of a goldfish. The flowers are spectacular with glorious orange, red, or yellow coloring. The plant's leaves are oval and small, attached to wiry stems that in all varieties other than C. *crassifolia* have a natural drooping habit, so they are good for hanging baskets and pots. By far the best variety is C. *banksii*, which produces masses of orange flowers from early spring on. The secret of successful flowering is to keep the soil as dry as possible during late winter without causing defoliation. Many columneas are much tougher plants than they are usually thought to be.

**Healthy Plant**
The Goldfish Plant is extremely striking, with its dark foliage and very bright flowers. It hangs in a luxuriant mass of straight, heavily laden stems.

### VARIETIES AND PURCHASING

Choose a plant with several cuttings in the pot so that it has a full appearance and is firm and healthy. The plant can be bought already in flower, but this need not be a condition of purchase.

*C. banksii* This is the finest variety and forms a full hanging plant with evergreen foliage and bright orange flowers. It is easily propagated from cuttings.

*C. gloriosa* The slender, less rigid stems of this variety carry soft, hairy leaves and can grow to 3 feet. The tubular flowers are vivid red with yellow throats.

*C. microphylla* The leaves of this plant are very small and abundant, but the orange flowers are produced rather spasmodically and this variety may be rather less attractive than the others.

## Pests and Diseases

Columneas seem generally to have a natural resistance to many common pests, but they are sometimes affected. As always, prevention is better than cure; remember that good plant hygiene helps to prevent pest infestation, and check your columnea regularly for signs of attack. Concentrate your search on the fresh new leaves and developing flower buds. Mist your plants frequently, especially in hot weather.

**Mealy bug** This small, white pest will be found only on older plants and can be removed with cotton soaked in denatured alcohol.

**Botrytis** This is rarely seen, but may attack a plant which is cramped and overwatered.

**Whitefly** These suck sap from the undersides of the leaves (see illustration).

## Ideal Conditions

### Light and Position

The columnea requires a position with good light to encourage flowering, but shaded from direct sunlight. It is best seen as a hanging plant, so it could be placed near the window in a bright room. However, it will not tolerate drafts.

### Temperature Range

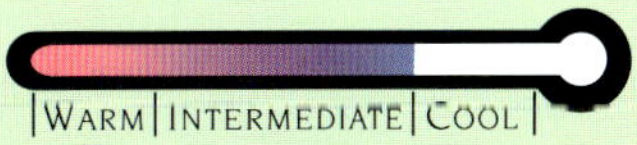


Few plants care for a large temperature range or periods of excessive heat or cold. A suitable range from the columnea is 59–70°F. Maintain steady but cooler temperatures during the winter flowering period.

### Watering

Water the plant regularly during the summer growth period, giving slightly less in winter. Water the soil from the top of the pot or pour it into the saucer, always avoiding the foliage. Keeping the soil almost dry during mid-winter will encourage better flowering. Provide high humidity at all times.

### Feeding

The plant is not too fussy in its feeding habits, but established plants should be fed about once a week in summer when they are active, once a month during winter. Cease feeding toward the end of winter when the watering is cut to a minimum.

### Seasonal Care

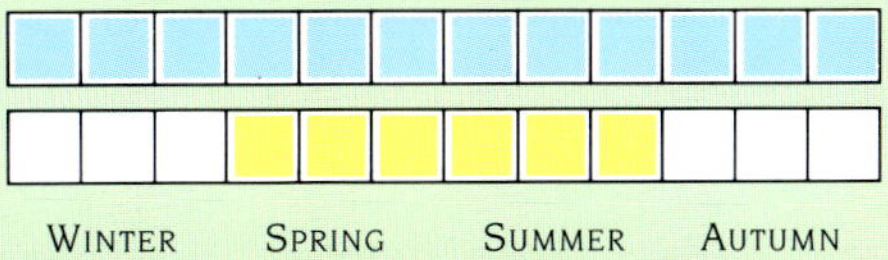


The columnea is quite easy to care for, and if the period of near starvation is followed in winter, the plant will flower more freely. The foliage can be trimmed to shape at any time when the plant is not in flower, but it is as well to cut back all stems to two or three leaf joints once every two years at repotting time. Beware of overwatering at all times, as this can ruin the leaves and ultimately whole branches.

### Soil

Cuttings from the plant will root quite well in moist conditions and a temperature of 70°F. When transferring them to a hanging basket, use a peat-based potting mixture and include at least five cuttings, to provide full and impressive growth.

# Cyclamen persicum

FLORIST'S CYCLAMEN OR SHOOTING STAR

Cyclamen are among the most beautiful of all flowering plants, whether they are grown in pots or not, but they are no longer simply seasonal flowers that only appear in the fall. Hybridists have made it possible for plants to be in flower throughout the year, although the plants still tend to be more popular during the winter months. Over the years, however, the development of C. *persicum* has been quite an achievement, as the plants today bear little resemblance to those initially collected in the eastern Mediterranean. The commercial grower raises fresh plants from seed each year, and for the main crop these are sown in mid-autumn in a temperature of around 70°F. The only time that plants need to be so warm is when they are germinating.

**Healthy Plant**
There is enormous variety to be found within this plant family, large and small, in colors in all shades of pink, red, and purple, as well as cool, elegant white. Look for those with interesting leaves, too; some are plain dark green; others have attractive pale borders delicately drawn into the center of the leaf by light-colored veins.

The secret of success with cyclamens is to keep them cool, always water from beneath, and only water when they really need it.

## Varieties and Purchasing

The main quality to look for when buying a cyclamen is that the stems, leaves, and flowers are all fresh and upright. Avoid a plant with leaves drooping over the side of the pot. Look among the leaves to make sure there are plenty of healthy flower buds, and inspect the whole plant for signs of botrytis, which will only become more and more troublesome. If the ends of leaves and flower stalks seem to be rotting, choose another plant. There are numerous strains and types among the many varieties of cyclamen. They are also available in many beautiful colors, so it is largely a matter of personal preference as to which should be bought, providing all the plants are equally healthy.

## Pests and Diseases

**Botrytis** This disease (see illustration, right) can quickly kill a plant, so deal with it as soon as it appears. Cut away affected parts, move to dryer conditions, and use an appropriate spray.

**Cyclamen mite** These tiny insects appear almost as dust on the reverse sides of leaves, which become stunted and very hard. Unfortunately there is no cure, and the plant must be destroyed.

**Aphids** These flies (see illustration, below) do occur on the cyclamen, but are quite easily controlled. Use a suitable spray and repeat the treatment as necessary.

**Vine weevil** The beetles attack the leaves of the plant, but the larvae in the soil cause the real damage. Use permethrin.

**Caterpillars** These are not usually found on plants kept indoors, but they may find their way into a sunroom. If you notice holes appearing in foliage, check for their presence and, if necessary, remove.

**Red spider mite** Check the leaves regularly if you have any suspicion that the plant has red spider. It is difficult to see and almost impossible to control. Spray the plant repeatedly with derris.

## Ideal Conditions

### Light and Position

Given cool, light, and airy conditions, these plants remain in flower for a longer period and have a bright, healthy appearance. Avoid subjecting them to direct sunshine.

### Temperature Range

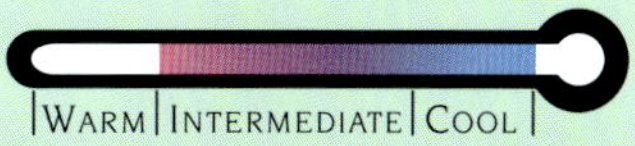


A temperature range between 55–65°F suits a cyclamen very well, and it will flower better if the temperatures are kept at the lower end of the range. If the surrounding environment is too hot and dry, the leaves of the plant will turn yellow. In common with many other plants, the cyclamen abhors cold drafts or sudden changes of temperature.

### Watering

A cyclamen will be damaged if the soil becomes sodden. Water from below to moisten the soil, but never leave the plant standing in water. The plant will come to no harm if it gets to a stage where the leaves droop slightly before watering is repeated. Make sure it has good humidity while flowering by standing plants in trays of horticultural aggregate.

### Feeding

A weak liquid fertilizer given through the soil with each watering is required while the plant is in leaf. As with the watering, any excess should be avoided. The plant must be given the most attention during winter and spring.

### Seasonal Care

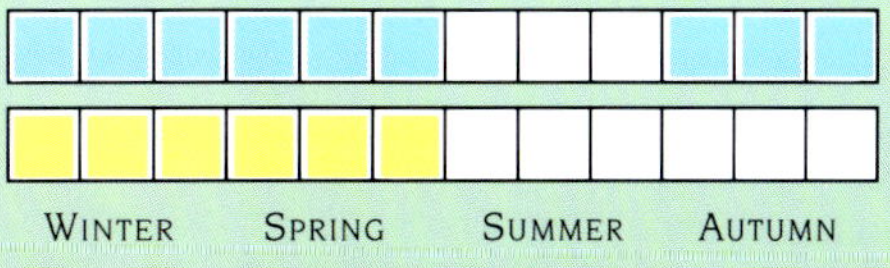


The flowering season of the cyclamen is fall to spring, and the growth dies down after the flowering. The plant can then be allowed to dry out slightly and rest in a cool, frost-free position until new growth starts in the summer. Repot in mid-summer when growth has re-started, leaving half the tuber above the level of the soil. At this stage the corm can be divided and the sections repotted for propagation of the plant.

### Soil

A good soil-based potting mixture is suitable at any stage and can also be used to raise plants from seed. Cyclamen flower well if slightly pot-bound.

# Cyperus

UMBRELLA PLANT, UMBRELLA SEDGE, EGYPTIAN PAPER PLANT, OR UMBRELLA PALM

The cyperus is one of the few water plants that can be recommended for indoor culture as, with reasonable care, it will do well. The plants grow in clumps and have rather thin, pale green, grassy leaves that are not in themselves attractive, but the 3-foot tall umbrella-like flower adds much to the general appearance. The simple way of producing new plants is to allow clumps to develop to a reasonable size, then to remove the plant from its pot and, with a large sharp knife, simply cut the clumps into sections. These can then be potted individually using a houseplant potting mixture.

**Healthy Plant**
Umbrella Plants grow wild all over the tropical and subtropical regions of the world. Their natural habitat is swampy conditions, and if they are allowed to dry out, their foliage will very quickly turn yellowish-brown.

## VARIETIES AND PURCHASING

Umbrella Plants can be quite difficult to obtain, but in the summer two varieties may be available.

*C. diffusus* This variety may reach a height of 3 feet. It is a striking plant with a wide spread of leaves.

*C. alternifolius* (main picture) This is a much smaller plant, usually growing to around 12–18 inches. It has narrow sparse leaves.

*C.a.* 'Albo Variegata' (see inset) This is a variegated attractive houseplant which has white-striped leaves.

## Pests and Diseases

As long as the Umbrella Plant is well-watered, it should remain quite healthy.

**Mealy bug** To check for these, look into the green flowers at the top of the plant. They can be removed with an insecticide.

**Greenfly** and **whitefly** These may attack young leaves.

**Danger signs** Brown edges or brown patches may mean that you are providing too little water or that the plant needs more light.

## Ideal Conditions

### Light and Position

The Umbrella Plant can be grown equally well in full, bright sunlight or slight shade. Highly adaptable, it will, with time, adapt itself to almost any location. If few stems are produced, however, the plant is getting too little light.

### Temperature Range

The Umbrella Plant will tolerate most temperatures between 50–70°F, provided there are no extreme fluctuations. In winter the temperature should not go below 50°F. *Cyperus papyrus* will need a minimum temperature of between 50–65°F.

### Watering

Being aquatic, the Umbrella Plant must be grown in pots placed in a shallow pan of water. The water should be changed daily. During growth periods, the plant will require more water than at times of rest. Do not totally immerse the pots, which can cause the stems to rot.

### Feeding

Because the plants sit in water, the best way to feed is with fertilizing tablets pushed well into the soil. Otherwise, a standard liquid fertilizer can be applied at monthly intervals during the active growth period.

### Seasonal Care

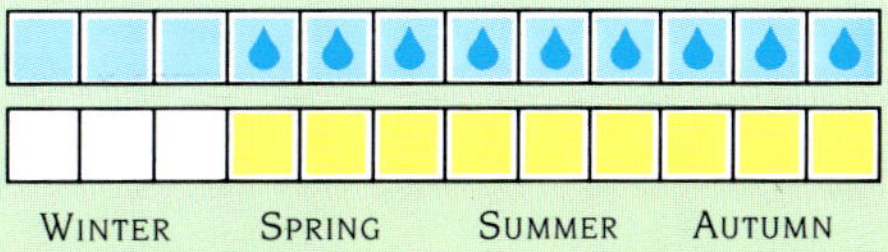


Throughout the year, the Umbrella Plant needs a constant source of water to keep the roots saturated. If kept in dry, heated environments, the water level should be checked frequently. Feed at regular intervals except in winter. The plants can be propagated by division in spring. As the green plants die, cut them off at intervals throughout the year to allow for new growth.

### Soil

The soil should have a high loam content to prevent it from disintegrating in the water. Pieces of charcoal can be added to the soil to keep it fresh and reduce odors caused by souring soil. As they grow, the plants will require larger pots.

# Dieffenbachia

## Dumb Cane or Leopard Lily

Although these plants do produce insignificant spathe flowers, they are grown almost entirely for their foliage. Some of the more robust forms can grow to a height of about 6 feet in only six years, but they are grown principally as compact plants that seldom get out of hand if confined to reasonable-sized pots. One of its common names, Dumb Cane, reflects the fact that all parts of this plant are poisonous. Wear gloves when tending these plants, and wash your hands well after handling.

New plants can be raised from pieces of stem cut into sections and placed in a peat and sand mixture at a high temperature, or by removing the small plantlets that cluster around their parents, potting them individually in smaller pots.

You can propagate dieffenbachia by removing the top portion of the stem tip (see illustration, left). Having done this, new growth will sprout from the cut.

**Healthy Plant**
*D. amoena* 'Tropic Snow' (left) is a variety of *D. amoena*. It is highly attractive, its dark green foliage being relieved by interesting white blotches. The sap of this plant is extremely poisonous; always wash your hands after handling it.

## Varieties and Purchasing

These highly attractive houseplants can produce flowers, but these are of little interest. Their main appeal is their attractive shape and their striking foliage. This is usually green, but it is often intermixed with shades of white or yellow. When you buy these plants, remember that dieffenbachias love heat. They originally came from Brazil and were given their name by Dieffenbach, the gardener to the Hapsburg rulers of Austria, in 1830.

*D. amoena* A vigorous-growing plant, this is popular since it is relatively easy to care for.

*D. camillia* This plant is noted for its combination of pattern and color.

*D. exotica* Striking blotched white and green foliage, with leaves spreading out and arching down make this an attractive plant.

*D. bausei* This has lance-shaped yellow-green leaves, up to 12 inches long, and marked with white spots and dark green patches and margins.

*D. bowmannii* This dieffenbachia has oval leaves 2 feet long and 18 inches wide on long stalks. The coloring is less striking than that of some varieties, being chiefly a mixture of pale and dark green.

*D. imperialis* This has leathery, oval leaves, splattered with yellow.

*D. maculata* Spotted Dumb Cane has many varieties, most with elegant pointed lance-shaped leaves, colored dark green, with irregular off-white markings.

*D. exotica* (above) and *D. camillia* (below) are both popular varieties, *D. exotica* being more compact in habit, with blotched green and white leaves. All dieffenbachias need warmth and humidity to thrive; increase humidity by standing them in trays of dampened horticultural aggregate.

*D. exotica*

*D. camillia*

## Pests and Diseases

**Scorch**
This problem is caused by placing the plant too near a radiator or too close to a sunny window. Move the plant to a more suitable location and, as the scorched leaves will never recover, it may be as well to remove them altogether.

**Symphalids** Treat with a soil insecticide such as malathion.

**Aphids** This common household pest will sometimes attach the dieffenbachia. Control with a soapy spray used at regular intervals.

**Stem rot** Cold, wet conditions may well cause this type of rot, either on the stem or on the foliage. Check your watering technique and make sure the temperature remains around the 60°F level.

**Overwatering** Brown edges on leaves can be caused by too much water. Provide water only when your plant really needs it.

Grown for their foliage, dieffenbachias offer a wide variety of leaf color. *Dieffenbachia camillia* (below) sports an almost cream leaf, delicately edged with green.

## Ideal Conditions

### Light and Position

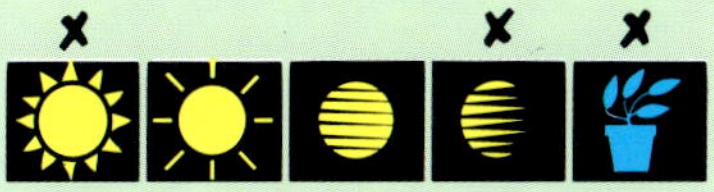

Place a dieffenbachia in a fairly light position, but shaded from direct sun. It should not be within range of heat from a radiator or cold drafts from a door or window. The color of a variegated plant will suffer if it has poor light.

### Temperature Range

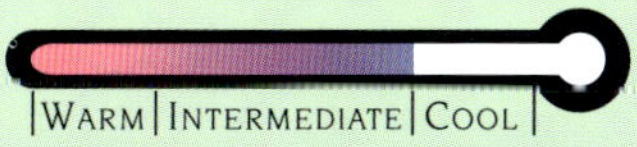


A dieffenbachia will live in a temperature of 59°F but would probably prefer nearer 70°F. In higher temperatures it is important to keep up a good level of humidity. A cool, moist atmosphere can be tolerated for a short period, but may cause some falling of the leaves.

### Watering

Moisture is required all year round, but the plant can be watered less in winter than in summer, when tepid water should be used. During spring and summer growth, watering should be generous and frequent.

### Feeding

While the dieffenbachia is producing new leaf growth it should be fred with every watering, using weak, liquid fertilizer introduced through the soil. Feeding with every other watering is sufficient at other times.

### Seasonal Care

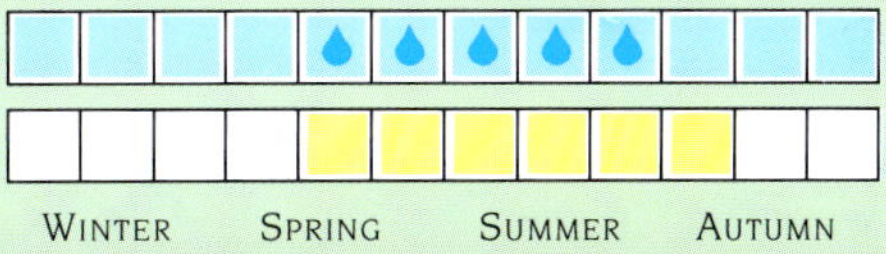


Light and moisture all year round are vital to the health of this plant. A dark location or cold drafts will result in general decline, spindly growth and loss of leaves. In cold and wet conditions the leaves will brown at the edges. Propagation is most successful from stem cuttings, placed in peat and sand and kept moist and in a high temperature of 70–75°F. The plant requires the most attention, receiving plenty of food and water, during the summer months.

### Soil

If the plant seems too large for its pot when purchased, it can be repotted immediately. Otherwise, wait until the plant is well established and repot in summer, using an open potting mixture containing loam and peat.

# Dracaena

## Silhouette Plant, Florida Beauty, Striped Dracaena, or Fountain Plant

This is a diverse group of plants that look as though they should be growing on a tropical island. Many are stately plants that grow on slender stems, but there are also those with a more prostrate habit, such as D. *sarculosa*, and the more colorful ones such as D. *terminalis*. Almost all dracaenas are a little difficult to care for in rooms where the light and temperature are inadequate.

Propagation methods vary; some plants can be raised from stem cuttings with a bud or two on each, and others from rooting suckers that develop as the plants age. Both these methods need temperatures in the region of 70°F, and to be kept humid and shaded while rooting takes place.

### Varieties and Purchasing

*D. deremensis* This variety may grow to 10 feet, but can be contained by pruning.

*D. marginata* 'Tricolor' (above right) At the top of this plant's stout stem is a cluster of narrow green leaves, edged with red.

*D. souvenir de Schriever* This plant has bold green leaves which have a margin of yellow.

*D. terminalis* (far right) This attractive plant may reach a height of 30 inches. Young plants have green leaves, but as they mature they turn a brilliant red.

*D. godseffiana* This has yellow mottled foliage on wiry stems.

**Healthy Plant**

Healthy dracaenas are most attractive plants. When buying, check that the leaves are not discolored. All varieties like light and will not achieve their best color and contrast unless given the maximum amount of light possible.

## Pests and Diseases

**Damaged leaves** Poor watering technique often leads to leaf damage. Take care not to overwater, particularly during the winter when the plant needs to be quite dry.

**Scorch** Although dracaenas need good light, their leaves will scorch when placed too close to a direct light source.

**Bacterial leaf spot** This is only a minor fungus disease; improve the ventilation. Remove leaves only if they become very blemished.

**Red spider mite** This is quite common. The pest will be found on the underside of the leaf, and brown patches may develop. Treat with insecticide.

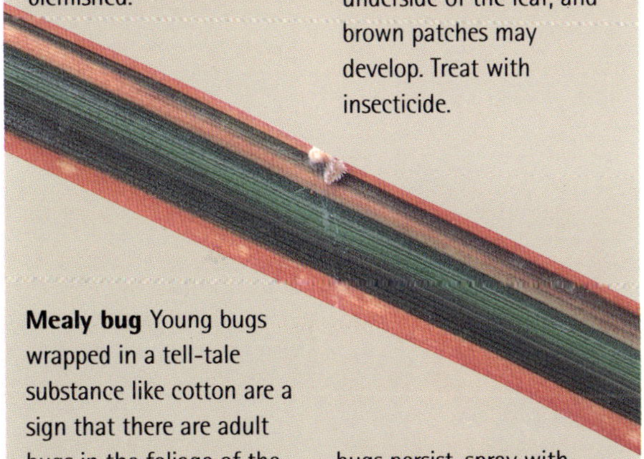

**Mealy bug** Young bugs wrapped in a tell-tale substance like cotton are a sign that there are adult bugs in the foliage of the plant. They are normally found among the topmost leaves. Clean the bugs from the foliage with a sponge soaked in denatured alcohol. If the bugs persist, spray with malathion.

**Root mealy bug** If these are found in the roots, immerse the rootball in malathion.

## Ideal Conditions

### Light and Position

All dracaenas need good light but care should be taken to avoid putting them in very bright sunlight as there is then a possibility of scorching. They should also be protected from cold drafts. Taller plants can be placed on the floor.

### Temperature Range

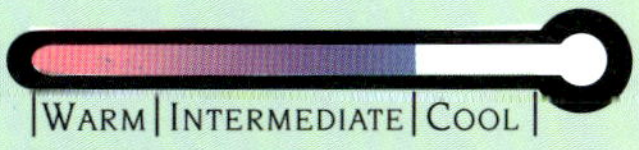


Dracaenas can survive quite low temperatures in the region of 50°F, although their leaves will droop in such conditions and eventually fall off. However, a couple of weeks in such temperatures will do no harm. The ideal temperature is somewhere between 59–70°F.

### Watering

The plant needs plenty of water, especially during the growing period, throughout which the potting mixture should be kept very moist. Be careful, however, not to stand the pot in water, and in the winter months, keep the soil fairly dry. They also need a humid atmosphere, so stand the plants on trays of damp horticultural aggregate.

### Feeding

Use a liquid fertilizer during the growing period, but it should not be fed during the winter. Do not use a foliar feed as dracaenas do not do well if their leaves become wet.

### Seasonal Care

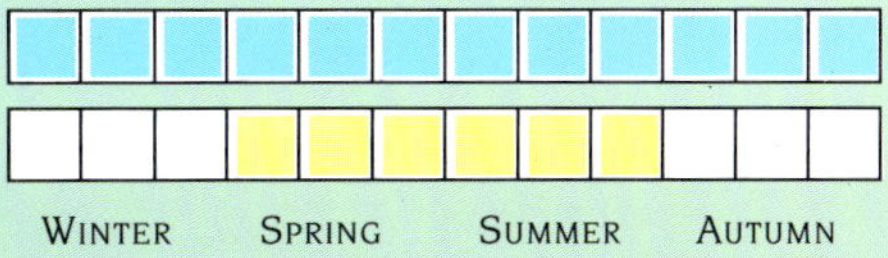


During the summer months, when the plant is growing, water is the most important thing to remember. Making the roots excessively wet should be avoided, so allow the plant to dry out to some extent between each watering. Do not allow it to get bone-dry in winter. Many of the taller-growing plants will need cutting back, and this can be done at any time of the year.

### Soil

Use soil-based potting mixture and pot the plants during the summer months, making sure that the new pots are not too large. It is a good idea with some plants to remove the top layer of old soil and replace it with fresh mixture. Pot on only when the plant is nearly pot-bound.

# Euphorbia pulcherrima

## Poinsettia, Lobster Plant, or Mexican Flame Leaf

In the past 25 years, Poinsettias have come from virtually nothing to being far and away the most popular winter-flowering plant. This is due to the development of greatly improved strains.

There are varieties with pink, creamy white- and bi-colored bracts, but the important color is the striking brilliant red version. The plant's leaves are pale green and the flowers uninteresting, but the brilliantly colored bracts are a magnificent attraction. The bracts are, in fact, colored leaves that begin to develop at the top of the plant in the fall.

Cuttings about 4–6 inches long are taken in mid-summer from top sections of the stem. Allow these to dry out before inserting them in a sandy soil. Keep them in humid conditions at a temperature of around 70°F.

### Varieties and Purchasing

Of this enormous family there is only one that grows really successfully indoors: *Euphorbia pulcherrima*, commonly known as Poinsettia. These eyecatching plants are brought into the shops for the winter season and, cared for correctly, will last for some considerable time. So great is their appeal that Poinsettias are not sold by variety but by color alone. As well as the familiar red, you may also find pink and white cultivars, which are on shorter stems.

**Healthy Plant**
A Poinsettia will always be striking because of its color, and is usually displayed alone (left) to considerable effect. The colored bracts that cluster around the plant's flowers can grow up to 10 inches long.

## Pests and Diseases

**Whitefly** This is by far the most troublesome pest and can easily be detected on the undersides of the leaves. It is notorious for increasing rapidly, and for being fairly difficult to kill There are numerous insecticides available, but start by trying a soap spray – remember they must be used intensively. Having killed off the parent flies, insecticide treatment must be repeated at four-day intervals to dispose of any larvae. A Poinsettia must be checked regularly for whitefly throughout its life.

**Botrytis** This can occur (see illustration, above), causing the plant to give off dust when it is moved or shaken. Household chemical sprays will cause spotting of a much smaller type than botrytis patches. To cure, remove badly affected leaves and treat with fungicide.

**Root rot** Another regular cause of discoloration in Poinsettias (illustration, above), this causes a dramatic fading in the color of leaves.

## Ideal Conditions

### Light and Position

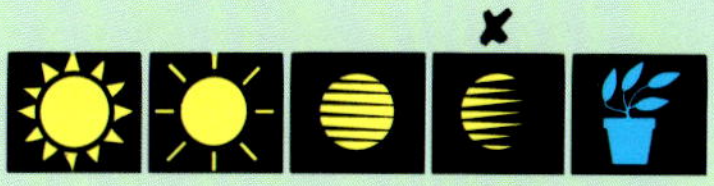

The Poinsettia must have plenty of light to maintain the color of its bracts. It will not be harmed by weak winter sunshine once established, but young plants should be protected from direct sun and cold drafts.

### Temperature Range

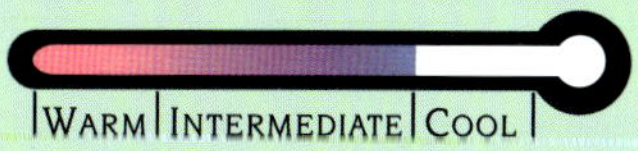


Keep the plant in intermediate temperatures. Room temperatures of 59–70°F are fine. When the Poinsettia is not in color, it will survive in a cooler atmosphere, but should on no account be exposed to frost. The plant appreciates a moist atmosphere and may be adversely affected if there is a gas heater in the room.

### Watering

Keep the soil moist and make sure it is not allowed to dry out while the plant is growing and in flower. The watering can be reduced once the plant has flowered, but return to the normal amount after pruning or re-potting in midsummer. Water from the top of the pot.

### Feeding

Add liquid fertilizer to the water during the active period for the plant. When the Poinsettia begins to die down naturally, stop feeding until signs of growth are resumed.

### Seasonal Care

When the plant begins to die down after flowering, cut back the main stems to a length of about 4 inches. Store the plant in a warm, dry place and wait until new growth is apparent. This will take about six weeks, and as soon as the plant resumes activity, it can be watered and repotted. Be careful not to overwater a Poinsettia, as this can cause root rot and leaf discoloration. To obtain well-colored leaves, subject Poinsettias to complete darkness for 14 hours a day during autumn.

### Soil

Use a soil-based potting mixture for repotting in late spring. Remove the old soil and replant in the same container. Water the plant after potting, but keep it only just moist until new growth has fully taken hold.

# Fatsia and Fatshedera

FALSE CASTOR OIL PLANT, JAPANESE ARALIA, IVY TREE, OR TREE IVY

The fatsia and the fatshedera are very closely related, inasmuch as the fatsia is one of the parents of the fatshedera – the hedera obviously being the other. Both are hardy outdoors, and are reasonably trouble-free plants in the home. While the fatsia has large, shallowly indented, fingered leaves, the fatshedera has similarly shaped leaves that are very much smaller. Both are green, but there are also variegated forms of each. In mid-autumn the fatsia produces rounded heads of creamy white flowers in large stalked clusters. *Fatsia japonica* is a compact bush, while the fatshedera is much more upright and will generally branch out if the growing tips are removed.

The best method of propagating the fatsia is by means of seed. To grow new fatshederas, tip or stem cuttings should be taken during spring and summer.

## Varieties and Purchasing

These are both robust plants which are quite easy to grow. Check the leaves when buying the plant and choose one with glossy, bright green foliage. An overall browning of the plant may indicate the presence of red spider mites, so avoid a plant which does not look in the peak of condition.

*Fatsia japonica* Being very tolerant of a wide range of temperatures, this plant is sold for outdoor and indoor display. It is widely available unlike its variegated form which is more attractive.

*Fatshedera lizei* This fresh green plant has upright growth and is an ideal climbing plant, for instance, on an open staircase where the temperature may be too low for other plants.

**Healthy Plant**
The spreading leaves of *Fatsia japonica* (left) form an attractive, almost tropical display. The mature plant remains rounded and bushy, unlike the fatshedera (right).

## Pests and Diseases

**Aphids** These greenfly are found on the younger leaves (see illustration, above) and are easy to see. Treat the plant by spraying with a soap spray.

**Mealy bug** It is not difficult to detect this pest. At an early stage, wipe off the white bugs with cotton soaked with malathion.

**Slug damage** Even if it is not kept outside, your fatsia may attract slugs and caterpillars. Remove the offenders and, if necessary, cut away damaged leaves.

**Red spider mite** Both plants are vulnerable to this pest, fatsia more than fatshedera. Browning of the leaves and hardening of soft new growth is the sign of spider mites. Thorough and repeated spraying with malathion is vital.

**Botrytis** If the conditions in which the plant grows are cold, dank, and shaded, it may develop mold. Remove badly affected leaves and spray the plant with propicanizole.

## Ideal Conditions

### Light and Position

These plants are quite tolerant of bad conditions, but prefer good light, so long as it is not harsh sunlight.

### Temperature Range

Warm | Intermediate | Cool

A temperature of below 59°F is required, but the plants are quite hardy and anywhere in the range 45–59°F is suitable. The lower temperatures in the preferred range are adequate in winter.

### Watering

Water the plants regularly, but do not let them stand in water. They will require less moisture in winter, especially if the temperature is low. Be quite generous with the watering, but allow the soil to dry out slightly before providing more. Too little water and the leaves will develop brown edges; too much and they will fall off altogether. Fatsias enjoy a humid atmosphere, so mist them regularly and stand the plants in trays of horticultural aggregate.

### Feeding

Established plants will need frequent feeding. Add liquid fertilizer to the water at regular intervals. As is usually the case, the plants may be fed less as watering is reduced, in this case during the inactive winter period.

### Seasonal Care

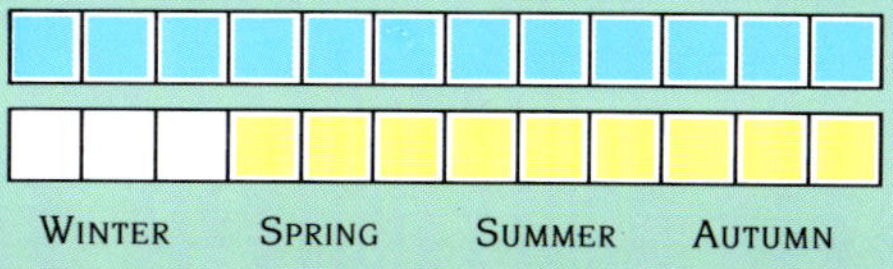


Both plants will enjoy being placed outdoors in summer, if they are placed in a sheltered position, though not in full sun, and if their need for food and water is not neglected. Spray the leaves regularly when the plants are indoors. Provide fatsias with good light during the winter and keep them cool. Cut back the stems if the plant becomes too leggy or the leaves have suffered from dry heat. The plants may be propagated from stem tip cuttings potted in the spring.

### Soil

Plants in small pots will need potting on soon after they are bought. Once the plant has reached its maximum pot size, it can stay there for two or three years. Use a soil-based mixture.

# Ferns

### Finer foliage ferns

The finer foliaged ferns must rank among the oldest of houseplants, and they are as popular today as they were in the other heyday of indoor plants, the Victorian age, when they were well adapted to the relatively dark rooms of most homes. There are some varieties with silvery variegation to their foliage, but the vast majority are grown and enjoyed for their cool, soft greenery.

### Coarse foliage ferns

It is probably more correct to say that these have large, rather than coarse, fronds as the Bird's Nest Fern, *Asplenium nidus avis*, has just about the smoothest and the most exquisite leaves of any green foliage plant.

**Healthy Plant**
The Bird's Nest Fern, *Asplenium nidus avis* (above), is one of the most popular varieties, its distinctive leaf pattern giving rise to its common name. Its fronds, which are undivided and glossy, spread themselves upward to form a bowl shape, similar to that of a bird's nest. The fronds themselves are delicate during the first few weeks of growth.

The Stagshorn Fern, *Platycerium alcicorne*, is coarser in appearance, on account of the waxy coating that completely covers the antler-shaped fronds. The asplenium has pale green fronds that in very mature specimen plants can be 3 feet long, arranged in the shape of a badminton birdie, which can be a most impressive sight. As the name suggests, the Stagshorn Fern has decorative leaves that have a definite antler appearance to them. The fern also has anchor leaves which attach it to trees and other forms of aerial support, where the plant makes its natural home.

*Platycerium alcicorne*, or Staghorn Fern (below), has decorative leaves that have a definite antler appearance to them. In time they may extend to 3 feet long.

*Adiantum capillus-veneris* (below) This delicate fern, commonly known as Venus Hair Fern, rarely grows to more than 12 inches indoors. It is particularly sensitive to changes in temperature and temperamental about watering technique.

*Nephrolepis exaltata* (left) The graceful, bright green, arching fronds of this fern grow from an underground rhizome. Their growth habit makes them perfect specimens for either hanging baskets or pedestals.

## Varieties and Purchasing

Though flowerless, ferns are extremely popular houseplants. The family consists of many different varieties, with common characteristics. Their method of reproduction is unusual; unlike most other plants, they reproduce by means of spores, rather than flowers or seeds. Ferns can be bought in many sizes, but, whatever, their size, they will grow at a prodigious pace, given suitable conditions. Small plants, therefore, can be just as good a buy as large ones. Check any plant carefully before you buy it. The leaves should be fresh and green. Any plant with dry and shriveled foliage should be passed over, although browning of leaf ends is only a sign that the plant was allowed to become too dry at some time and is not, in itself, a reason not to buy it. Watch out for signs of scale insects and mealy bugs, the chief pests. Their presence is normally easily detectable if you examine the leaves. Any asplenium should be checked for blemishes along the margins of its leaves which are very susceptible to damage. The anchor fronds of a platycerium should be green, fresh, and not dried out; the latter is a sign of neglect. All ferns orefer shaded locations and deteriorate quickly if exposed to strong sunlight. Grouping plants together is a good idea; they will invariably grow and look better.

*Blechnum* Many different varieties of fern are included in this genus, ranging from small creepers through to upright plants with small trunks. The most popular is *B. gibbum*, an attractive plant with a neat rosette of fronds crowning its trunk. Other popular versions are *B. brasiliense*, whose pinnae are copper-colored when young, turning green as the plant ages, and *B. occidentale*.

*Pellaea rotundifolia* The Button Fern is one of the two species of pellaea grown as houseplants. The other is *P. viridis*, or Green Cliffbrake. The former's fronds arch downward, carrying pairs of button-like pinnae. *P. viridis* has a bushy look.

*Cyrtomium falcatum* The Holly Fern is extremely decorative and long-lasting.

*Phyllitis* Only one species, the Hart's Tongue Fern, is commonly grown as a houseplant.

*Polypodium* The fronds of *P. aureum* rise from a long rhizome part-embedded in the potting mixture.

*Davallia* Two popular

**Healthy Plant**
*Asparagus setaceus* Given support, this fern will climb. The climbing stems are often bare at first, but they will eventually produce the familiar bright green branchlets.

varieties are *D. canariensis* and *D. fejeensis*. The rhizomes are furry and will spread over the pot so that it is hidden.

*Platycerium alcicorne* The easiest of this family to grow indoors, it needs to be acclimatized gradually. It does best growing on bark or in a basket.

*Pteris* Three species do well as houseplants – *P. cretica*, *P. ensiformis*, and *P. tremula*.

Although these may look like scale insects, they are in fact spores, which may well be found on the underside of healthy nephrolepis fronds.

**Healthy Plant**
A fine example of an adiantum (below left); next to it (below right) is a *Pteris cretica* or Table Fern, which produces light-to medium-green upright fronds. They are borne on slender black stems and can grow quite tall, arching over the top.

## Pests and Diseases

Coarse foliage ferns are relatively easy to care for, being less temperamental than some houseplants. Remember that an open, peaty potting mixture is essential and that pots and containers must be well drained. Some varieties, notably the platycerium, like to be rooted in bark. Do this by wrapping the roots in sphagnum moss soaked with liquid fertilizer. The roots can be attached easily to the bark and, eventually, will cling naturally by their anchor fronds. Such plants make very fine specimens. They are watered by plunging the plant and anchorage into a bucket to soak them thoroughly. With all coarse foliage varieties, use rainwater for preference, plus a weak liquid fertilizer. When the plant is well soaked, allow it to dry out a little before repeating the process. At no time should the roots be allowed to become excessively dry. All fine foliage ferns prefer shaded locations and quickly deteriorate if exposed to strong sunlight. Keep the plants moist at all times; in dry conditions, it is a help if plant pots can be plunged up to their rims in moist peat. It is important to maintain humidity in the surrounding atmosphere, though the potting medium should never be allowed to become sodden for a long period. Feed weak liquid fertilizer at every stage of potting and follow by watering the soil and the foliage of plants well with a fine nozzle. Guard against too wet winter conditions when temperatures are low. A thorough cleaning out of the centers of plants each fall will reduce the risk of leaves rotting and falling off.

**Scale insect** These present by far the most serious problem as far as pests are concerned, since they can soon infest plants if left unchecked. To start with, they mostly trouble the reverse sides of the leaves. These should therefore be examined carefully as a matter of routine, so that remedial action can be taken at the earliest possible stage. A chemical treatment might be best, but check carefully first to make sure the necessary insecticide, dimethoate or malathion for example, will not damage the plant itself, as many of the ferns are sensitive to chemicals. Treat a specimen section of the plant to see if there is any reaction. The fronds of the asplenium can be wiped gently with a damp cloth to remove scales; this, however, is not recommended for the wax-covered fronds of the platycerium. When treating fine foliage ferns, wipe the insects carefully off the infected plant; brown scales may be scraped with a thumbnail. Again, check that the insecticide is suitable before using it on the whole plant. Test a leaf, waiting about 10 days to see the result.

**Change of environment**
All ferns are susceptible to changes in their environment (see damaged leaf, left), so ensure in particular that temperatures remain stable at all times.

**Mealy bug** This is a less serious problem. The bugs can be eradicated by soaking a cotton swab in denatured alcohol and dabbing directly onto the powdery white adult bugs.

Take care also to treat the young bugs in their waxy white protective coverings. Mealy bugs are difficult to locate in older fine foliage ferns. Part the foliage for close inspection and, if bugs are present, remove them as for the coarse ferns.

**Watering problems** The two illustrations above show the results of underwatering, while below is an example of an overwatered plant. Watering technique is not easy with ferns. Remember, they are shade lovers, so they will not take up as much water as those that thrive in the sun. Only water ferns when they need it; they will react dramatically to the wrong treatment.

## Ideal Conditions

### Light and Position

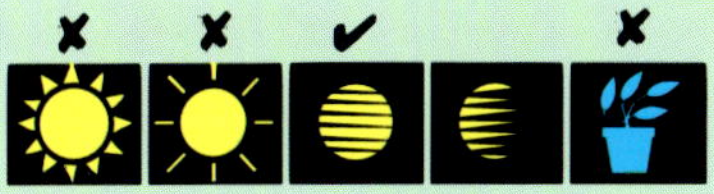

Most ferns prefer a fairly shady location and will deteriorate quickly if exposed to strong sunlight. Position ferns in the natural shade of other plants or in a room with diffused natural light.

### Temperature Range

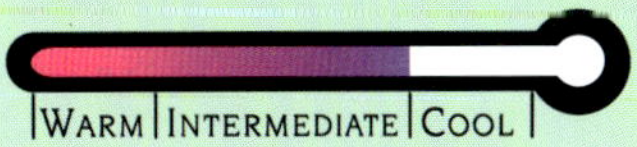


There are a great number of different ferns, and as a group they cover quite a wide range of preferred temperatures. In general, fine foliage ferns such as the nephrolepis and pteris need intermediate conditions of 55°–65°F. The ferns with coarser foliage, such as the platyceriums, require more warmth, in a range of 59°–70°F. Some ferns are quite hardy.

### Watering

All ferns enjoy a moist atmosphere. Spray them generously – this will also keep their lovely foliage clean and dust-free. Watering should be frequent to help maintain humidity, but the plant container should not be allowed to become waterlogged. Avoid overwatering, especially in lower temperatures.

### Feeding

Feed the plants with weak liquid fertilizer at every watering while they are active and producing new foliage. Little or no food is needed in the winter.

### Seasonal Care

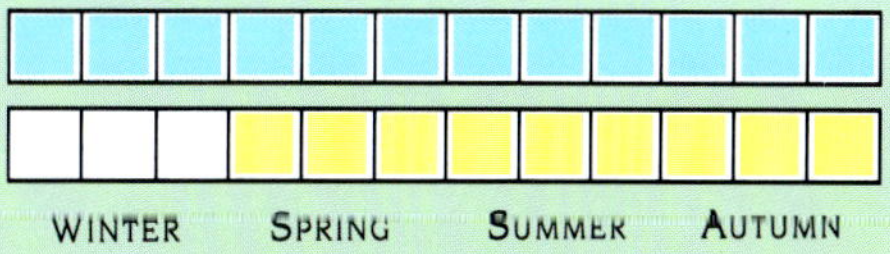


The plants must be kept moist throughout the year and may prefer to be given rainwater. Although you must guard against overwatering, it is also important to take care that the roots are not allowed to dry out. Thorough cleaning in the center of each plant during the fall will reduce problems with rotting leaves which clog the plant and make it unsightly

### Soil

An open, peaty mixture is essential to the well-being of all types of ferns. The containers must be well-drained, and a plant which is newly potted should be wetted mainly on the leaves and the soil kept only just moist.

# Ficus

Many houseplants are drawn from this diverse family of plants whether they are large, small, or creeping. Most have green foliage, although there are some variegated forms. All are propagated by means of cuttings of one kind or another, and need temperatures of around 70°F to get them under way.

The leaves of the F. *benjamina* have a weeping habit and can be most attractive in many settings – especially placed over water by an indoor pool. The plant's small, oval-shaped, glossy green leaves are produced in abundance – and lost in abundance as well if the light levels are inadequate.

**Healthy Plant**

*F. benjamina*, the weeping fig, grows into a large, graceful tree. As it grows, its "weeping" appearance becomes more pronounced. The plant does not have a definite rest period, but its leaves often turn yellow and drop off in winter. The leaves are 3–4 inches long, and are light green when young, darkening with age.

## F. Benjamina Ideal Conditions

### Light and Position

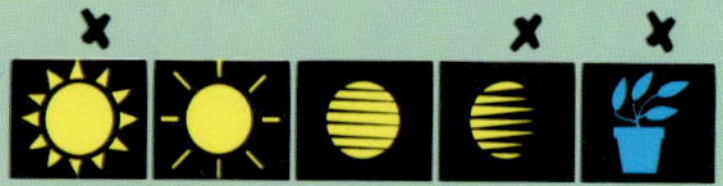

*F. benjamina* is one species of this family which requires plenty of light, but not direct sunlight. If adequate light is not provided, the leaves will turn yellow and drop off.

### Temperature Range

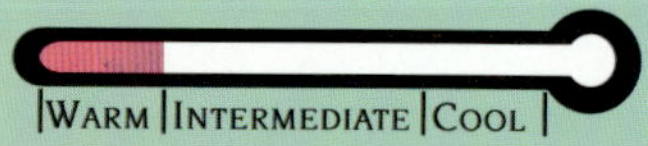


The Weeping Fig is happiest in temperatures between 65°–70°F. The maximum temperature it will tolerate is 75°F. This plant does not like drafts, so if it is near a window, make sure there are no cold breezes coming through.

### Watering

As with all the ficus varieties, *F. benjamina* should not be overwatered, or the leaves will inevitably turn yellow and drop off. Water no more than twice a week in summer and every 7–10 days in winter.

### Feeding

Established plants will need copious feeding in whatever form you chose. Less feeding is required in winter, but plants that continue to produce new growth will need a small amount.

### Seasonal Care

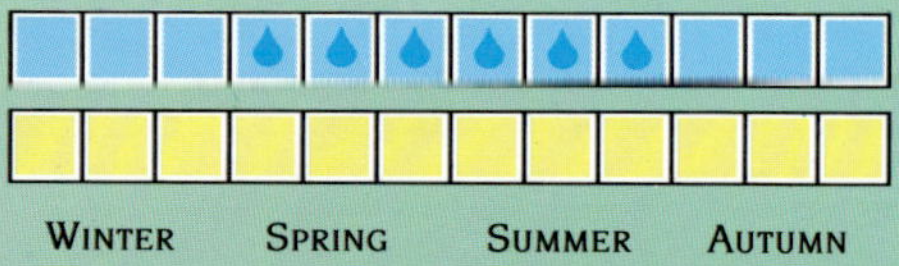


Liquid fertilizer should be added to the water during the active growth period. A daily spraying of water will benefit this plant throughout the year. Repot, once a year at most, in the spring. Mature plants need not be repotted but can have the topsoil replenished. Prune in spring, but do not remove any aerial shoots. The plant can be propagated from stem cuttings taken in the spring.

### Soil

Like many of the strong ficus plants, it will soon push its roots through the bottom of the pot. Withdraw the plant from its pot and carefully tease back the roots through the drainage holes. When the rootball is a mass of roots, repot in a soil-based mixture.

**Healthy Plant**
*F. robusta*, the Rubber Plant, (above) is surely one of the most familiar houseplants. The central stem usually grows straight, but branching can be induced by cutting off new growth. When purchasing, make sure the leaves are free from blemishes and dark green, shiny, and leathery in texture.

New plants are made by removing tip cuttings that are reasonably firm and about 4 inches in length. In moist peat and a temperature of 70°F, rooting is not too difficult.

The well-known ubiquitous Rubber Plant is one of the most popular houseplants. *F. robusta* is the name of the modern version of an earlier plant, *F. elastica*, which has long been discontinued. The Rubber Plant today is a much tougher individual than its predecessor and is more able to withstand the vicissitudes of life in the home.

New plants are raised from cuttings prepared from individual leaves with a small section of stem attached, and, as a rule, are inserted in the fall when plants are either dormant or at least less active. For rooting, a temperature of around 70°F is needed.

## F. Robusta Ideal Conditions

### Light and Position

Although the Rubber Plant will tolerate fairly shady conditions, it grows more quickly in good light. It will also benefit from direct sunlight for a few hours a day. *F. robusta* prefers cool environments to dry and hot; otherwise, it is a very adaptable plant.

### Temperature Range

Warm | Intermediate | Cool

Temperatures between 50°–59°, are best, but the Rubber Plant will tolerate a minimum of 40°F in winter. In very hot rooms, above 85°F, the leaves tend to lose their turgid appearance.

### Watering

With most houseplants, the temptation is to overwater. This is one plant that should never be overwatered. In winter the soil should be just moist, in summer water twice a week at most.

### Feeding

When plants are first purchased and brought indoors, they should be fed immediately. Feeding should continue thereafter, using a weak fertilizer with each watering. Less is needed in winter. Plants which have just been repotted need no food for at least three months.

### Seasonal Care

Winter Spring Summer Autumn

Overgrown, larger plants can be pruned in autumn by cutting through the stem just above the leaf. Check the resultant flow of sap by covering the wound with moist peat. Clean the leaves by wiping them with a damp sponge. Less watering is required in winter when the plant is inactive.

### Soil

A soil-based houseplant mixture is essential. Once in pots 7 inches in diameter, sustain with regular feedings. The plant should be well rooted before repotting. Water after potting and keep on the dry side for one month to allow the plant to root in the new soil.

## Varieties and Purchasing

Because there are so many varieties of ficus, there is sure to be one to fit each personal requirement. When purchasing, look for clean, blemish-free leaves. The plants should have a little sparkle to them, too. Those with dull and dowdy foliage will have less chance of surviving when introduced to the conditions of the average living room. Look also for missing leaves, which are a sign of old age and poor culture. Besides *F. benjamina* and *F. robusta*, the most popular varieties, there are other members of the ficus family which make excellent houseplants.

*F.* 'Europa' This cream and green variegated form of the Rubber Plant is one of the most attractive of all the many ficus plants.

*F. pumila* This is also called the Creeping or Climbing Fig. It has little in common with the other plants, being a small, creeping variety with thin, heart-shaped leaves which are usually pale green. *F. pumila* is generally used as a trailing plant, and it grows very well in moist, shady locations.

*F. lyrata* The Fiddle Leaf Fig has violin-shaped leaves attached to woody stems. The plant can reach tree proportions in time and will require regular pruning to keep it under control. It grows quickly and tends to stay on a single stem. In poor conditions, rapid shedding of the leaves will occur.

*F. benghalensis* The Banyan Tree is valued for its branching habit and dark, oval leaves which can grow to 12 inches in length.

*F. retusa* This ficus, the Indian Laurel, may occasionally bear small inedible fruit. The plant has dark green, elliptical leaves which grow to about 3 inches on stems which branch profusely.

*F. rubiginosa* This plant is the Rusty Fig, a small tree with leathery, oval leaves which are rust-colored underneath. *F.r.* 'Variegata' has leaves which are marbled with yellow markings.

*F. sagittata* This is a good trailing plant with leaves 2–3 inches long.

**Healthy Plant**
*Ficus pumila* This little ficus (above) is a creeper with shape and habit quite unlike larger members of its family. It likes a moist, shady atmosphere, and given this, it will produce aerial roots, enabling it to climb. There is a variegated variety available.

Plant breeders have really gone to town with this very popular and handsome houseplant. Until recently, there were only two varieties available, those with the familiar apple-green weeping foliage and their near relative with creamy variegations. Now you will find many forms of *Ficus benjamina*; in particular, one with deep, almost olive-green foliage, and another lovely variety with a slightly serrated leaf.

## PESTS AND DISEASES

All these plants can contract pests and diseases, but which type will depend on the individual plant.

**Scale insect** (below) These can become a major problem if left unchecked to go about their destructive business. Black, crusty adult scale insects, or softer, pinkish-beige young insects attach themselves to leaves, branches, and almost every other part of the plant. *F. benjamina* is especially prone to these pests, so check the undersides of leaves frequently. For minor attacks, remove the scales with an old toothbrush. Bad attacks may need treating with dimethoate.

**Sooty mold** Dark mold on a *F. benjamina* leaf grows on the excreta of scale insects into which fungus mold then settles. To cure, wipe the leaves clean with soapy water.

**Root rot** (below) This is aggravated when roots are deprived of oxygen, which in turn is caused by soil that is too wet and does not allow air to penetrate it. Because the plant is deprived of moisture and nutrition, the roots will turn brown and lifeless, and the plant will shed its foliage. Let the soil dry out thoroughly so the plant can produce new roots. The obvious precaution is never to overwater the plant nor let the plant stay wet for long periods of time.

**Mealy bug** (right) These usually appear on older plants. Remove adults and their nests using cotton soaked in denatured alcohol or use chemicals like malathion or dimethoate.

**Underwatering** To maintain healthy, lush growth, *F. pumila* needs careful watering. Never allow the plant to become too dry or the paper-thin leaves will shrivel. Allow only the top ½ inch of soil to become dry between waterings.

**Overwatering** This is a common mistake with *F. robusta*. A symptom of overwatering is drooping, lifeless leaves which will soon turn yellow and drop off. These plants need only moderate watering, even in active growth.

**Brown leaf** When leaves die naturally, brownish spots appear on them and continue to spread until the leaves are dead and finally drop off.

## General Ideal Conditions

### Light and Position

There are many ficus varieties, each requiring slightly different lighting and positioning. All, with the exception of *F. pumila*, require good light and shade from direct sun. Healthy specimens will grow quite large and thus need ample space.

### Temperature Range

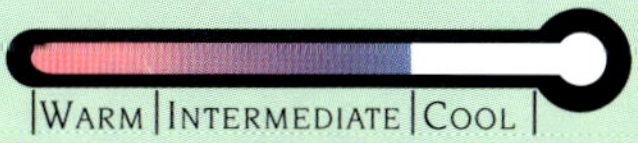


All except *F. diversifolia* require a minimum temperature of 59°–70°. *F. diversifolia* can withstand temperatures down to 45°F, provided watering is infrequent. The maximum temperature for all these plants is 75°F.

### Watering

None of these plants like to be overwatered. A symptom of overwatering is yellowing and falling leaves. Water twice a week in summer and once a week in winter. Never let a plant stand in a dish of water.

### Feeding

Liquid fertilizer can be added to the water every few days during the active growth period. Generally, ficus plants should be given larger and stronger doses than those recommended by the manufacturer or retailer.

### Seasonal Care

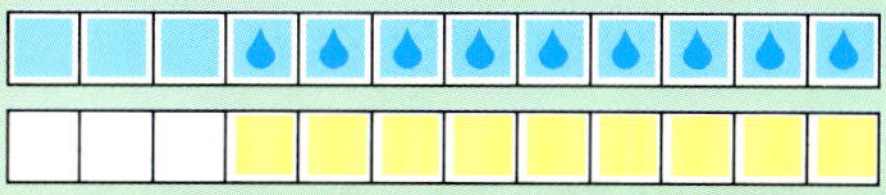


All varieties need to be kept moist throughout the year, although less water is needed in winter than at other times. Water thoroughly and allow the soil to dry out before repeating. Repotting can be done annually in spring. Mature plants which do not need repotting can have the topsoil replenished. Prune the plant in spring and remember to dust the cuts with charcoal to prevent bleeding. As they age, some of these plants will develop aerial roots which should never be cut. Instead tie them back.

### Soil

All large specimens need soil-based mixtures. The plants should be repotted when they have a solid rootball. Larger plants tend to push their roots through the pot bottom. Draw these back by carefully removing the rootball, pulling the roots with it.

# Gardenia jasminoides

CAPE JASMINE

This is a real old-fashioned flowering shrub. There was a time when no self-respecting indoor gardener was without one. There were then teams of greenhouse gardeners in the background to coax these rather temperamental plants into flower. However, they are not that difficult to grow, but they do need particular attention if they are to fill a garden room or sunroom with their glorious perfume, which some people do not like.

As with all plants that need this combination of high temperatures and high humidity, the rooting process can be slow, so propagation requires concentration and patience. Start by taking 3-inch tip cuttings in spring or early summer. Dip the cuttings into a rooting hormone and place them in small pots of damp "acid" peat-based soil. There are specialized mixtures on sale for these acid-loving plants. Secure the potted cuttings within plastic bags, or place them in a propagator, and maintain temperatures between 61–65°F.

Once new roots have started to grow, there will be fresh green top growth. Remove the cuttings from the propagator and place them in a warm shady spot to grow on. During this time, water them moderately, enough to wet the soil thoroughly, but allow the top ½ inch to dry out before watering again. When the roots have filled the pot, the young plants can be moved into pots one size larger using a similar potting mixture.

**Healthy Plant**
Although mature gardenias may reach 6 feet indoors, they are more often bushy shrubs. Their glossy evergreen foliage is not unlike that of a camellia, but it is softer and less rounded. The flowers are startlingly white seen against the deep green leaves and can be single, double, or semi-double.

## Varieties and Purchasing

*Gardenia jasminoides*
Although there are other varieties, this is the one most commonly seen on sale. It will be generally available during the summer when it is in flower. However, this is the most inappropriate time to move it from place to place, so take great care when doing so otherwise, you may lose some or all of the buds. Make sure that the plant is well protected within a draft-free carrier and never take it home in the trunk of a car.

## Pests and Diseases

Gardenias are prone to scale insect, red spider mites, and mealy bug. As these plants like high humidity and glasshouse pests dislike a moist atmosphere, stand gardenias on trays of damp horticultural aggregate and mist-spray them daily. While doing so, check them carefully for signs of attack.

**Aphids** (above) These sap sucking insects may be green, brown, black, or a grayish-pink, the most common being greenfly or blackfly. They collect and feed on new leaves, flower buds, and soft stems. Remove them manually, improve humidity, and spray the plant forcibly with water. Use a soapy spray or permethrin if the aphids are a persistent problem.

**Scale insect** The adult scale insects live protected within a waxy scale, which you will find attached to the undersides of leaves. Remove them with an old toothbrush and spray the plant with soapy water. Check again in a week and repeat the spraying if necessary.

**Red spider mite** Evidence of these will be found under the leaves, too, as it is here where they weave their webs. Remove parts of the plant that are affected and spray with derris. Red spider infestations are hard to keep under control – you may have to discard the plant altogether.

**Mealy bug** Check all over the plant for mealy bug, as they appear everywhere. They look rather like tiny woodlice. Remove both adults and their wooly nests by hand or with a cloth soaked in denatured alcohol. Chemicals like malathion or dimethoate may be needed for total control.

## Ideal Conditions

### Light and Position

Provide good light, with some direct sun during the winter months. During the summer gardenias will do well in the dappled shade provided by other taller plants.

### Temperature Range

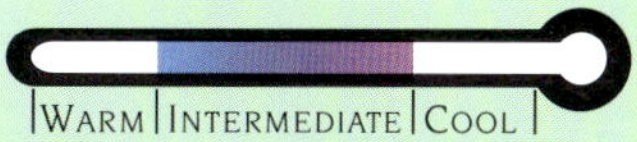


Pay great attention to the detail of temperature where these fickle plants are concerned. When buds are forming, make sure they have a steady day and night temperature of 61°F. Swings in either direction are likely to cause bud drop. The temperature can rise by 10°F when buds are not forming.

### Watering

Always use soft, tepid water for gardenias. Water moderately for the majority of the year, giving enough to make sure that the soil is thoroughly moistened, but allowing the top ½ in to dry out between waterings. From October to February provide less water, allowing the top 1–2 in to dry out before watering again.

Humidity is a high priority with gardenias; provide too little and the buds will drop. So mist daily with soft, tepid rainwater, taking care to avoid any open flowers as this will mark them.

### Feeding

Provide liquid fertilizer in standard doses once every two weeks from March to September.

### Seasonal Care

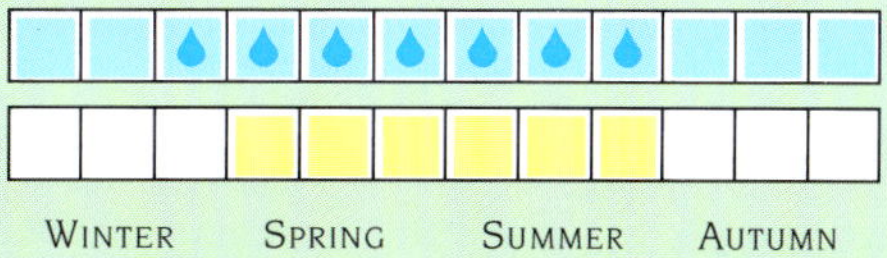


Remember to maintain an even temperature of 61°F while buds are forming in the spring; to make sure of high humidity by misting regularly; and to provide the plants with good light during the winter months and dappled shade while the plant is in flower.

Prune into shape, if necessary, in late winter.

### Soil

Gardenias are lime-haters, so when repotting, once every two or three years, use a special soil.

# Gloriosa rothschildiana

GLORY LILY

This tender climber comes from Africa and tropical Asia. It grows from a tuber which lies dormant during the winter and needs to be started into growth each spring. In its season it grows fast to 6 feet or more. If there is space or support, it will happily cover a pillar or a wall, attaching itself by tendrils. Its flowers are elegant and showy – brilliantly colored, the petals scarlet with a golden yellow base and golden margins. Each of the six petals curves back so that it touches the stem; emerging at right angles from the center of the petals are long eye-catching stamens.

It is very easy to increase the stock by removing "offsets," or small tubers, from the parent tuber when growth has started in early spring. These should be potted up and grown on in 5-inch pots containing a soil-based potting mixture. The young plants may not flower in their first season.

## Pests and Diseases

**Aphids** Gloriosas are really only troubled by greenfly. These will congregate on mature leaves, on the underside of young leaves, and on the soft stems. If the plant becomes infested, the leaves below the invaded growth become sticky with honeydew, a secretion from the greenfly. Remove as many of the flies as are visible, spray the plant with a diluted soap solution, repeat in three days, and once again in another ten.

## Varieties and Purchasing

*GlorIosa rothschildiana* is readily available in tuber form from good garden centers in the spring. These are usually pre-packed by reputable bulb and tuber specialists.

*G. superba* Slightly more unusual, but worth looking for.

It is also possible to purchase the plants already started into growth. Take care when selecting these, as gloriosas are very susceptible to changes in temperature. They should have a green and healthy look. Leaf loss without discoloration is a sign that temperatures have not been correct. Make sure, too, that they are securely packed in a draft-free container for the journey home.

**Healthy Plant**
The showy Glory Lily is an easy-going, fast-growing climber. They grow from small tubers started into growth during the spring. For a display like this, you will probably need 3 or 4 tubers planted in an 8-inch pot using a soil-based mixture.

## Ideal Conditions

### Light and Position

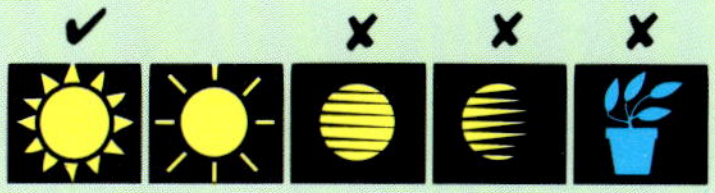

Gloriosas need good light with some direct sun during the spring. During the summer when the sun is at its most intense, they will need some protection from midday heat.

### Temperature Range

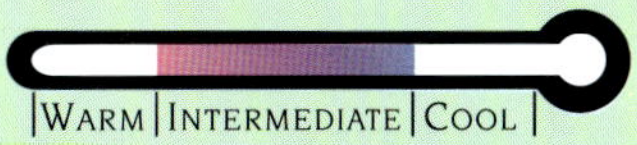


These plants need quite a high temperature to start them into growth, around 68°F. Once growth has commenced, a temperature of about 61°F will be fine. It is very important that the temperatures remain stable, particularly in the early stages of growth; any violent swings will cause a growth check from which the plant may not recover.

### Watering

During dormancy the tubers should be kept completely dry. When they are repotted in early spring, make sure the soil is moist. As growth begins to emerge, gradually increase the amounts of water provided. In full and active growth gloriosas will need to be kept moist at all times. When growth shows signs of slowing down, the foliage will begin to yellow, then gradually reduce the amounts of water provided until finally watering is stopped altogether.

### Feeding

Once growth is established, gloriosas will need a liquid feed once a week.

### Seasonal Care

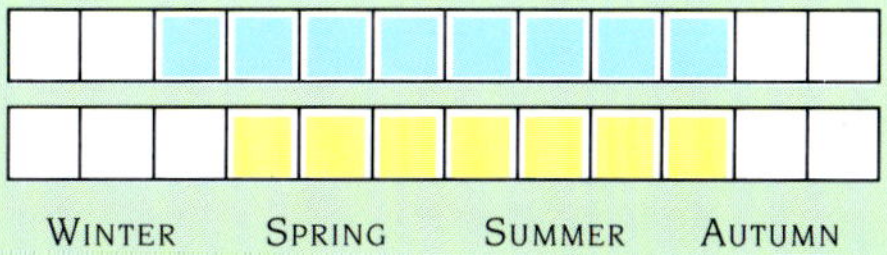


A warm, completely dry position is necessary during the winter dormancy period. Check watering technique during the spring and summer and make sure that the soil is kept thoroughly moist at all times while the plant is in strong active growth. Dead head regularly to encourage further flowers.

### Soil

Gloriosas need plenty of water but do not like to be saturated. Good drainage is therefore essential so a soil-based compost must be used. Increase the drainage facility further by adding washed shards to the bottom of the pots.

# Gynura sarmentosa

PURPLE PASSION VINE

### VARIETIES AND PURCHASING

As a plant grown chiefly for its foliage, *Gynura sarmentosa*, or the more shrubby *G. auranticica*, should be available at good garden centers all year round.

Unlike many plants with hairy, colored foliage, this one needs good light to maintain it. It is really only grown for its brilliant leaf color because, although it bears clusters of bright orange flowers which look great with the leaves, they do not smell too good. As the buds form, they can be removed.

Gynuras can be grown as a trailer or trained up a support, but they are seen at their best when planted, several to a hanging container, and hung just at eye level.

These little plants are easy to propagate. Simply take 3–4-inch tip cuttings at any time between March and September and plant them in groups of four in pots containing potting soil. Keep them warm, but out of direct sunlight, and water them just enough to keep the potting soil moist. They should root within three weeks. When they have made about 6 inches of new growth, pot them on and treat them as mature plants.

## Pests and Diseases

**Aphids** This is the only pest really to trouble gynuras. Keep an eye on the shoot tips and young foliage, as this is where they will cluster together doing their worst. They multiply at an astonishing rate. Wipe off all the visible adults and spray the plant with a strong jet of water, or a diluted soap solution.

**Healthy Plant**
Make sure they have a good strong color, as this is a sign that they have been growing in the right type of light. Well maintained, they should appear bushy.

## Ideal Conditions

### Light and Position

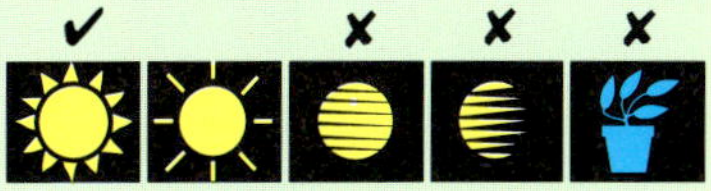

Gynuras need good light; a position where they will receive some direct sunlight every day will guarantee their intense coloring. Without this, growth will become leggy, and the growing tips will begin to pale. They will trail or climb, given support; either way, they are best planted three or four to a pot.

### Temperature Range

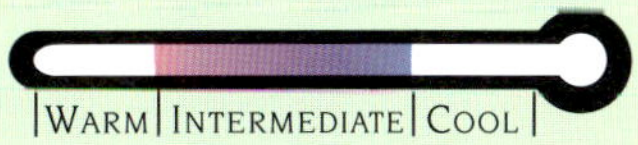


A minimum temperature of 50°F is adequate, but they will do better kept around 55°F.

### Watering

Provide enough water to make sure that the soil becomes moist, allowing the top ½ inch of soil to dry out before watering again. Less water is necessary during the winter. Try to avoid wetting the leaves while watering, as the fine hairs are likely to trap water droplets which can cause leaf marking.

### Feeding

Provide liquid fertilizer in the recommended dose once a month throughout the year.

### Seasonal Care

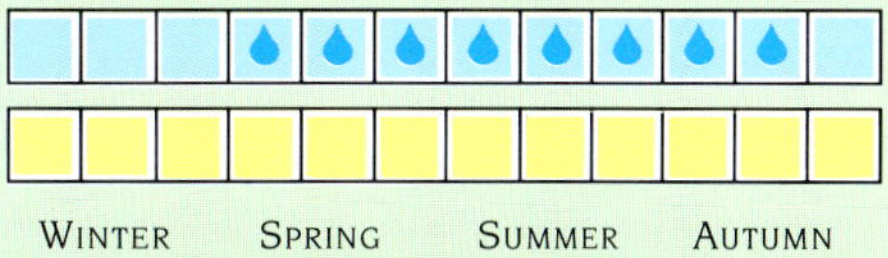


Good light throughout the year is essential for this plant; without it a gynura will lose its dramatic coloring.

Pinch out the shoot tips regularly to encourage bushy growth and to prevent the plant from becoming leggy.

If the scent of the flowers is disliked, remove them while they are still in bud form.

Maintain a collection of young, strong plants by taking cuttings at six-monthly intervals.

### Soil

Gynuras grow fast and will need to be moved annually into larger pots in the spring, using a soil-based mixture.

# Hedera

IVY

These are among the most popular of plants sold for indoor decoration, although they are not particularly suited to rooms that are heated. Perhaps one of their most appealing qualities is that once they appear to have failed indoors, they can be planted out in the yard where they are likely to flourish.

There are many different varieties, and almost all of them are propagated from easily rooted cuttings taken during the spring and summer months. Firm pieces of stem with two sound leaves attached are put into small pots filled with a peat-based soil and placed in a close atmosphere at a temperature in the region of 65°–70°F. Several cuttings should be inserted in each pot to help make sure that the eventual plant looks quite bushy.

**Healthy Plant**
*Hedera helix* 'Glacier' A very popular houseplant – no surprise – it is easy-going and will climb or trail, providing an excellent foil for its more showy neighbors. However, it can quickly become straggly and unattractive; to avoid this, pinch out the growing tips two or three times a year.

## Varieties and Purchasing

Never buy an Ivy with long lengths of leafless stem at the top of each stalk, as this indicates the plant has already been attacked by pests. What is more, all the other plants in the store are likely to be infested as well. There are only a few hedera species, but many varieties, with a wide range of leaves.

*H. canariensis* This is one of the tallest plants. It has large leaves 5 inches long and 6 inches wide, which are the shape of a rounded triangle. The leaves are dark green with pale green veins. There is also a variegated form called 'Gloire de Marengo,' which has leaves bordered in cream and blotched with gray-green.

*H. helix* This is the English Ivy, of which there are many varieties. Its familiar leaves have three or five lobes.

*H.h.* 'Chicago' This has medium-sized green leaves. There is a variegated form H.h. 'Chicago Variegata' which has creamy-bordered leaves. It is a little more difficult to manage but worth growing as it is a very colorful plant.

*H.h.* 'Glacier' This is perhaps the hardiest of all the variegated Ivies. It is light and dark gray.

*H.h.* 'Little Diamond' This also has gray-colored variegated foliage. Its leaves are a particularly pleasing diamond shape. The stems have a twisting appearance.

*H.h.* 'Sagittaefolia' As its name, derived from the Latin for "arrow," suggests, the dark green leaves of this Ivy are arrow-shaped. There is also a variegated form, *H.h.* 'Sagittaefolia Variegata,' which has green and pale yellow leaves. This makes an excellent trailing plant.

*H. ivalace* This hedera has glistening green leaves and reddish-brown stems. It is excellent for both indoor and outdoor use. It is seen to its best effect when grown as a hanging plant in the window of a cool room or outdoors on a sheltered patio where there are no cold winds.

## Pests and Diseases

**Mealy bug** Check the leaves of your hedera regularly for mealy bug. Remove and destroy any adults and nests you see, or wipe the infested leaves with a pad of cotton soaked in denatured alcohol.

**Black spot** Ivies are particularly susceptible to this. It will appear on plants that have been kept crowded together or in very damp conditions. It is a damaging fungus which should be treated immediately with a reliable fungicide.

**Thrips** These insects, which are also called thunderflies, are sometimes present in Ivies. They can be detected by gray streaks on the softer leaves. Remove any very badly damaged leaves, and spray thoroughly with an insecticide such as pyrethrum.

**Scale insect** These will lodge on the stem of the plant, or under its leaves. They should be brushed off with an old toothbrush. It might be necessary to spray the plant with dimethoate.

**Aphids** One of the most common houseplant pests, aphids may be detected on the leaves. Treat with a soapy spray. Aphids may also spread virus.

**Botrytis** The spores of this fungus are constantly in the air, and they only become a problem in a cool, damp atmosphere. Check the environment and move the plant if necessary. Remove and destroy affected parts.

## Ideal Conditions

### Light and Position

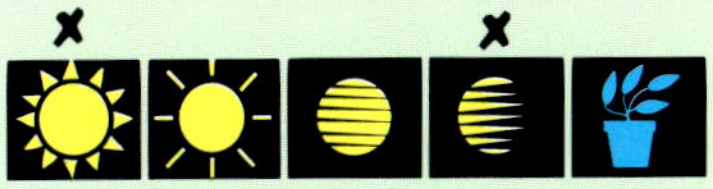

Ivies require light, cool environments. If poorly lit, variegated types will lose their coloring and should thus have 2–3 hours of sunlight each day. Keep other types out of direct sunlight and away from dry heat which can encourage red spider mites.

### Temperature Range

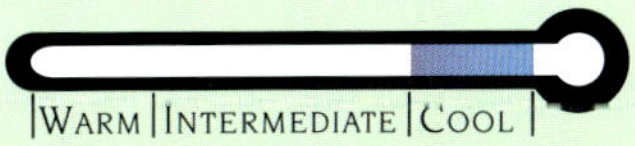


Ivies are generally sturdy enough to withstand a broad range of temperatures but they do not like wide fluctuations. Most respond well to temperatures between 50°–59°F. In temperatures higher than 65°F, provide a moist environment. In winter, let the plants rest in a cool temperature of 50°F.

### Watering

Keep the compost moist n summer with regular waterings. In winter, water sparingly but do not let the compost dry out. Ivies like humidity, especially if the atmosphere is dry, as in summer. Mist frequently at these times, and also in winter if the room is dry and warm.

### Feeding

Ivies are not fussy about feeding, and any fertilizer recommended by the manufacturer may be used. Feed actively growing plants with a standard liquid fertilizer every two weeks.

### Seasonal Care

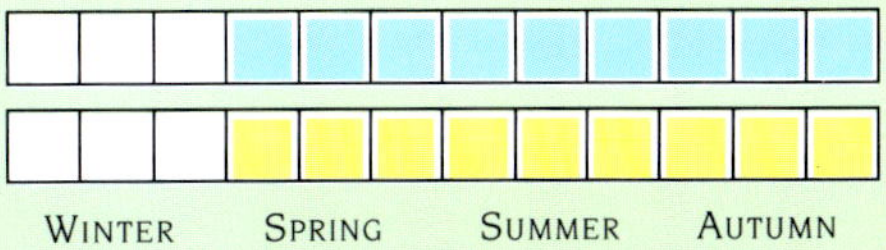


In their growth period, Ivies can create dense foliage which should be cleaned out in autumn and spring by removing all dead or dying undergrowth. Water frequently in all seasons except winter when the soil should be kept fairly dry. Repot Ivies every two years in the spring in pots no larger than 4–6 in in diameter. Plants which are not repotted should have the top layer of soil replenished annually.

### Soil

Peaty mixtures tend to produce soft growth, so use a combination of a peat-based potting mixture and a soil-based one. This will also eliminate the need for frequent repotting in a mixture of moistened peat moss and coarse sand.

# Heptapleurum

## Parasol Plant or Green Rays

Heptapleurums make handsome foliage plants. They are reasonably easy to care for and free-growing. In the right circumstances they can grow into small trees. There is a variegated form and also varieties with smaller leaves, but they all grow in a similar way. Naturally glossy green leaves, elliptic in shape, are arranged like fingers on slender stalks attached to a stout central stem. By removing the growing tip at an early age, plants may be encouraged to branch quite freely and take on a very bushy form. Alternatively, they can be left to grow on, in which case they simply extend to about 8–10 feet as slender specimens.

Stem cuttings can be rooted in a temperature of around 70°F if the conditions are close and moist. At potting time, three plants put into a 5-inch pot will provide plants of considerable beauty as they mature.

**Healthy Plant**
*H. arboricola*, or Parasol Plant, is a beautiful plant to display, particularly when it is allowed to grow tall and slender. The *H.a.* 'Variegata' (below) has yellow markings on its leaves and has been encouraged to take on a more bushy shape. The coloring can be shown to advantage when the foliage is dense.

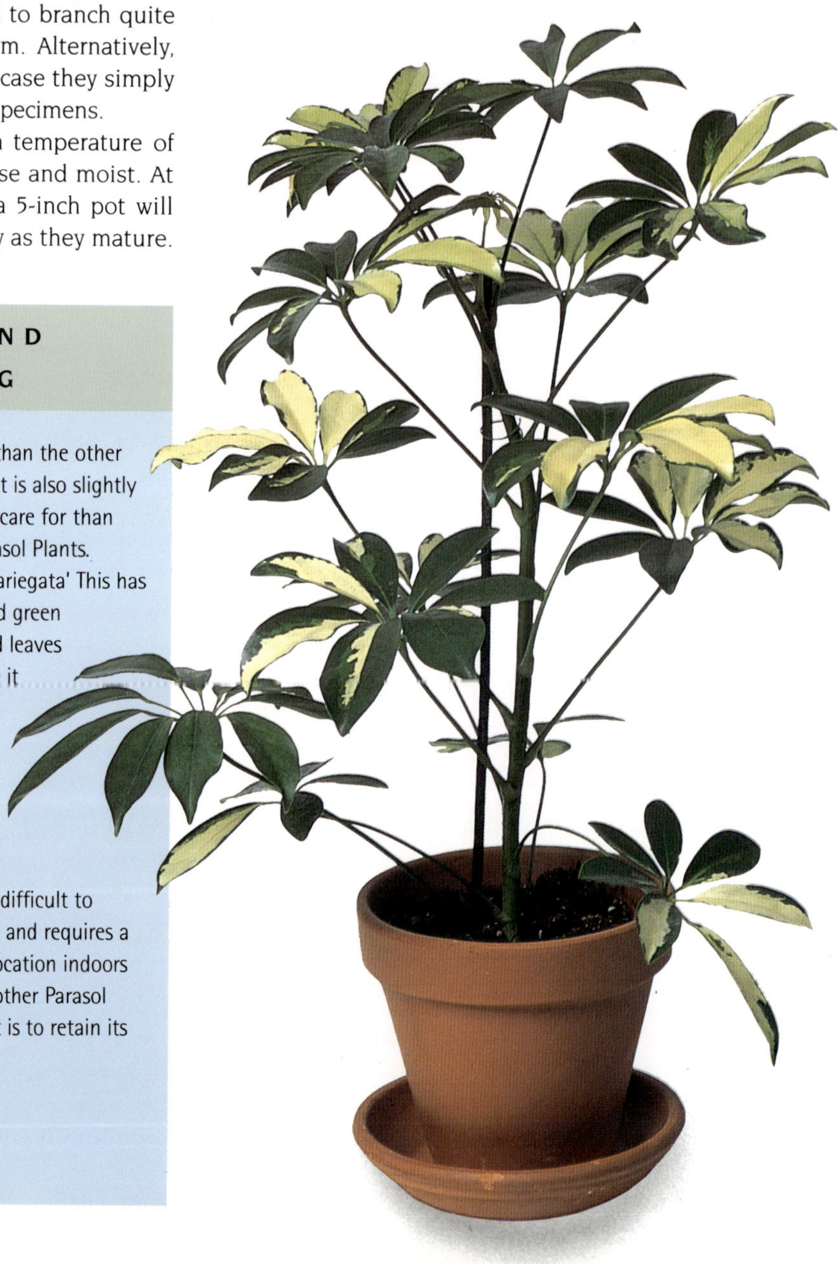

### Varieties and Purchasing

Inspect young leaves for aphids and avoid plants with yellowing foliage or any other leaf discoloration. Parasol Plants that have been very wet and cold will wilt, and should also be avoided.

*H. arboricola* The original variety, this is the most elegant plant and is probably the best type to choose.

*H.a.* 'Geisha Girl' With more rounded individual leaves, this is less free growing, although it is similar to the original *H. arboricola* in other respects.

*H.a.* 'Hong Kong' This has green foliage, too, but is much smaller and more compact than the other varieties. It is also slightly harder to care for than other Parasol Plants.

*H.a.* 'Variegata' This has yellow and green variegated leaves that make it more colorful than the other varieties. It is fairly difficult to propagate and requires a brighter location indoors than the other Parasol Plants if it is to retain its coloring.

## PESTS AND DISEASES

**Mealy bug** This is normally only found on larger plants with a tangled mass of growth in which it can go undetected. Wipe bugs off the plant with a sponge that has been soaked in denatured alcohol or spray thoroughly with insecticide. Large yellow blotches often appear on the topmost leaves of heptapleurums. There is no simple explanation or cure, but fortunately most plants seem to grow out of this condition.

**Red spider mite** These may attack heptapleurums, particularly if the surroundings are unusually hot or dry. They are very small and hard to detect with the naked eye as a result. Light brown leaf discoloration is a sign of their presence, which can be confirmed by thorough scrutiny of the undersides of the leaves with a magnifying glass. Remove and destroy damaged parts of the plant. Treat with insecticide.

**Aphids** These occasionally attack young leaves and cause spotting. They can be controlled by using a soapy spray.

**Stem rot** This can affect Parasol Plants, causing them to become slimy, black, and rotten near the base.

## IDEAL CONDITIONS

### LIGHT AND POSITION

All heptapleurums require good light. At least two to three hours a day are needed, but avoid direct sunlight. If lighting is poor, the leaves will grow abnormally long. Position the plant well away from radiators and drafts.

### TEMPERATURE RANGE

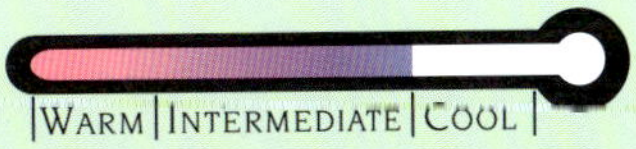


*H. arboricola* requires a minimum temperature of 59°F all year long, and a maximum temperature of 70°F. In winter, keep the plant warm at not less than 59°F. Heptapleurums also enjoy a moist, humid environment which can be created by standing the plants on trays of pebbles covered with water.

### WATERING

*H. arboricola* needs moderate watering. Allow the top 1 in of soil to dry out between waterings. The soil should not dry out more than this, nor should it be watered so that it is thoroughly wetted. The plants also enjoy frequent misting.

### FEEDING

Feed only when the plants are well rooted in their pots. This can be determined by turning the plant out of its pot to check the amount of root growth. A standard fertilizer may be used every two weeks from spring until late autumn.

### SEASONAL CARE

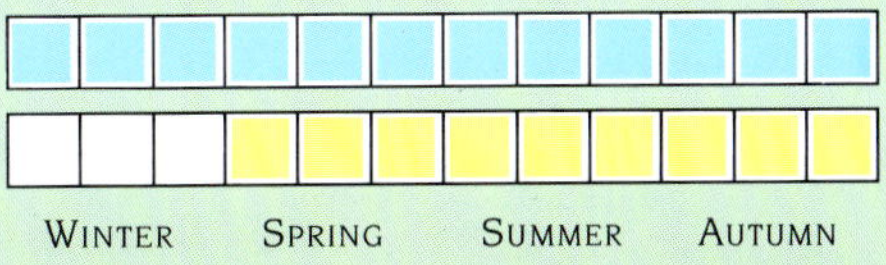


Heptapleurums should never be overwatered, but they should be watered more frequently during the active growth period between spring and summer. In spring the plants should be moved to pots 2 in larger. Continue to repot during the growth period as required. The plants can be propagated in spring from tip or stem cuttings.

### SOIL

Peat mixtures with a small amount of loam are best. Press the mixture down firmly in the pot, but not too tightly. Before repotting, make sure the plants have enough root growth to justify the move. When propagating, plant cuttings in a mixture of moistened peat moss and coarse sand.

# Herbs

Culinary herbs used to be grown only outdoors. Now potted herbs can be bought from the supermarket. They are ready to use and only need to be kept alive. Too often they are brought home, perhaps given a little water, and then stood in the kitchen. It should be no surprise that they keel over within a week. A kitchen is probably the most inappropriate place to keep plants like these. Most of them survive quite happily outside in the yard, where they benefit from relatively stable temperatures and, more important, cool air moving around them. A kitchen is almost certainly warm – too warm for many herbs; the air will be dry and the ventilation poor – a place for humans, not plants. Even those herbs that come from warmer parts of the world will not like it very much, unless they are given a little consideration.

Although many of these plants like different growing conditions, they can still be displayed together by using a large bowl or planter filled with a horticultural aggregate. Dampen the aggregate and then plunge the potted herbs into it. This will provide a permanent home for perennial herbs, and exhausted parsley and basil can be removed and replaced easily, thus extending your herb growing season.

**Healthy Plant**
There is a wide variety of herbs available. They may be grown for practical uses in cooking, or purely as decorative plants. A group of herbs (below) can also be grown together in a single container to great effect.

**Healthy Plant**
English parsley (left and above) is widely used for culinary purposes. Its tightly curled leaves make an attractive display.

**Healthy Plant**
A pot of basil (below) is commonly available from garden centers.

## Annual Herbs Varieties and Purchasing

**Basil** – *Ocimum basilicum* This can be bought in many places, so great is its general popularity. Basil needs more warmth than the other herbs and is very definitely an annual – it will grow for its season and then die. It can be bought as a small plant or grown from seed. Simply sprinkle the seeds onto the surface of some dampened seed mixture. Cover with a plastic bag, or keep in a propagator. When the seeds have germinated, remove them from their protection and let them grow on until they are large enough to handle. Then plant four or five together in 3-inch pots.

**Parsley** – *Petroselinum crispum* Strictly speaking, this is a biennial, but the foliage is at its best in the first season, so treat it as an annual, growing fresh seeds each year. Unlike many seeds, these need to be really cool to germinate. In March sprinkle them on the surface of dampened seed mixture, cover them very thinly, and stand outside until germination has taken place. Keep them cool while they are growing on. When they are large enough to handle, transplant into 3-inch pots of potting soil. Of course, this ever-popular herb is easily available as a small plant at many retail outlets through the spring and summer.

**Healthy Plant**
Aromatic herbs such as rosemary (left) are a popular choice for the herb garden, being both practical and easy to grow. Bay (right and below) is a common herb often used in cooking.

## Perennial Herbs Varieties and Purchasing

**Thyme** Plenty of varieties to choose from, all strongly aromatic, some with variegated foliage, for example: *Thymus vulgaris aureus, T. citriodorus* – Lemon Thyme, or *T. serpyllum* – Wild Thyme.

**Marjoram** – *Origanum marjorana* A basic herb with many uses, it is an ingredient of mixed herbs, together with sage and thyme. When dried, it has a stronger flavor.

**Tarragon** – *Artemisia dracunculus* This is a bushy, tangled herb, with a delicious, spicy, fragrant flavor. It bears flowers that do not mature or bear seed. The foliage may well die back during the winter.

**Rosemary** – *Rosmarinus officinalis* More space is needed for this popular herb. It really benefits from regular picking, which encourages a lush dense foliage.

**Bay** – *Laurus nobilis* This is a really worthwhile herb to grow. Like rosemary, it will need a bit of space, but properly cared for in a cool environment, it will grow into a small tree and live for years.

You should be able to buy all these from your garden center or nursery during the early spring and summer.

## Pests and Diseases

Happily, perennial herbs do not seem to be troubled by glasshouse pests. Basil and Parsley are sometimes invaded by whitefly or greenfly. You will find the greenfly clustering around the fresh new growth. The adult whiteflies generally settle on the undersides of leaves, their presence obvious: when you touch the plant, the white wedge-shaped flies will all take to the wing. Obviously, you can only use a safe form of control – so remove all greenfly you can see with a dampened cloth, and spray plants with a dilute soap solution.

Always remember to wash your freshly picked herbs before you use them.

Stand them in trays of moist aggregate, which will keep the air around the plants humid and help them to keep cool and produce plenty of fresh foliage.

Water them regularly, never allow them to dry out completely, or indeed to become waterlogged. Harvest the herbs as often as possible. Pick out the growing tips, which will encourage them to make good bushy growth, once again providing plenty of fresh herbs to use.

Dry any surplus herbs in a light airy place and store them in airtight jars, ready to use in the dark days of winter.

Keep indoor herbs cool; around 59°F would be perfect, but if warmer than this, they must be kept well ventilated. Keep all herbs in good light, but out of direct sunlight.

**Powdery mildew** This fungus thrives in cool damp conditions. Check environmental conditions and allow the plant to dry out slightly between waterings.

## Ideal Conditions

### Light and Position

Although all herbs need good light to make the required fresh leaf growth, they will not do very well indoors if they are placed in direct sunlight, except perhaps early morning sun. Hot, direct sunlight will scorch the foliage and even if it has been properly watered, the plant will very probably wilt.

### Temperature Range

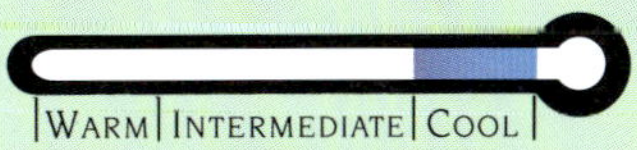


Many of the familiar perennial garden herbs, such as thyme, marjoram, bay, and rosemary, can happily tolerate temperatures as low as freezing. Of course indoors this is an impossibility, but keep them as cool as possible.

The more tender herbs, such as basil, parsley, and tarragon, should be kept warmer.

### Watering

During the summer months, provide enough water to moisten the soil thoroughly, allowing the top ½ inch to dry out between waterings. Remember, if herbs are kept in a warm place, they will dry out very fast.

During the winter, the perennial varieties will only need enough water to prevent them from drying out completely.

### Feeding

Provide all herbs with a dose of liquid fertilizer only every two weeks during the summer.

### Seasonal Care

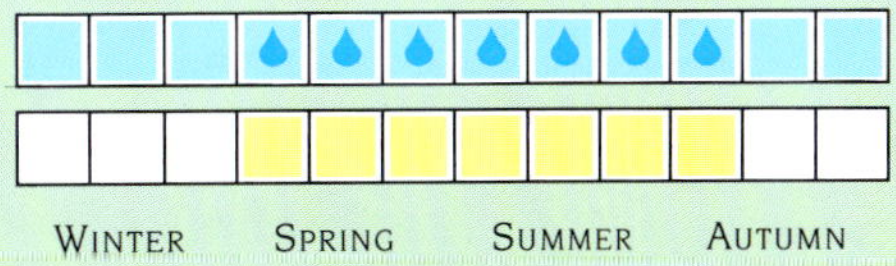


Any flower buds must be removed as soon as they appear, because the flowers will diminish the strength of flavor in the foliage. Harvest the herbs regularly by pinching out the growing tips, but do not overpick. Turn the potted herbs once a week so they get full advantage of the available light.

### Soil

Perennial herbs will do well if planted in a soil-based mixture. They will need repotting annually. Annual herbs bought ready for use will not need transplanting. Annual herbs raised from seed will need a peat-based mixture.

# Hibiscus rosa sinensis

ROSE OF CHINA, BLACKING PLANT OR CHINESE ROSE

This is another much improved potted plant for indoor decoration, owing much of its undoubted success to the scientist rather than the grower of the plants. The discovery of growth-retarding chemicals has made it possible to grow these plants so that they can be in full flower when they are little more than 15 inches high. This makes them ideal for the average room, ideal for handling and packing, and ideal in that they require less heated space in the greenhouse than many other houseplants. H. *rosa-sinensis* is woody, has glossy green leaves, and produces quite superb flowers in both single and double forms.

**Healthy Plant**
A hibiscus has glossy leaves and brilliant flowers. The leaves should grow right down to the top of the pot. When choosing one, check the buds and undersides of the leaves for aphids.

**Healthy Leaves**
Despite the differences in shape, these four leaves all came from the same plant.

## VARIETIES AND PURCHASING

*H. rosa-sinensis* This is the original Rose of China from which many hybrids have been produced. The flowers may be crimson, pink, yellow, or white, and have long golden stamens.

*H.r-s Cooperi* This is a variety of the Rose of China. Its leaves have olive green, pink, and white markings, and its flowers are red.

*H. schizopetalus* This is the Japanese hibiscus. Its delicate stems support orange-red flowers.

*'Hawaian hybrids'* This group of hibiscus all have very large flowers. They include 'Surfrider,' 'Elegance,' and 'Firefly.'

## Pests and Diseases

**Aphids** These insects will attack both the buds and the open flowers, as well as the upper leaves. Remove aphids by running a finger and thumb along the plant, but if the attack is severe, immerse the plant in insecticide.

**Dehydrated plant** This hibiscus has not been given enough water with the result that the leaves are wilting.

## Ideal Conditions

### Light and Position

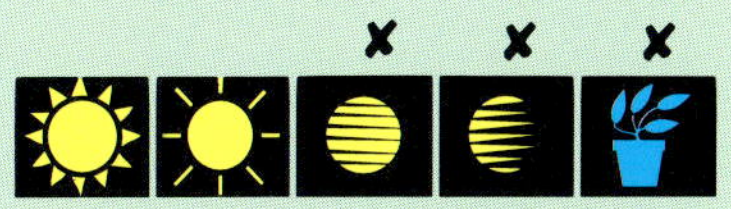

In common with all flowering pot plants, the hibiscus needs very good light to retain its buds and go on to produce a satisfactory flowering. Keep the plant away from drafts and maintain an even temperature.

### Temperature Range

The plant prefers an even, moderate temperature of around 59°F although the range in which it can exist without problem is 55°–65°F. Any radical change in the temperature to either end of the scale may damage the plant and cause the buds to drop.

### Watering

Water the plant well during dry weather and evenly all year round, allowing the top of the soil to dry before watering again. Do not make the plant waterlogged or the roots will rot. When the plant is in bud, it benefits from a daily overhead spray.

### Feeding

Feed the hibiscus with weak liquid fertilizer, given at each watering, while the plant is in active growth. This can be discontinued in winter while the plant is resting.

### Seasonal Care

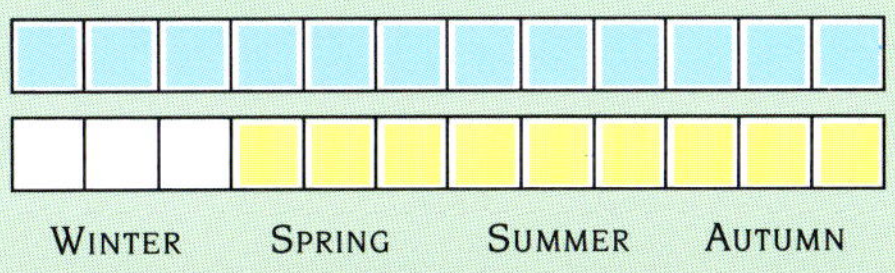


When the plant is being well watered in the summer months, it is important that it should drain quickly through the soil when applied at the surface. In winter, even though the soil is kept at the right moisture content, some leaves will fall from the plant, but the new growth in spring refurbishes it. Pruning is only needed if growth is really out of hand and is best done when the plant has just finished flowering.

### Soil

The hibiscus does not do well in soil, but will enjoy a soil-based potting mixture. Pot the plant into a slightly larger pot each spring. It is not good practice to transfer a small, new plant into a large pot and wait for it to fill it.

# Hoya

## Wax Plant

Two lovely varieties, *Hoya bella* and H. *carnosa*, have thick, fleshy foliage and drooping heads of waxy, scented flowers.

Propagate either variety by taking a 3-inch portion of stem, making the cut immediately below a pair of leaves. Dip the cuttings in a rooting hormone and place two or three together in a pot containing a mixture of peat and perlite. Maintain humidity by securing all inside a plastic bag, or by protecting within a propagator. Rooting usually takes place within six weeks, after which the cuttings can be removed from their protection. Grow on in good light, but out of direct sunlight, and provide enough water to keep the potting mixture moist. Feed once a month, until the roots have filled the pot, when the young plants can be planted individually into 3-inch pots containing a soil-based potting mixture.

**Healthy Plant**
Quite the reverse of its climbing relative, *H. bella* is a well-contained elegant trailing plant. It doesn't begin to trail until it is about 12 inches tall. Its fleshy stems bear many 1-inch long pointed, pale gray/green leaves – these always look a bit unhealthy, but this is their normal color. The flowering clusters have the same formation as *H. carnosa*, only much smaller.

### Varieties and Purchasing

Either of these varieties should be available through the summer.

*H. bella* Often sold in a specialized hanging container.

*H. carnosa* With its much more rampant growth, it is trained around a wire hoop. This will not be difficult to remove if the plant is to climb, but it does require time and patience.

*H. australis* A slightly more unusual larger relative, probably only available through specialist growers.

## Pests and Diseases

**Aphids** Check the shoot tips every day for evidence of these pests. If any are visible, remove them with a cloth soaked in a dilute soap solution and then spray the plant with a fine jet of water.

**Scale insects** Check under the waxy Hoya leaves for these insects, which live quite protected underneath their "scale." This protection is easily removed with an old toothbrush and soapy water.

**Mealy bug** If mealy bugs have invaded your plant they are easily spotted; they look rather like tiny pinkish woodlice. They lay their clutches of eggs in conspicuous wooly nests; both adults and nests must be removed as soon as possible using cotton soaked in denatured alcohol. If your treatments are not effective, the plant may have to be sprayed with malathion or dimethoate.

**Mildew** This is a fungus that infects the leaves of plants. White powdery patches appear on the upper surfaces of the leaves, and in bad cases the fungus may spread to flower buds and stems. Its presence generally reflects poor ventilation, so check that the plant is not too hot and dry, and improve ventilation and humidity levels.

**Healthy Plant**
*H. carnosa* comes from Australia. Its flowers are pink and strongly fragrant, especially at night.

## Ideal Conditions

### Light and Position

Hoyas need good light with some direct sunlight every day. *H. bella* will be seen at its best if planted in a hanging container. *H. carnosa* will cover wall space if it is provided with wires or a trellis; otherwise, a moss pole or wire hoop will suffice.

### Temperature Range

Warm | Intermediate | Cool

A winter minimum of 45°F is quite sufficient for these plants.

### Watering

Hoyas are rather temperamental about water; it is very easy to give them too much. Water moderately, allowing the top ½ inch to dry out between waterings. During the winter, water only enough to prevent the soil from drying out completely. Whenever watering hoyas, make sure that the soil is never allowed to become waterlogged and that the plants never stand in trays full of water.

Despite these dire warnings, these plants do need a high degree of moisture in the air around them, so they will need daily misting with soft tepid rainwater.

### Feeding

Provide hoyas with liquid fertilizer once every two weeks during the summer months. Do not feed those plants that have recently been repotted.

### Seasonal Care

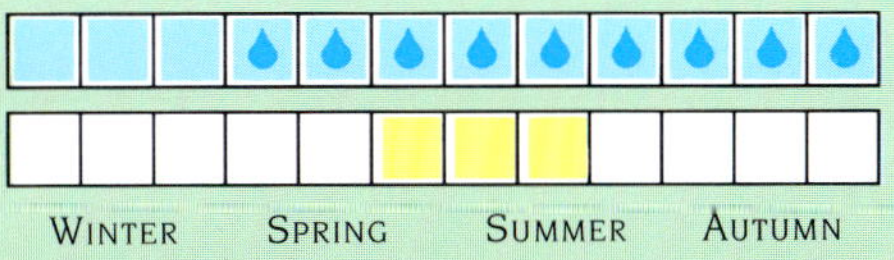


If possible, train stems of *H. carnosa* horizontally, as this will encourage flowering shoots to break.

Cut back in late winter if necessary.

Allow dead flowers to drop naturally, as next year's flower buds nestle at the base of the short flower stalks.

### Soil

Hoyas dislike being disturbed and often appear to be in pots that are too small for them – they like it. Repot every two or three years using a soil-based potting mixture, adding clean shards to the base of the pots.

# Hydrangea macrophylla

**HYDRANGEA**

Hydrangeas are available in the spring in white, pink, and blue, the latter in fact being pink plants artificially treated with alum to persuade them to change color. Blues will often vary, sometimes being nothing more than washed-out pink. This happens when the coloring chemical is used incorrectly. These plants will be outdoors most of the year, coming inside in the middle of winter to be forced into flower. If they are to do well for years after they have been bought, hydrangeas should be outdoors all summer, coming into a cool place in the fall and then to a warmer place in mid-winter to encourage flowering for the spring.

## Varieties and Purchasing

Hydrangea plants are available from early until late spring. Look for fresh green coloring and sturdy leaves. Avoid plants that are thin and weak with discolored foliage. Multi-headed plants are usually a better buy. Try to obtain plants with both flowers and buds. Hydrangeas are not usually offered by name, but by color and general appearance.

*H. macrophylla* One of the best varieties for growing indoors, this has much larger flowers than other types. The flowers are either pink, red, blue, or deep blue.

**Healthy Plant**
Hydrangeas are attractive, but need careful attention. The many different colors of the plant flowers are produced by the acidity of the soil in which they are grown. By changing the acid content, the owner can alter the color of the flowers to blue (see illustration, left), purple, pink, red, or deep blue. Group hydrangeas in pots of differing soils to produce a delightful rainbow of colors.

## Pests and Diseases

**Aphids** These are found on softer leaves and should be treated with a soapy spray.

**Red spider mite** These appear on the underside of leaves. In time, the mites produce tiny webs. Remove the worst leaves and treat with pest control.

**Mildew** This is seen as a powdery white deposit on the top of leaves. Remove the worst leaves and treat with a fungicide.

**Botrytis** This fungus develops in large, wet patches on the leaves. Remove affected leaves and spray with a solution of propicanizole.

**Underwatering** The normally thick and healthy leaves will turn brown and curl under (below). In extreme cases (bottom), the whole plant will wilt dramatically. To revive, immerse the pot in water and continue watering regularly.

## Ideal Conditions

### Light and Position

Hydrangeas prefer to be positioned in a light, cool place. Leaf scorch may result if the plant is placed too close to a window, but this is usually minimal. If put out-of-doors, keep in light shade.

### Temperature Range

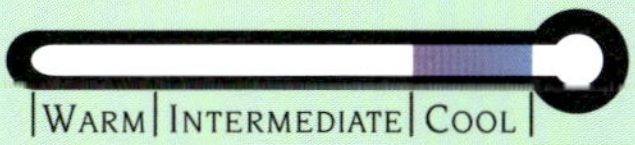


Keep in farily cool conditions of 50°–59°F. This will ensure that the plant will go on flowering much longer than if placed in a hot, dry location. Avoid direct sunlight and heat. When properly situated, hydrangeas will produce abundant, lush growth.

### Watering

During active growth, the plants will need frequent watering. Allow the topsoil to dry out before watering, but avoid letting the plants wilt. Pots should have large drainage holes and a healthy layer of shards at the base of their pots to aid drainage.

### Feeding

Hydrangeas usually have an abundance of strong foliage and will need weekly feeding to keep them strong and healthy. The acid in some soil can cause the flowers to go blue; adding alum will ensure that the flowers remain blue and do not revert to pink.

### Seasonal Care

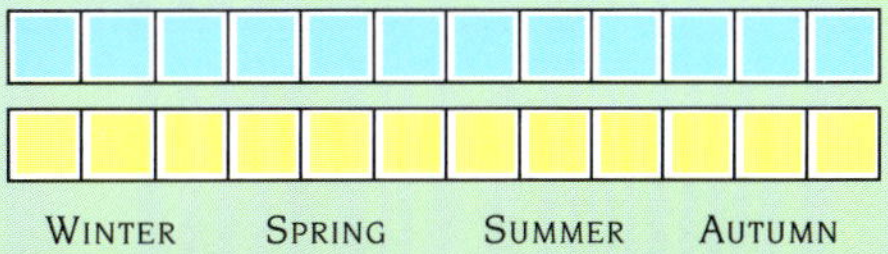


Copious watering is required when the plants are in active growth, but none while the plants are in their dormant phase towards the end of the year. After flowering, shoots should be cut back to about half their length. Top sections of shoots that have not flowered can be treated in a heated propagator. The cuttings should have two leaves attached. Prune in early spring, removing any dead material, as well as dead flower heads.

### Soil

Hydrangeas prefer heavier soil and a soil-based mixture is best. Pot in the spring when flowering is over. An all-purpose potting soil can be used. Make sure enough room is left at the top for heavy watering. The pots should also have good drainage.

# Impatiens

## Busy Lizzie, Patience Plant, Patient Lucy, or Touch-me-not

This is another very familiar, easy-going little houseplant. They are generally robust in habit, the flowers colorful and attractive, and the variegated foliage of many of the varieties is as colorful as the flowers. Cuttings about 4 inches long, with the flowers removed, will root very readily either in water or in a peaty potting mixture. The cuttings should be provided with moist conditions, shade from the sun, and a temperature in the region of 65°F. When the cuttings have rooted and started to grow, the tips should be removed to encourage branching.

### Varieties and Purchasing

*I. petersiana* This one has burgundy-colored foliage and rich red flowers. It grows to a height of 2–3 feet and can attain a very attractive shape.

*I. wallerana* The flowers of the hybrids can be all shades – white, pink, orange, or a combination of any two.

*I.* 'Red Magic' This is similar in appearance to *I. petersiana.* However, it is not as vulnerable to red spider. It usually grows to a height of 2 feet and has scarlet flowers. It is a hybrid of *I. wallerana.*

*I.* 'Arabesque' This is another hybrid of *I. wallerana.* Its leaves are veined with red and have yellow centers.

*I.* 'New Guinea' hybrids These are the latest version of Impatiens.

**Healthy Plant**
Impatiens are too often straggly, with yellow foliage and few flowers. A healthy plant (below) should be compact, with glossy leaves and a profusion of bright flowers. When choosing one, make sure the leaves are clean and fresh, the flowers open, and lots of buds are visible. A well-cared-for Impatiens will hardly ever stop flowering.

## Pests and Diseases

**Whitefly** These are easy to spot as they fly away from the plant when it is moved. Treat with soapy sprays.

**Aphids** Like all sucking insects, aphids love Impatiens. They are usually found on the new growth, and they should be treated with a fine spray of soapy water.

**Sooty mold** This is a fungus which develops on the honeydew of the aphids. Remove with a damp sponge.

**Stem rot** Wet and cold conditions may cause this – parts of the stem will be black. Remove the affected parts and treat with fungicide.

**Red spider mite** Treat with insecticide, paying particular attention to the undersides of leaves.

**Biological control** A really safe way to control houseplant pests is by using biological controls. They come in the form of tiny insect predators which feed on adult pests and their offspring. Most of them are small enough to be almost invisible to the naked eye, and they won't fall into your coffee or fly out of the window. By using biological controls, you will never completely eliminate a pest, only control it so that it does little or no harm. Once the pest disappears completely, so too will the predator, of course, having nothing to feed on.

## Ideal Conditions

### Light and Position

If the Impatiens is to produce a lot of flowers, it must have the lightest possible position, although it is wise to protect it from very strong sunlight. It does not like drafts and will not do well in a shady position.

### Temperature Range

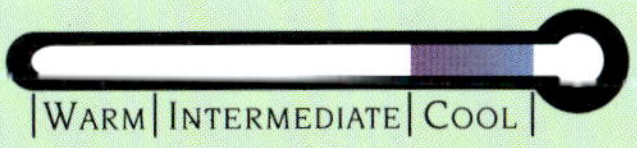


The Impatiens will not flourish in temperatures below 55°F. Normal room temperatures are ideal. It is possible to put the plant outside in summer, provided it is in a warm and sheltered spot. At temperatures over 75°F, the plant needs a humid atmosphere, so stand it on a tray of damp pebbles or moss.

### Watering

The Impatiens should be given moderate amounts of water at rest times, and plentiful supplies while it is growing. Never let the potting mixture dry out, and never let the plant stand in water for too long.

### Feeding

This vigorous plant responds well to liberal feeding. During the spring and summer, which are periods of fast growth, it can be fed once a week with a standard fertilizer. Extend the interval to three weeks during the rest of the year.

### Seasonal Care

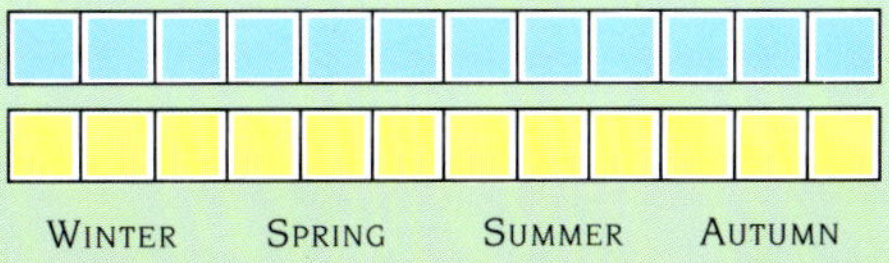


Because the Impatiens is so susceptible to pests, it is important to keep a regular lookout for invaders. Never neglect its water or feeding if the plant is to remain at its best. In winter it should be kept a little warmer. In the fall, trim large plants back hard; otherwise, they will be difficult to care for. Cuttings should be taken and rooted to replace older plants when they are past their best.

### Soil

For the vigorous growth of this plant, use a peat-based mixture. Young plants can be put into 5-inch pots on purchase. In the first year, plants can be potted on twice.

# Jasminum

## Jasmine

This is another familiar plant family, some of which will grow outside and quite happily tolerate several degrees of frost. Growing them indoors means that they can quickly get out of control, but this does not seem to spoil their short-term popularity stakes. Those grown indoors are good, if rather messy, climbers, but they are given house room for their long-lasting flowering display and of course for their scent.

Although neither *Jasminum officinale* nor J. *polyanthum* are difficult to propagate, it is especially worthwhile to take cuttings from J. *polyanthum* because young plants flower so quickly. Do so by taking 3-inch cuttings from side shoots. Plant the cuttings in 3-inch pots containing a mixture of dampened peat and sand. Secure the pots within plastic bags and keep in bright light. Rooting should have taken place within four weeks. The cuttings can then be removed from their protective plastic bags and grown on until the roots have filled the pot. The young plants can be moved into 4-inch pots containing a soil-based mixture.

**Healthy Plant**
The main attraction of these climbing plants is their mass of scented white flowers.

### Varieties and Purchasing

*Jasminum officinale*
(Common White Jasmine)
Widely available almost all the year round. Although its natural flowering time is from midsummer to mid-autumn, the growers seem to be able to make it flower at any time. It is at its most appealing when seen fresh, young, and green, the delicate stems and tendrils escaping from their meager support and the tiny tubular white flowers filling the store with their unmistakable scent. If kept indoors, it will grow extremely fast and will need to be kept in a cool spot for it to survive for any length of time.

*Jasminum polyanthum*
A great deal better behaved than *J. officinale.* It, too, is a climber which will eventually branch profusely, but initially it has only a single long stem which bears oval dark green leaves. It is on sale toward the end of the summer, its flowering season being mid- to late-autumn and winter. Don't worry if the single stem looks small; this is one of the few plants that flowers well while still only a few months old.

## Pests and Diseases

**Aphids** Any greenfly present will be easy to see clustered around the growing tips and on the flower buds; wipe them away with a cloth soaked with soapy water.

**Scale insect** Signs will be found on the undersides of the leaves, the adult insect living protected under a scale which is attached firmly to the leaf. These scales will need to be rubbed, or brushed off; once this is done, you must spray the whole plant with a dilute soap solution. Where an infestation has gotten out of control, you may have to consider spraying your plant with a multipurpose insecticide.

**Red spider mite**
Although the red spider mite is almost invisible to the naked eye, its activity is not. As with all sap-sucking insects, it secretes honeydew, so you may have reason to become suspicious if the upper leaf surfaces become sticky. Look underneath the leaves and between the leaf stalks and stems, where the red spider mites weave fine white webs. As with any other pest, you must act immediately; left unattended, the insect will gradually kill off your plant, and the honeydew will cause a fungus called sooty mold. So, move the jasmine well away from your other house plants and cut away any affected parts of the plant, burn these cuttings if possible, if not, dispose of them in a sealed plastic bag. Having done this, spray the affected plant with derris.

## Ideal Conditions

### Light and Position

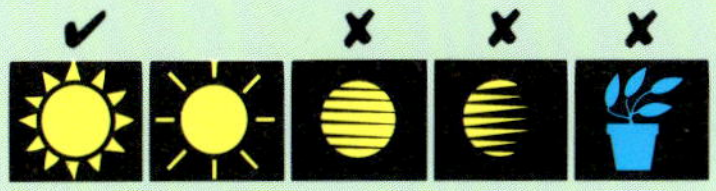

All jasmines need to be in a position where they receive some direct sunlight every day. If possible position these plants so that they can climb – they will need wires or trellis to do so. If there is no suitable space, provide them with some means of support within their container.

### Temperature Range

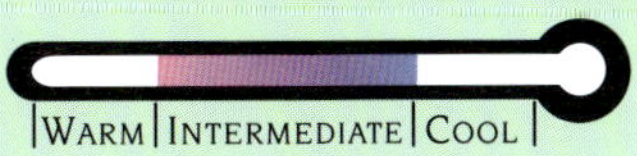


For *J. officinale* a winter minimum of 45°F is quite sufficient. Do not subject these plants to temperatures much higher than 55°F as they will grow out of control and stop flowering. *J. polyanthum* prefers a winter minimum of 55°F.

### Watering

While these plants are growing and flowering, give them plenty of water, enough to keep them thoroughly moist at all times. While they are resting, only provide them with enough water to prevent the soil from drying out completely.

### Feeding

Provide a liquid fertilizer once every two weeks from late spring to late autumn.

### Seasonal Care

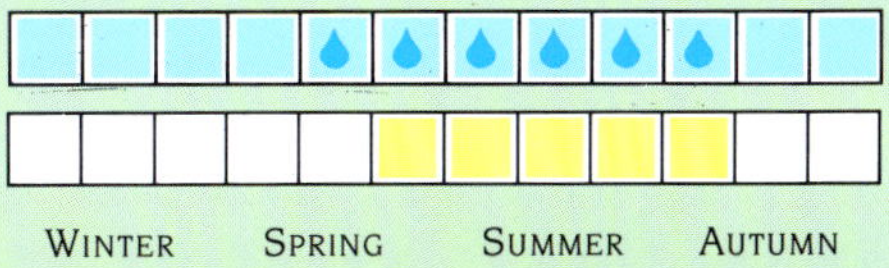


Jasmines are strong growers and will therefore need hard pruning to keep them under control. Cut back stems that have flowered as far as necessary but not completely as they flower on growth made the previous season, so some new shoots should be left unpruned. Pinch out the growing tips of *J. polyanthum* when young to encourage bushy, branching growth.

### Soil

Use a soil-based potting mixture for jasmines. Repot *J. polyanthum* during the summer, *J. officinale* in the early spring.

# Lantana camara

YELLOW SAGE

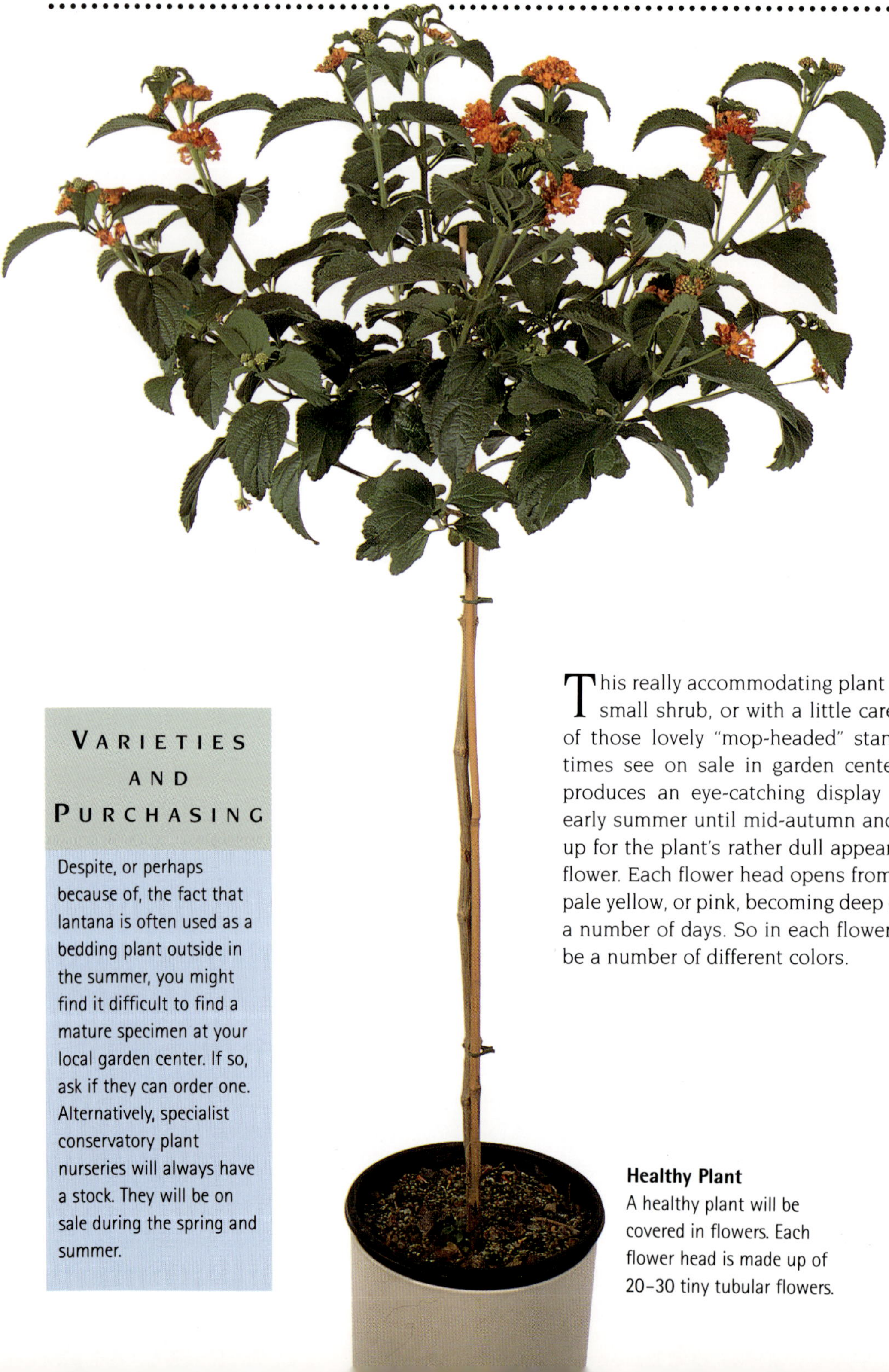

This really accommodating plant can be grown as a small shrub, or with a little care trained into one of those lovely "mop-headed" standards you sometimes see on sale in garden centers. Either way, it produces an eye-catching display which lasts from early summer until mid-autumn and definitely makes up for the plant's rather dull appearance when not in flower. Each flower head opens from the center white, pale yellow, or pink, becoming deep orange or red over a number of days. So in each flower cluster there will be a number of different colors.

## Varieties and Purchasing

Despite, or perhaps because of, the fact that lantana is often used as a bedding plant outside in the summer, you might find it difficult to find a mature specimen at your local garden center. If so, ask if they can order one. Alternatively, specialist conservatory plant nurseries will always have a stock. They will be on sale during the spring and summer.

**Healthy Plant**
A healthy plant will be covered in flowers. Each flower head is made up of 20–30 tiny tubular flowers.

## Pests and Diseases

**Red spider mite** These sap-sucking pests concentrate their attention under the leaves, where the adults are hard to see with the naked eye, but their fine white webs are not. The leaves below the webs where red spider are active may also become sticky. This is honeydew, a secretion from the mite. Remove infected parts of the plant and spray with derris.

**Whitefly** It is easy to tell if a plant has been attacked by whitefly as these are the most physically active of all glasshouse pests. Although they settle to suck sap on the undersides of leaves, they will swarm up as the plant is brushed past. Treat with a soapy spray immediately, repeat in three days, and again in another ten.

**Aphids** These are much less excitable; although they can fly, they are much less active once they have settled on the shoot tips and flower buds of your plant. Remove them manually with a cloth soaked in soap solution.

If you want a standard or mop-head, this is the way to get one, as the garden center varieties are usually rather expensive. Simply take 3-inch shoot "tip" cuttings at any time during the summer. Plant individually in 3-inch pots in a mixture of dampened peat and sand, and stand in a warm, bright spot with no direct light. Rooting should take place within two or three weeks. Allow the cutting to grow on for another three or four weeks before potting into a soil-based mixture. The plant will stay in this pot until the following spring.

Meanwhile, the stem needs to make strong straight growth, so provide it with a small support and pinch out any side shoots that appear, leaving only those at the growing tip. When it has reached the required height, pinch out the growing tip and allow the side shoots in the top 5–6 inches of stem to develop freely; below this level, keep the stem clean by rubbing out any new growth that appears. The length of these top side shoots rather depends on the height of the tree. For a time, the plant will look slightly strange, but gradually the stem will thicken and become quite woody and strong as the mop-head increases in size.

## Ideal Conditions

### Light and Position

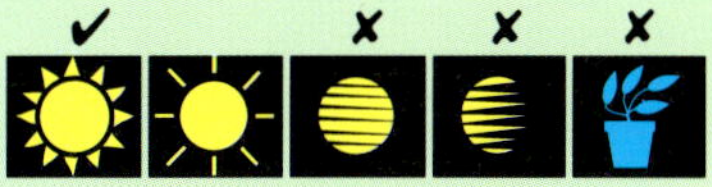

Lantanas need a position where they receive as much direct light as possible; the only time they cannot tolerate direct sunlight indoors is in mid-summer.

### Temperature Range

Lantanas can winter at near-freezing temperatures, but if subjected to those, they will almost certainly lose their leaves for the season. In order to prevent this, provide a minimum temperature of 50°F. These plants dislike high temperatures and poor ventilation, so it is often a good idea to put them outside for the hottest months of the year.

### Watering

Give enough water to wet the potting mixture thoroughly, but allow the top 1 inch to dry out between waterings. During the winter months, provide only enough to prevent the soil from drying out completely.

### Feeding

Give liquid fertilizer once every two weeks from early summer to mid-autumn.

### Seasonal Care

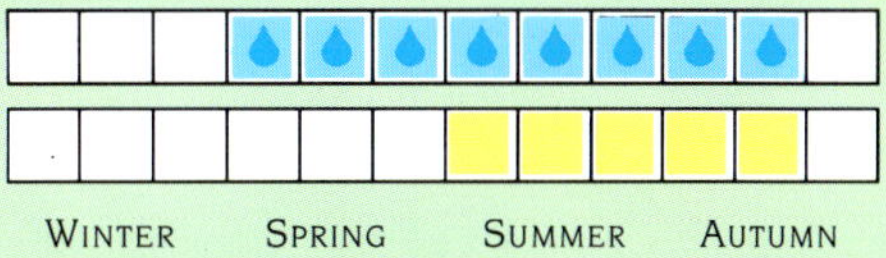


Prune in late winter to required shape. Repot every second year; otherwise top-dress. As these plants dislike high temperatures, poor ventilation, and the effects of direct midsummer sun through glass, it is as well to give them a summer vacation outside, where they will continue to grow and flower. Don't forget to water them and still maintain a watchful eye for pests.

### Soil

Always use a free-draining, soil-based potting mixture for lantanas. Add clean shards to the base of pots.

# Mandevilla splendens

DIPLADENIA

**Healthy Plant**
Seen on the staging at a garden center, a mandevilla should have an abundance of glossy, bright green leaves and showy, rose-pink, trumpet-shaped flowers. Naturally a climber, it should be anchored to some form of support, and if it is growing well, one or two of the twining stems will have escaped control.

It can grow to 10 feet or more, but being very adaptable, it will still produce masses of flowers if kept short and bushy.

Although this flowering beauty is now called mandevilla, it is still frequently referred to, and sold as, dipladenia. Whatever it is called, this self-contained little plant is really easy-going, and the combination of bright glossy green leaves and brilliant rose pink flowers is irresistible.

It is, however, difficult to propagate, needing a combination of high humidity and high temperatures 75–85°F – to be successful. Start by taking 3-inch ripe side shoots. Place them in a mixture of moistened peat and sand, and stand them in a propagating case. They are very slow to root, but new top growth will begin to appear when this has occurred. Remove them from the protection of the propagator and keep them in a warm, shady spot. Then begin to add a little water, not very much, just enough to prevent the potting

## Pests and Diseases

It is not just the human element that find mandevilla attractive; it is prone to scale insect, mealy bug, greenfly, and red spider mite. Be on the lookout for all these, and check the foliage regularly not just for a sight of the pests, but also for the familiar sticky honeydew some of them produce.

**Aphids** These will collect in bulk on the fresh green shoot tips and flower buds.

**Mealy bug** This pest will lay its wooly bundles of eggs simply anywhere.

**Red spider mite and scale insect** These will concentrate their efforts on the undersides of leaves; watch out for their fine webs and waxy scales respectively. Whatever the problem, act immediately by removing the visible adults, washing the whole plant with a diluted soap solution – the removal of scales might need a stiff brush, something like an old toothbrush would be perfect. With a mass infestation, it may be as well to isolate the plant and spray with malathion, following the manufacturer's directions exactly.

mixture from drying out completely. While the cuttings are growing on, they will also need feeding every two weeks. When the roots have finally fully filled the pot, repot in a container one size larger, using a soil-based mixture, and treat like an adult plant.

## Varieties and Purchasing

These plants are easy to find at good garden centers, and they do not need to be big and expensive, as mandevillas will produce plenty of flowers while still young.

*Mandevilla laxa* This variety is just as beautiful, but more subtle, producing masses of white scented flowers all through the summer.

## Ideal Conditions

### Light and Position

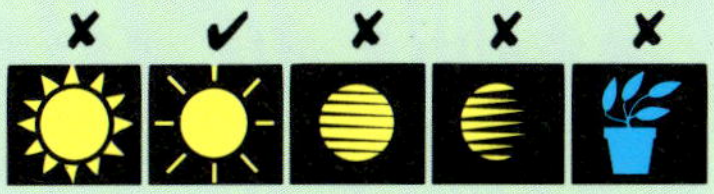

Mandevillas need good light as insufficient amounts of light will lead to poor flowering. Direct sunlight, however, will scorch the leaves and cause bud drop. If the mandevilla is to climb, it must be given some means of support, such as trellis or wires.

### Temperature Range

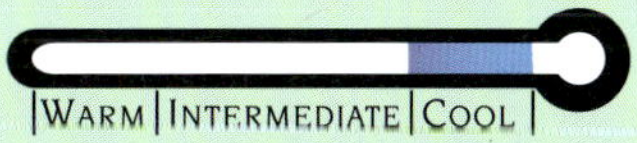


Despite the need for high temperatures during propagation, adult mandevillas only need a very mean 40°F minimum temperature in winter. This will encourage the plant to take a much needed seasonal rest. Spring and summer minimums are a little higher at 55–65°F.

### Watering

While the plants are actively growing, they need only moderate amounts of water. Give enough to wet the compost thoroughly but allow the top ½ in to dry out between waterings. During their winter rest, only water enough to prevent the soil from drying out altogether.

Keep the air moisture levels around the plant high during the summer months by misting daily. Alternatively, stand the plants in trays of a dampened horticultural aggregate.

### Feeding

No fertilizer is necessary during the winter months. Provide liquid fertilizer in the recommended amounts once every two weeks during the summer.

### Seasonal Care

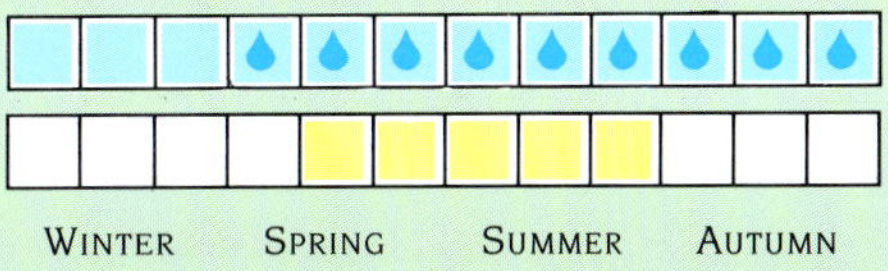


Mandevillas flower on the current season's growth. Encourage plenty of this by cutting away nearly all the flowering stems in the autumn when growth and flowering has noticeably slowed.

Ensure the correct winter minimum temperature.

### Soil

When transplanting mandevillas use a soil-based potting mixture and line the base of their containers with well-washed shards or horticultural grit. If necessary move them into pots one size larger in the spring when growth commences. If the plant has reached its final pot size, simply top-dress with the recommended mixture.

# Medinilla magnifica

Found growing in the forks of trees in the wild, this plant can grow to 8 feet. Happily, indoors it never normally grows to more than about 4 feet. But beware: medinilla is not for the learner: as a house plant, it needs perfect conditions. Despite this, they are fascinating plants, particularly when in flower. Although it is possible to grow them from cuttings, this is not advisable for the amateur to try. Even if the high temperatures and humidity levels they require at this time can be provided, the new leaf growth is very large, and it quickly becomes awkward and unwieldy.

## Pests and Diseases

**Red spider mite**
Medinilla is particularly prone to this pest. The regular spraying required to maintain high humidity levels will help to deter them, but be on the alert. They will be found underneath the huge leaves, weaving their fine webs in between the natural ridges. Spray these and the rest of the leaves with derris for instant, if not lasting, control – derris will only eliminate the adults, not their eggs.

With such a special, expensive beauty, it may be worth ordering a biological control. These minute predators called *Phytoseiulus persimilis* cannot fly. On receipt, distribute them among the infested foliage and leave them to do their business. They feed on all stages of the red spider mite – indeed, the more they eat, the more eggs they lay, making control very effective, but of course when there are no more red spider mites on a plant, the predator will also die. This is a very efficient, completely safe method of control, but meanwhile only safe sprays can be used to control other glasshouse pests.

**Healthy Plant**
A healthy plant is a bulky plant. It will be 3–4 feet high with a similar spread, so you will need plenty of space for it, too. The woody angled stems and numerous branches carry large, coarsely textured, ridged leaves. The flowering heads appear at the ends of drooping pink stalks. Papery bracts are carried in tiers along the length of the stalk, with a huge descending cluster of bright pink flowers in between each tier.

## Varieties and Purchasing

Despite the fact that they are difficult to grow and not cheap to buy, they are often seen in garden centers and florists' windows in the late summer and early fall so it will not be hard to find.

## Ideal Conditions

### Light and Position

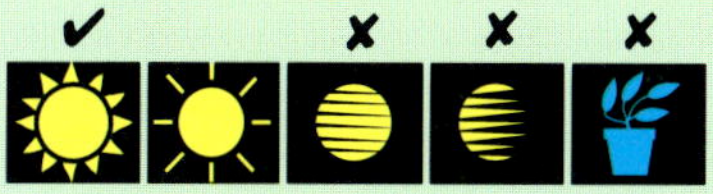

Medinillas need good light at all times. They also need plenty of space. If possible, elevate them slightly so that the flowers can be really appreciated.

### Temperature Range

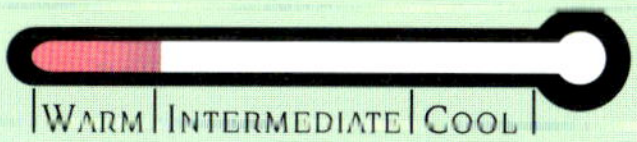


These plants need a winter minimum of 61°F and summer temperatures of 61–90°F. The spread of summer temperatures may seem wide, but the chosen temperature must be maintained steadily. Medinillas do not like temperatures higher than 90°F – during exceptionally hot weather, extra ventilation must be provided in order to prevent this from happening.

### Watering

During the summer, provide enough water to wet the soil thoroughly, allowing the top ½ inch to dry out before watering again. During the winter water only enough to prevent the soil from drying out completely. Do not begin to give more water until the new flower stalks start to appear in the spring. High humidity levels are vital to medinillas, so stand them in trays of moist horticultural aggregate and mist-spray them daily with soft rainwater.

### Feeding

Use liquid fertilizer as soon as flower buds start to open, then feed once every two weeks until early autumn, even if the flowering display is not finished.

### Seasonal Care

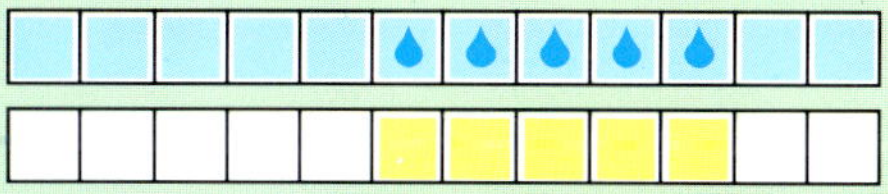


Prune into shape immediately after the last flowers have faded. Cut out spindly growth altogether, and shorten long branches by half.

### Soil

Repot using a dampened soil-based mixture with a little peat and perlite added. Move the plant in early spring, taking great care not to damage the roots. If the plant has reached the desired size, simply top-dress.

# Monstera deliciosa

## Swiss Cheese Plant, Mexican Breadfruit Plant, or Hurricane Plant

Blessed with numerous common names, the monstera has immense appeal. Indigenous to Mexico, it now grows naturally in most tropical regions, and in almost every collection of tropical and indoor plants. Easily raised from seed, the monstera is therefore an ideal plant for the commercial grower, who can produce uniform quality plants with little difficulty, as long as the reasonably undemanding cultural requirements are provided. Indoors, the naturally glossy green leaves, interesting habit of growth, and ease of culture mean that the monstera will always be one of the most popular houseplants.

Endless questions are asked about this attractive plant, chief among them being what should be done about the natural aerial roots that protrude from the main stem of the plant. Where there is an excessive amount of these roots, it will do no harm to remove some of them, but it is really much better to tie the roots neatly to the main stem of the plant so that they may grow naturally into the soil in the pot when they are long enough. The important thing to remember is that these roots will draw up food and moisture to nourish the plant, so any drastic removal of the roots would weaken it.

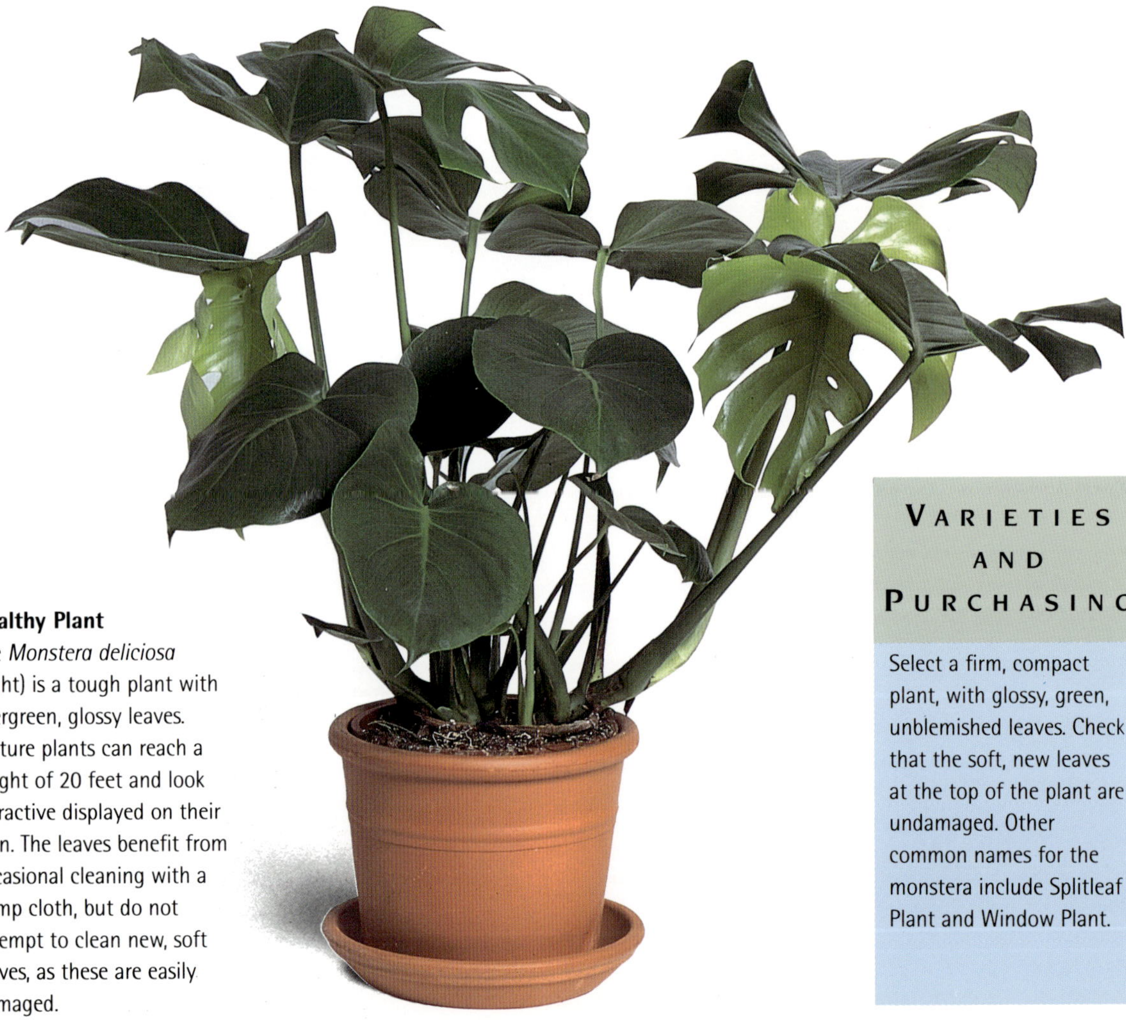

**Healthy Plant**
The *Monstera deliciosa* (right) is a tough plant with evergreen, glossy leaves. Mature plants can reach a height of 20 feet and look attractive displayed on their own. The leaves benefit from occasional cleaning with a damp cloth, but do not attempt to clean new, soft leaves, as these are easily damaged.

### Varieties and Purchasing

Select a firm, compact plant, with glossy, green, unblemished leaves. Check that the soft, new leaves at the top of the plant are undamaged. Other common names for the monstera include Splitleaf Plant and Window Plant.

## Pests and Diseases

**Pests** It is extremely unusual for the monstera to suffer from pests.

**Overwatering** Always make sure of the correct temperature for your monstera: 60°–70°F. A plant kept at the lower end of the scale will need a great deal less water than one growing in a warmer room. The plant only needs moderate amounts of water, provide enough to keep the compost moist, allowing the top two-thirds to dry out between waterings. Yellowing leaves are an indication that the plant is both too cold and too wet. These damaged leaves will never recover and should be removed.

## Ideal Conditions

### Light and Position

Ideal conditions will produce a large, healthy plant. Avoid strong sunlight and dark corners. Sun will scorch the leaves, while poor light will restrict growth and result in smaller, less serrated leaves. Monsteras are happiest in locations with ample space.

### Temperature Range

Warm | Intermediate | Cool

A temperature range of 59°–70°F is ideal. Excessive heat should be avoided or the lush leaves will begin to curl and droop. Avoid wet conditions around the roots if lower temperatures are likely to prevail which may cause the roots to rot.

### Watering

Monsteras should be kept moist, especially if in dry surroundings. The roots which grow from the main stem can be put into containers of water, reducing the plant's need for frequent watering. Sponge the leaves with water to keep them clean.

### Feeding

This plant produces masses of roots in its active period, so it must be given regular feeding at this time. During less active periods, feed only if new leaves are being produced. Large plants which have been in their pots a long time need frequent feeding.

### Seasonal Care

Winter Spring Summer Autumn

When in the active growth period, feed and water monsteras generously. Give less of both at other times. Clean the leaves occasionally, but never wipe soft new leaves at the top of the stem because these are easily damaged. If the plant is healthy, potting can be done at any time of year but should be avoided during the colder months.

### Soil

The potting mixture for monsteras should be peat-based. As plants mature, they will benefit from a little soil-based mixture being added to the basic mix.

# Nerium oleander

## COMMON OLEANDER OR ROSE BAY

Oleanders seem to grow like weeds on little more than sand in the hot sun of the southern Mediterranean countries. Grown as house plants, they need a cool, very dry winter and a position where they receive as much hot sun as possible all the year round. If an oleander fails to flower, the cause will almost certainly be lack of strong light, which is needed to ripen the wood. Only sun-ripened wood will produce flowers.

All parts of these plants are poisonous, especially the sap, which will ooze from any cut parts of the stem and leaves. Those with sensitive skins should always wear gloves when handling and cutting these plants; others must always wash their hands thoroughly after touching them.

Cuttings can be taken from oleander at any time during the spring and summer. These need to be about 3 inches long and taken from new growth. Allow the ends of the cuttings to dry out before putting them into individual pots containing a mixture of moistened peat and sand. Keep them warm, damp, and out of direct light, and repot using a soil-based mixture when roots show at the bottom of the pot.

## Pests and Diseases

**Red spider mite** Evidence of this glasshouse pest is to be found on the undersides of leaves where their fine webs appear. They spread very fast and can do a lot of damage to your oleander and any nearby plants as well. Remove and destroy any affected parts of the plant; then spray the whole plant thoroughly with derris.

**Mealy bug** Always be on the alert for house-plant pests. The best form of pest control is efficient plant hygiene. Check under the leaves and on the stems where mealy bugs often lay their wooly balls of eggs. Wipe these and adult bugs off the plant with a cloth soaked in denatured alcohol.

**Scale insect** The waxy scales that conceal and protect the scale insect are easy enough to remove from the tough leaves of oleander. Soak an old toothbrush in soapy water and remove them as soon as possible.

**Honeydew** All sap-sucking insects produce a sticky secretion which drips and collects on surrounding leaves. Clean it off with a soapy spray. If it is not removed, sooty mold, a blackish-colored fungus, will grow on it. Sooty mold must be sponged off carefully; while you are doing this, check the plant for the pests that might be producing the secretion.

**Healthy Plant**
Given the right care and conditions, oleanders can grow into quite large evergreen shrubs with narrow, leathery, dark green leaves. The flowers 1–2 inches across, appear in groups of six to eight at the ends of stems. When not in flower, these plants are really quite unattractive, but as their flowering season is a long one – early summer to mid-autumn – they are well worth finding space for.

## Varieties and Purchasing

Only one variety is easily available, but there should be a choice of flower colors from white to rose pink and crimson with many shades in between.

## Ideal Conditions

### Light and Position

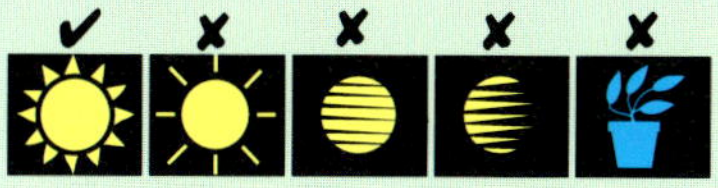

Oleanders will not flower unless they are in a position where they receive as much direct light as possible throughout the year. They can be used to shade other plants that need shade from direct sun.

### Temperature Range

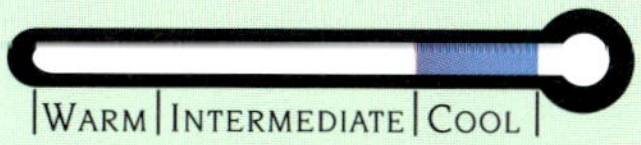


A winter minimum of 45°F is quite adequate for oleanders, the trick being to provide them with both this low temperature and full sunlight. Although they thrive naturally under the hot Mediterranean sun, oleanders do not like summer temperatures above 70°F. This is because they need air moving around them. When the indoor temperature rises too high, extra ventilation must be provided, or the plants can be moved outside for a while.

### Watering

During spring and summer, oleanders need enough water to moisten the soil completely, allowing the top ½ inch to dry out before watering again. Winter watering must be kept to a bare minimum, just give enough to prevent the soil from drying out completely.

### Feeding

Give a liquid fertilizer once every two weeks through spring and summer.

### Seasonal Care

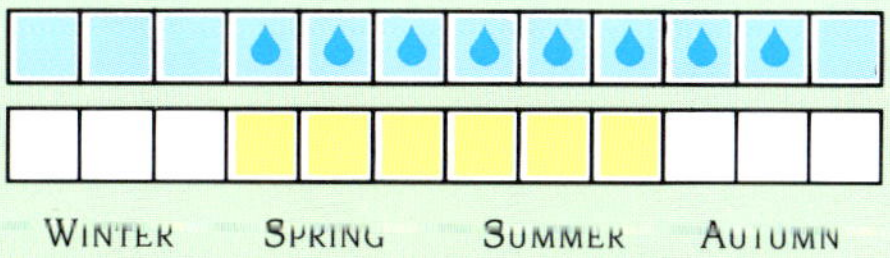


If possible, give oleanders a summer break outside; if not, ventilate freely during warm weather. Prune hard back in mid-autumn, cutting back the current season's growth to within 4 inches of its starting point.

### Soil

These stout, top-heavy branching plants need to be grown in a large tub or heavy pot. Use a soil-based mixture for top-dressing or re-potting, lining the base of the pots with clean shards for extra drainage. Repot annually in spring until the maximum pot size is reached, thereafter top-dress.

# Ophiopogon jaburan

WHITE LILY TURF

Grown chiefly for its foliage, this very easy-going evergreen house plant looks rather like chlorophytum, the well-known spider plant, but ophiopogons are more upright and the foliage more attractive.

Multiply a stock of ophiopogon by dividing any overcrowded clumps during the spring. When doing this, make sure that each new plant has at least 10 leaves and as many of the cord-like roots as possible. If the roots are very tangled, wash them gently under running water. Using a combination of moistened soil-based mixture and clean river sand, plant the divided stock individually in 5-inch pots.

## VARIETIES AND PURCHASING

You should be able to buy ophiopogons from good garden centers during the summer months. Look for the varieties with variegated leaves. The attractive striping comes in white, cream, or yellow.

## Pests and Diseases

These plants are usually not troubled by pests, but the plants should still be checked regularly. Efficient plant hygiene is a good way of preventing attack, so remove any dying foliage and flowers as soon as they lose their healthy bloom; wipe the leaves regularly, or give them a summer shower with soft rainwater.

**Healthy Plant**
The tufted, leathery, strap-shaped, dark green leaves arch up from a clumpy root stock. Each of them grows to about 2 feet long, but they are never more than ½ inch wide. The flattened flower stalks appear during the summer, rising from the center of the clump of leaves. The flowering heads appear in loose clusters, each bearing between six and 20 tube-shaped white or whitish-pink flowers. Sometimes these flowers are followed by pea-sized berries.

## Ideal Conditions

### Light and Position

Although these plants need good light in order to flower, only ever subject them to the most diffuse direct sunlight. Position them near to, but not pressed up against, an east-facing window. In the early morning the sun is at its weakest, so will not damage the plant unduly, and here it will receive good light for the rest of the day.

### Temperature Range

WARM | INTERMEDIATE | COOL

Provide these plants with a winter minimum of 50°F. They will tolerate a wide range of summer temperatures but they do best kept on the cool side – 55–65°F.

### Watering

During the summer provide enough water to moisten the compost thoroughly, allowing the top ½ in to dry out between waterings. Ophiopogons have a very clearly defined winter rest; during this time they will only need enough water to prevent the compost from drying out completely.

### Feeding

Provide a liquid feed once every two weeks throughout the spring and summer.

### Seasonal Care

WINTER SPRING SUMMER AUTUMN

Take care that winter watering is kept to a scant minimum. Provide enough light for these plants to flower but ensure that they are only subjected to the weakest sunshine.

### Soil

Use a soil-based mixture with some additional sand, which provides the extra drainage that ophiopogons need. Repot during the spring, dividing the clumps if necessary.

# Orchid

Until quite recently, orchids were only grown by real plant specialists; they were definitely not recommended for amateurs. Today it is difficult to find a garden center where they are not on sale. Within this enormous plant family, there are more than 25,000 species. With a little ingenuity, it is possible to provide suitable growing positions for a variety of these beauties in almost any room in the house. Temperatures that are comfortable for people are fine for these home-grown orchids. Light on a sunny windowsill is adequate for many species, but others prefer a shadier position.

Orchids have developed very specialized root systems according to their needs in the wild. Some have roots which are often completely exposed to the air. Others have swollen stems called pseudobulbs which act as water storage areas. This combination of specialized roots and/or swollen stems makes it possible for orchids to survive in their natural environment. Their rather unusual growing habits have to be accommodated if they are to live, and, most important, flower indoors.

Sometimes orchids are sold potted on "rock wool" or oasis, both frequently used by commercial growers. To

**Healthy Plant**
All leaves and their flowers should be unblemished and firm; their coloring should be clear.

**Healthy Plant**
The flowering spikes appear from the base of the crown; they take 6 or 8 weeks to grow and mature.

**Healthy Plant**
The sophisticated flowering display is not difficult to achieve. Cymbidiums like a summer outside, a cool fall, and a warmish winter; given this, they should grow and flower for years.

make the plants easier to care for at home, repot them as soon as flowering is over in a recommended orchid soil.

Frequent watering means that soils need changing, often on an annual basis. As the plants grow too large for their containers, it is easy to increase the collection by division.

Use clay or plastic containers for potting and repotting. For drainage and stability, fill one-third of the container with well-washed shards or stones. Hold the plant in its new pot with one hand, with the base of the pseudobulbs, or the top of the rooting surface, ¾ inch below the rim of the container. Use the other hand to ease fresh soil around the roots. During repotting, the old soil must be carefully removed and thrown away, together with any soft or brown (dead) roots. Great care should be taken when handling the healthy roots, which are usually white.

All orchids have a high humidity requirement, so stand their pots on trays of damp horticultural aggregate. The moisture from this will evaporate gradually and create a humid atmosphere around the plants.

## Varieties and Purchasing

Choose plants that are in bud or flower. A good buy is a plant that is firmly potted, not wobbly. Orchids like to be tight in their pots but there should be room for growth. It may be necessary to visit an orchid specialist for the more unusual varieties.

*Cymbidium hybrids* Of all the orchids, cymbidiums are the most easy-going, adaptable, and available. There are plenty of varieties to choose from, color and size depending on the individual, but a mature plant may bear as many as 100 blooms in a single season. Cymbidiums are renowned for their clumps of swollen stumps, pseudobulbs, which are surrounded by leathery strap-like leaves. Flower spikes appear from around the base of the swollen stems. They mature gradually and bear one or many flowers along the length of the spike.

To encourage flowering, cymbidiums need a cool period at 55–61°F for four to six weeks in late fall. They can then be returned to their normal position.

Cymbidiums will happily spend summers "resting" outside on the patio or balcony. During this period the sun will ripen the plants and encourage them to flower later in the year.

*Paphiopedilum maudiae* The Ladies Slipper orchids have the most stunning green and white flowers which rise from fans of marbled green leaves. They grow well in plastic pots or in slatted orchid baskets in a position where they get good light but no direct sunlight.

*Phalaenopsis hybrids* The Moth Orchids are real beauties, the common name referring to the shape of the flowers. They prefer to grow in slatted orchid baskets, but will adapt to life in a pot. The stems bear two rows of dark green leaves from which the flowers appear. The flower spikes may be simple or branched, and may bear a few, or many, long-lasting showy flowers in summer or fall. Like paphiopedilum, they like bright light, but not direct sunlight.

**Healthy Plant**

As with all Orchids, the air around phalaenopsis must be kept moist at all times. Spray the flower spikes regularly using soft rainwater; aid humidity still further by standing plants in trays of dampened aggregate.

## Pests and Diseases

**Aphids** Sometimes a nuisance on flower spikes and buds during the winter. Treat immediately with malathion.

**Red spider** Occasionally a problem. Treat with malathion as soon as a population becomes apparent.

**Mosaic virus** Sadly, there is no cure for this disease, and the plant should be destroyed as this disease is spread very quickly by aphids.

**Group infestation** Although Orchids are rarely troubled by pests, you should still check them regularly. House plant pests dislike humidity, so make sure the air around the plants remains damp at all times.

## Ideal Conditions

### Light and Position

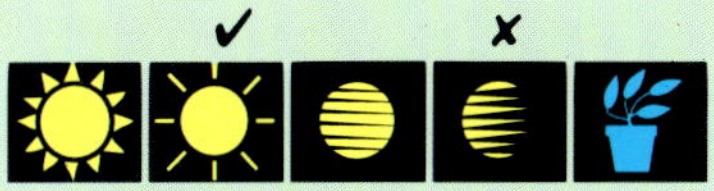

**Paphiopedilum and phalaenopsis** Although these orchids will survive in the weakest sunlight, like that found near an east-facing window, they will really do best in the shade. Position your plants where they receive no direct light at all.
**Cymbidium** These varieties need good light at all times and will benefit where they receive direct sunlight during the winter, but they must be protected from the hottest summer sun.

### Temperature Range

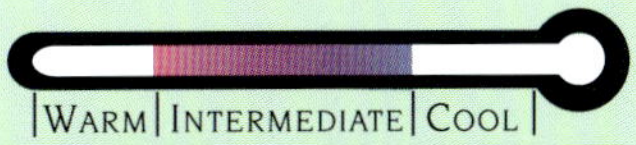


**Paphiopedilum** These orchids have a minimum temperature requirement of 50°F, but will flower best if the daytime temperatures are a fairly stable 61–65°F.
**Cymbidium and Phalaenopsis** Both these orchids need a cool winter, so keep the temperatures around 45°F. During the summer the temperature should not rise above 68°F.

### Watering

If possible, use rainwater at room temperature. Water in the morning on sunny days so that the plants begin to dry out as the temperature rises. Watering once a day, especially for mounted plants, may be necessary during the summer. Once or twice a week will be more usual at other times of year, reducing to weekly or two-weekly intervals in winter.

### Feeding

Most orchids need supplementary feeding during the growing season. Liquid fertilizer is easiest to apply, but always dilute to half the recommended strength. Feed regularly, every two or three feeds in summer, not at all during the resting phase.

### Seasonal Care

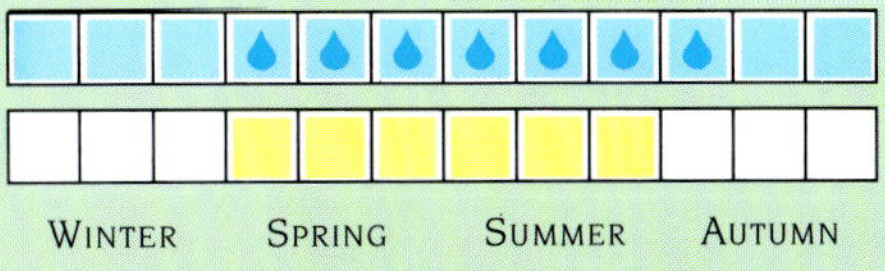


Most orchids have a resting phase. While they are resting, they need little or no water and no feed at all.

### Soil

Several commercially made orchid mixtures are available. They are all based on a mixture of fibrous peat, grit and/or perlite, and pieces of charcoal to aid drainage.

# Palms

There are many types of palm, almost all of them fairly tough, but the majority are rather too vigorous for today's average living accommodation. The best known is the Parlor Palm, *Chamaedorea elegans* (*Neanthe bella*). This is a neat, slow-growing plant that many people have in their homes and which is very easily produced from seed by the commercial grower. Although there are many palm varieties, most of them require similar treatment and temperatures, and they all attract the same sort of pests.

There are two howeas which are available – the Howea Palm, (H. *forsteriana*), by far the most popular, and the Sentry Palm (H. *belmoreana*). The first has broader and fewer leaflets to each individual set of leaves, but they both attract the same culture and pests.

Howeas have been popular for indoor decoration since Victorian times and, in spite of their high cost, there seems to be very little change in their popularity today.

**Healthy Plant**
*Howea belmoreana* syn. *Kentia belmoreana* The Curly Palm can grow up to 8 feet tall with a 6-foot spread. As it ages, the stem forms a short trunk which thickens at the base.

**Healthy Plant**
*Chamaedorea elegans* – the Good Luck or Parlor Palm – will take several years to reach its final size of around 3 feet. Insignificant yellow flowers may be produced in small sprays on plants over three years old.

**Healthy Plant**

*Chrysalidocarpus lutescens*
Sometimes called the Areca Palm, it produces many reedlike stems in clusters. The arching fronds are yellowish-brown and up to 24 inches long. Older stems are marked like bamboo canes, with notches where fronds were formerly attached to them.

## Varieties and Purchasing

Palms fall into two main divisions – those with pinnate (feathery) fronds and those with palmate (fan-like) ones. Always choose plants that are free from blemishes and have a bright, fresh look to them. Check carefully for the presence of pests, such as the red spider mite and scale insect.

*Caryota* – There are two common varieties, *C. mitis*, the Burmese Fishtail Palm, and *C. urens*, the Wine Palm. They like warmth, should be watered plentifully, and fed once a month during the active growth period.

*Howea* – The slender build of *H. belmoreana* and *H. forsteriana* belies their stamina. They are able to thrive even in difficult conditions, though they do not like temperatures below 55°F.

*Phoenix* – *P. canariensis* is hardier than *P. dactylifera* or *P. roebelenii*. The last needs frequent repotting, as it grows quickly. Suckers can be used for propagation.

*Chamaedorea* – As well as *C. elegans*, *C. erumpens* and *C. Seifrizii* are also popular. They all need plenty of water in the active growth period. In winter, however, water only just enough to moisten the potting mixture.

*Microcoelum* – *M. weddellianum* must not be potted in a pot that is too big for it and must be kept at a minimum temperature of 59°F.

*Trachycarpus* – *T. fortunei*, the Windmill Palm, is a slender-stemmed plant, bearing attractive, fan-shaped leaves. These must be removed when age makes them unsightly.

*Chrysalidocarpus* – *C. lutescens*, the Yellow Palm, produces clusters of reed-like stems. The small suckers that grow at its base can again be used for propagation.

*Rhapis* – *R. excelsa*, the Little Lady Palm, and *R. humilis*, the Slender Lady Palm, are slow-growing, producing fan-shaped dark green leaves. They will both do well in pots that seem a little small for them.

**Propagation** You can try to germinate the seeds of *Chamaedorea elegans* (see illustration, left). Gather them in spring, place in a moist, humid environment and maintain a temperature of around 27°C (80°F). It is easier to multiply your stock using palm varieties that produce offsets. Having allowed these to develop leaves and roots, carefully remove them from the parent plant and place them in a moist compost. Ensure a humid atmosphere while the plant becomes established.

## Pests and Diseases

**Red spider mite** This is the chief enemy of all palms. As a preventative, keep the plant in fairly humid conditions and mist-spray regularly. Check the undersides of fronds for their fine webs or remove a sample and examine it under a magnifying glass as, in its initial stages, this tiny pest is easy to miss. Treat by thoroughly spraying the foliage with derris.

**Scorched leaf** Although palms tolerate some direct light their leaves will easily scorch if placed too close to glass, or if the leaves are sprayed while the plant is in direct sunlight.

**Scale insect** These infest the stem and underside of the leaves. Like red spider mites, they are difficult to spot. Treat with dimethoate.

**Mealy bug** Look for their woolly nests on any part of the plant. Remove nests and adults with cotton wool soaked in methylated spirits.

## Ideal Conditions

### Light and Position

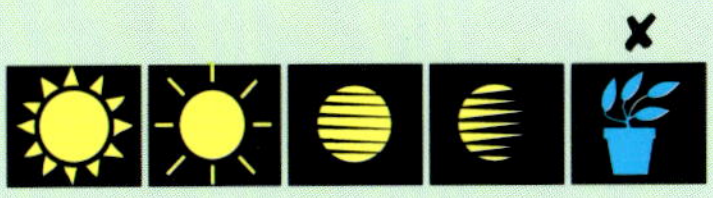

Most palms grow naturally in places where there is intense heat and sunlight. So, to encourage them to grow well indoors, place new plants where they will enjoy 2–3 hours of direct sun a day.

### Temperature Range

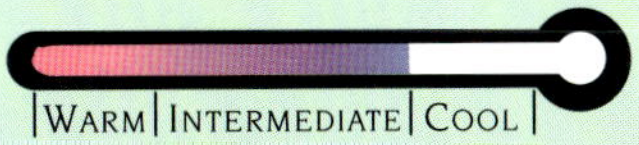


During the active growth period a warm environment of 15°–25°C (59°–70°F) is best. During winter, hardier varieties, such as chamaerops, livistona and washingtonia, can tolerate temperatures down to 7°C (45°F). Other types should not be subjected to temperatures below 13°C (55°F).

### Watering

The amount of water needed will depend on the individual palm. In general, water thoroughly during the active growth period. In winter, the cooler the room, the less water required. All palms like to be sprayed occasionally with tepid water. water.

### Feeding

Smaller plants will do well with a weak feed every watering, but phoenix palms must have heavy feedings at weekly intervals during summer, and fortnightly in winter. For all palms, in winter use a weak feed or else stop feeding.

### Seasonal Care

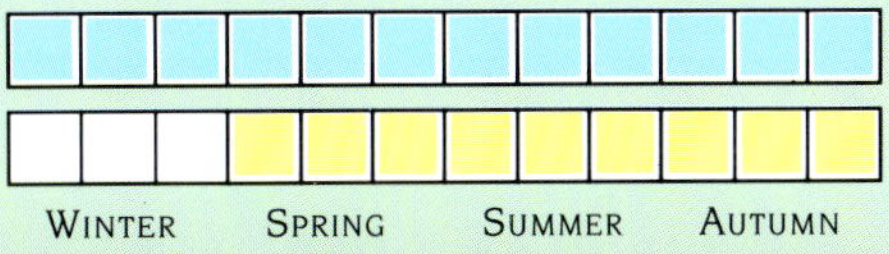


All palms should be watered and fed thoroughly during the active period. Stop feeding and water only moderately during the rest period. Do not clean leaves with chemical mixtures; use a sponge and water instead. Most palms are very difficult to propagate and the seed can take up to two years to germinate. Palms are sensitive to changes in environment so if moving the plant out-of-doors in summer, acclimatize it gradually. Be sure to bring the plant back indoors before the temperature drops.

### Soil

Smaller plants can be potted every two years using a soil-based mixture. Good drainage is essential for all palms. Repot only when the roots have filled the pot and have begun to protrude through the drainage holes.

# Pelargonium

GERANIUM

## Varieties and Purchasing

There are so many varieties of pelargonium that it is impossible to give a full list. The flower colors and leaf markings are hugely varied. When selecting a plant, look for a full, bushy specimen and check the undersides of leaves to make sure there are no pests already at work.

*P. domesticum* Otherwise known as the Regal pelargonium, this is the most popular of domestic varieties, and when well kept it is a pleasing and impressive sight.

*P. zonale* This has red-brown markings on the leaves and bears its flower heads for several months.

Most pelargoniums, which commonly tend to be called Geraniums, will do well indoors, but they must have the lightest possible position if their flowers are to open satisfactorily, and they are to continue to flower well. There are many types, but the Regal pelargonium is most associated with indoor culture. Cuttings can be taken at almost any time during the summer, but it is best to leave them until late summer so that young plants are overwintered and ready for potting on and getting under way in the spring. Cuttings 3–4 inches long root very easily and need no special treatment. Older plants that have flowered should be pruned back in the fall and kept on the dry side until the following spring.

**Healthy Plant**
Part of the great pleasure of these plants is the fresh and vigorous effect of the contrast between the clear, bright colors of the flowers and the rich green leaves, enhanced if several plants are kept together.

**Aphids** These little greenflies can be a nuisance on young plants. They suck the sap from soft growth and deposit sticky honeydew on the foliage.

**Whitefly** This is a more prevalent problem and also more difficult to treat. The small white insects sit on the undersides of leaves and dance about when the plant is disturbed. Spray the leaves with a soft soap spray and repeat the treatment every four days until the plant is clean. Repeated spraying also kills the young flies which are hatching out.

**Black leg** This is a fungal disease which attacks the stems of pelargoniums. It occurs in conditions which are too wet and airless. There is no useful treatment, and the plants must be destroyed.

**Vine weevils** Adult beetles can be damaging to the leaves, but the grubs attack the roots of the plant. As soon as you notice this condition, treat with permethrin.

**Rust** A disease which is not common in houseplants, this may appear on pelargoniums in dank, airless conditions. You will notice brown spores on the undersides of the leaves. Remove the diseased leaves and treat the plant with propicanizole if necessary.

**Virus** If certain areas of the plant are distorted or stunted, or the leaves develop pale green or yellow patches, it may have a virus. Sadly, there is nothing to be done, so you must dispose of the plant.

**Mealy bug** These white bugs, the adults large and waxy and the young wrapped in cottony fluff, are easily seen on the plant (see illustration, below). Treat by spraying the leaves generously with malathion, or wipe them off carefully with cotton soaked in denatured alcohol.

**Botrytis** This is a gray mold caused by cold, wet conditions. Cut away affected leaves and spray with propicanizole.

## Ideal Conditions

### Light and Position

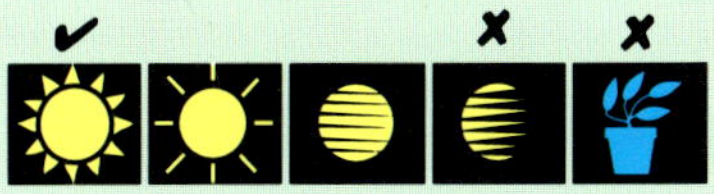

Full light is essential for pelargoniums, and they prefer an airy atmosphere, although they do not care for drafts. There are many varieties, and they all enjoy sunshine, especially when flowering, but guard against scorched leaves in really hot weather.

### Temperature Range

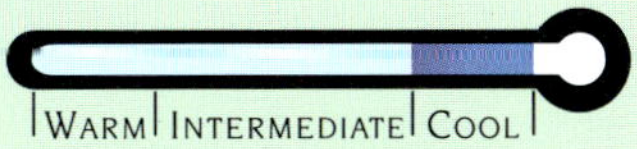


Pelargoniums appreciate a cool or moderate range of temperature. They will exist happily in 50°F, but prefer a slightly higher temperature, nearer to 59°F. In summer they can tolerate rather warmer conditions for a while, and a dry, rather than humid, atmosphere is best.

### Watering

Introduce water at the top of the pot and let it sink down through the soil. After 15 minutes, empty the excess water from the saucer. The plants do not like overhead spraying, and this may cause rotting in the leaves.

### Feeding

Excessive feeding will encourage a leafy plant, but at the expense of the flowers. Give no more than an average amount of liquid fertilizer in summer as the plants are watered. They will not require winter feeding.

### Seasonal Care

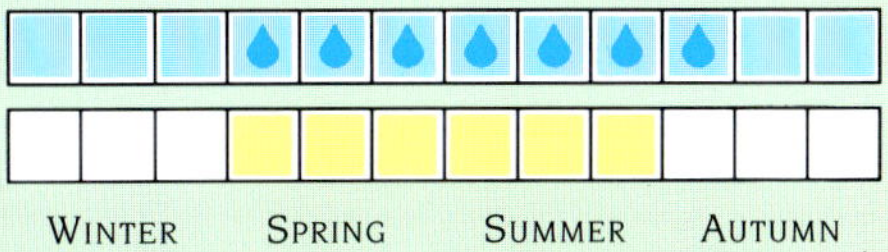


Water the plants quite generously in summer, moistening the soil often, but keep them fairly dry during the winter and in the lower temperature of 50°F. The top growth of the plant can be severely cut back during the winter rest. This reduces the likelihood of disease in congested foliage and also allows for more attractive growth in spring. Cuttings taken in late summer provide plants for the following year.

### Soil

Use a soil-based or peat-based mixture. Repotting should not be done too frequently, as the plant can benefit from being slightly pot-bound. Young cuttings should be potted on, but do not repot fully grown plants.

# Peperomia

## DESERT PRIVET OR LITTLE FANTASY

These plants seldom reach a height of more than 10 inches. The Desert Privet has attractive cream and green variegation on rounded leaves that are attached to succulent stems. The Little Fantasy plant is very dark green with crinkled leaves that are small and rounded, sprouting not from stems but from soil level. This is a dwarf variety that rarely grows above 6 inches in height.

Little Fantasy is propagated from individual leaves, while the Desert Privet is propagated from leaves with a piece of stem attached. They should be inserted in a peat and sand mixture in small pots, and the temperature should be in the region of 70°F.

**Healthy Plant**
*Peperomia magnoliifolia*, the Desert Privet, is a small plant which generally grows to a height of 6 inches. It has attractive rounded leaves which are variegated in cream and green. The leaves grow from thick, fleshy stems.

### VARIETIES AND PURCHASING

When purchasing peperomias, select sturdy, compact plants with distinct markings. Look for damaged leaves and any discoloration. Carefully inspect the soil area for rot, which could quickly lead to irreversible problems.

*P. magnoliifolia* 'Variegata' This is also known as Desert Privet. It has green leaves with cream markings.

*P. hederifolia* has pale gray leaves which are indented.

*P. scandens* 'Variegata' has small green and cream leaves.

**Healthy Plant**
*Peperomia caperata* There are more than a dozen species and varieties of peperomia. This one rarely grows to more than 10 inches high. The leaf stalks are red or pink, bearing white flower spikes of varying lengths which appear through summer and fall.

## Pests and Diseases

It is fairly easy to tell when something is wrong with most peperomias. Botrytis (above) starts at the base of the plant. Treat with fungicide and cut out any rotting leaves. If the leaves of the plant turn dull and pale, it is receiving too much sun. If the leaves begin to drop off, the plant could be sitting in a cold draft. Leaves that develop blisters are suffering from overwatering. Besides regulating the water supply, check to make sure the plant is not standing in water and that proper drainage is provided. Let the plant dry out thoroughly and water only moderately thereafter.

**Red spider mite** An occasional problem. On variegated types, red spider can be difficult to see, and a magnifying glass might be necessary to locate them. This should be carried out regularly anyway, because once the pests appear, they usually maintain a firm foothold. In advanced stages, the plant will have a thick, dry appearance. Close inspection at this point will probably reveal fine webs on the undersides of leaves and the stems of the plant. If the plant is overrun with the pests, it could prove pointless to attempt total recovery. Drastic as it might seem, the best action is to burn the plant to prevent the pests from spreading onto other nearby plants.

## Ideal Conditions

### Light and Position

Because of their neat size and shape, peperomias are essentially windowsill plants. The window should provide good light, but not direct midday sun. These are excellent plants for mixing with other types. They are not, however, suitable for bottle-gardens.

### Temperature Range

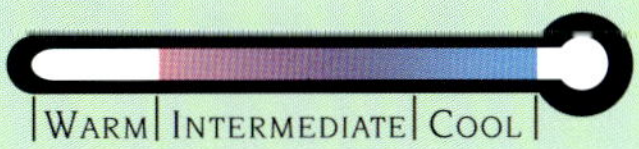


A modest temperature of 55°–65°F is best although this can drop to 50°F in winter if watering is also reduced. The maximum summer temperature should be 75°F.

### Watering

Peperomias should be watered only sparingly, every 10 days in summer and every two weeks in winter. Use lime-free water. The plants store water in their leaves, and if overwatered, these will quickly rot.

### Feeding

Peperomias will usually be growing in a soil-less mixture which lacks essential nutrients, so feed with a weak fertilizer with each watering. In summer, feed every two weeks using half the recommended dosage.

### Seasonal Care

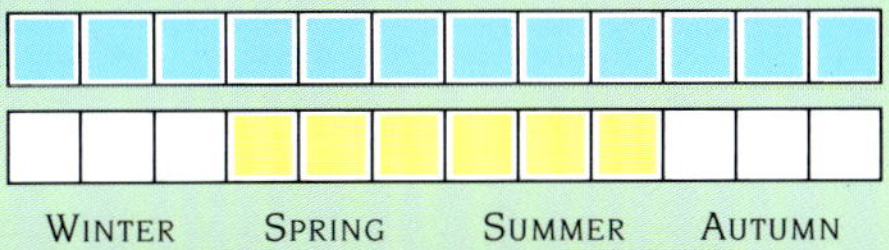


These can be difficult plants to keep growing from year to year, but it is well worth the effort. Peperomias should be watered very moderately throughout the year. Generally, these plants do not develop extensive root systems and will not require repotting. If necessary, repot only in the spring. Propagate from cuttings.

### Soil

These plants do well in peat-based mixtures. Repotting should be done every second year at most. When repotting, use shallow containers rather than deep pots. Never repot in winter.

# Philodendron

SWEETHEART PLANT, HEARTLEAF PHILODENDRON, OR PARLOR IVY

Philodendrons are certainly some of the most important foliage houseplants. Although there are a few variegated forms, they are mostly green to reddish-brown in color. Some are majestic and upright, others are radiating and equally majestic, while some are plants that are content to creep along the ground.

All philodendrons produce aerial roots of some kind from their stems, or trunks, which are used in their natural jungle habitat for entwining around tree trunks, enabling them to climb into the upper air. Besides their climbing facility, these roots can also spread out over the floor of the jungle and provide the parent with nourishment and moisture. Bearing this in mind, it is important not to remove too many of these roots from plants that are growing indoors. It is much better to tie them neatly to the main stem of the plant or its support and allow the tip of the root to enter the soil when it is long enough. With the low-growing, radiating types, any very long roots can be wound around the base of the plant on top of the soil by

**Healthy Plant**
*P. scandens* (left and above) is known as the Sweetheart Plant because of its distinctive heart-shaped leaves. These can be allowed to climb or trail, depending on requirements. The plant does particularly well in hanging baskets, where the trailing effect of its growth is most attractive.

**Healthy Plant**
*P.* 'Red Emerald' (above) is a hybrid, noted for its burgundy-red leaves. It is a slower climber than other philodendrons, but makes up for this by an increased spread.

making a hole with a pencil and carefully inserting the root into it.

New plants can be raised by a variety of methods. The most productive is from seed that is reasonably easy to germinate in a temperature of around 70°F. The seed should be sown in shallow boxes or trays filled with peat and sand that is not allowed to dry out. Most seed will be large enough to sow at approximately ½-inch intervals before being covered with a very thin layer of the propagating mixture. Seedlings can be left in the propagating mixture until they have made several small leaves, when they can be transferred to small pots filled with a peaty potting mixture.

Almost all the philodendrons, other than the stockier radiating kinds, can be propagated from pieces of stem with one or two leaves attached. Use a peat and sand mixture; a temperature of around 70°F is necessary if the plants are to do well.

## Varieties and Purchasing

Philodendrons are available throughout the year and are easy plants to handle and care for, as they do not require much in the way of special attention. Keep the moss moist and remember to apply enough to allow for the eventual growth of the plant. Your new plant should have no damaged or missing leaves. Remember, too, that the leaves of young plants can be entirely different in both size and shape when they reach maturity, so it is well worth a little research before you buy.

*P. bipennifolium* Commonly known as the Panda Plant, this is one of the many varieties whose leaves change as the plant becomes older. At first, they are heart-shaped; as the plant matures, they shape themselves like a violin. The plant can grow to a height of 6 feet and needs to be supported securely.

*P. bipinnatifidum* This is a radiating type, with fingered green leaves spreading from a central trunk. It can reach a height of 10 feet, but this is seldom attained indoors. Its aerial roots are very strong. These should be directed into the soil when they are long enough. This will help support the trunk as well as providing added moisture and nourishment.

*P. hastatum* This is an attractive plant, with broad arrow-shaped leaves, ideal for display. The stems of the plant must be well supported.

*P.* 'Red Emerald' This hybrid has red stalks and stems. Its new leaves are totally red at first, but after a few weeks, the tops turn green.

*P. scandens* This is one of the easiest philodendrons to cultivate. Pinch out some of the growing tips regularly or the plant will straggle.

*P. wendlandii* A non-climbing species, this has leaves arranged in the shape of a "birdie."

*P. imbe* A fast climber, this can reach a height of 8 feet in a couple of years if it is supported securely. Its heart-shaped leaves are thin, but firm, in texture. They are carried on long stalks, which lead off vertically from the plant's stems, so the plant looks layered.

*P. pedatum* This is a slow climber, with shiny green leaves divided into five lobes.

## Pests and Diseases

Once in their final pots, most philodendrons need little more than regular feeding and watering. The larger the plant, the more food it will require, though only moderate amounts of water are needed. All philodendrons should be protected from direct sunlight, while they are happiest at around 65°F.

**Mealy bug** These can be troublesome on some plants as they get older, but, fortunately, the open growth of most philodendrons makes it easy to deal with the pests. Remove adults and their nests manually. If necessary spray with malathion.

**Black leg** This attacks cuttings during the propagation stage in unhygienic conditions. There is no cure, so the cuttings must be burned.

**Root failure** Due to wet and cold conditions, this can cause the plant's collapse. The same can happen in too dry conditions, but this can be avoided with care.

**Slugs** These can be troublesome on plants with soft, tender leaves. Use a recommended slug repellant around the base of the plant to eradicate them.

**Sooty mold** This is a black fungus which grows on the sticky secretions – honeydew – produced by the various sap sucking insects. You must sponge it off with a dilute solution of soapy water and check for pests.

**Too dry** Drooping leaves are an indication of underwatering. The best solution to this problem is to stand the plant in a bucket of water until the earth is quite saturated, then remove and allow to drain. The holes in these leaves may well be snail or slug damage; check the plant and control with a safe slug bait if necessary.

**Healthy Plant**
*P. hastatum* (below) is distinguished by its broad, arrow-shaped leaves (above). These are bright green in color and attached to long stalks. They must be staked if the plant is to remain erect. It can reach a height of 20 feet in optimum conditions.

## Ideal Conditions

### Light and Position

All philodendrons must be given locations that will provide them with protection from direct sunlight and drafts. Choose a suitable position for each type. Radiating plants will need ample space around them.

### Temperature Range

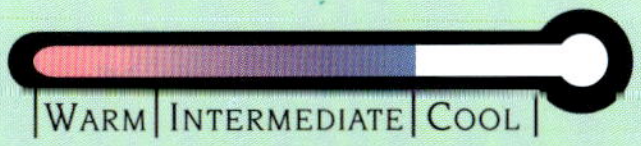


Philodendrons will thrive best in temperatures between 59°–70°F but above all should not suffer a drop in temperature below 55°F. The maximum summer temperature at which they are comfortable is 75°F and at all times they will appreciate occasional mist-spraying.

### Watering

Water these plants in the growing period enough to moisten the potting mixture and then allow the top layer of the soil to dry out before watering again. In the short mid-winter rest period give them just enough water to prevent the soil from drying out completely.

### Feeding

The larger the plant and the longer it has been in the same pot, the stronger or more frequent fertilization it will require. For smaller plants, best results are obtained by including weak fertilizer in the water each time the soil is moistened.

### Seasonal Care

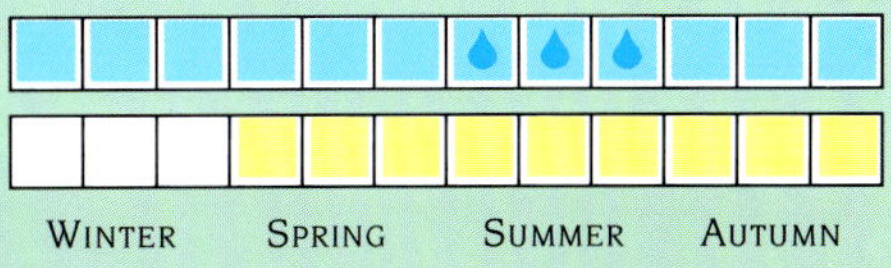


These are plants for all seasons but they should be kept out of colder areas at all times. They have a short mid-winter rest period during which time they should have just enough water to prevent the soil from drying out. Water in moderation for the rest of the year while the plants are in active growth and new shoots are being formed.

### Soil

Use a peat-based mixture and repot only when the roots completely fill the pot. Many of the larger plants (in pots over 10 in in diameter) are best left where they are. Extremely large plants or those that will climb readily if tied to a stake should be started in tubs.

# Pilea

## Aluminum Plant, Watermelon Plant, or Friendship Plant

Many of these plants are compact, easy to propagate from cuttings, and not too difficult to manage. Cuttings can be taken at any time if suitable conditions are available. Sound pieces about 3 inches in length should be taken from the ends of plant stems, and inserted in a seed potting mixture at a temperature of 65°–70°F. As an alternative to pure peat, the cutting can be inserted straight into 3-inch pots filled with a good houseplant soil – at least five pieces should go into each pot.

### Varieties and Purchasing

Go for younger, smaller plants.

*P. cadierei* Also known as the Aluminum Plant or Watermelon Plant, this is the most popular variety of pilea. It grows to approximately 12 inches in height, whereas the very similar dwarf variety, *P.c.* 'Minima' only reaches 6 inches.

*P. involucrata* This plant is more frequently called the Friendship Plant and is thought by some to be identical to another pilea, *P. spruceana*. In the summer it should produce minute pink flowers, and it adapts to different conditions quite easily.

*P. mollis* The leaves on this pilea have bronze markings and are a brighter green than the leaves of *P. cadierei*. The rough surface of the leaves gave rise to the plant's common name, Moon Valley.

*P. muscosa* This pilea resembles a fern. It never grows higher than 10 inches and usually blooms throughout the summer.

**Healthy Plant**
Pileas come in creeping as well as upright-growing varieties. They are popular for mixed displays because the different varieties encompass a wide range of size, color, and leaf texture. They look attractive when displayed with other small plants, and they are suitable for bottle gardens. The *P. cadierei* or Aluminum Plant (right) is perhaps the best-known, and it is relatively easy to care for. It can be distinguished by the silver patches on each leaf (above).

**Healthy Plant**
The Silver Tree *P. spruceana* derives its common name from the broad silver stripe of the leaf marking (below).

## Pests and Diseases

Pileas usually make healthy houseplants, but a few things may trouble them from time to time. Strong, direct sun or cold drafts will inhibit them and cause damage. Leaves pressed against a windowpane during a cold winter are especially at risk and may turn black when chilled.

**Mealy bug** These are quite a common pest in pileas, mainly found among the lower stems of the plant. Left to their work, they will cause so much damage that in time the plant may lose its leaves completely. Mealy bugs are easy to see on the stems or under the leaves, being white against the green and brownish coloring of the foliage. Young bugs wrapped in their wooly protection are particularly visible. Spray the whole plant with a soapy solution. Paint the leaves with denatured alcohol or spray with malathion.

**Red spider mite** This is not usually troublesome, but may occasionally be present and, when it is, must be dealt with immediately. Check regularly for spider mites by examining the undersides of leaves. Use a magnifying glass, as the insects are tiny and easily missed. Because the foliage of a pilea is quite dense, isolate it. Remove and destroy infested foliages. Spray with derris.

**Botrytis** This grayish-brown mold (see illustration, below) attacks the leaves of the plant, causing them to rot. The whole plant may also become dusty-looking. This fungal disease is encouraged by damp cold conditions and exacerbated if dead leaves become trapped in the living foliage and start to rot. Treat by removing badly affected leaves and dead or rotten matter, then spray with a fungicide.

## Ideal Conditions

### Light and Position

Pileas flourish in shady surroundings and should never be placed near a bright light or in direct sunlight. They grow best in the summer, positioned at a short distance from a window.

### Temperature Range

Warm | Intermediate | Cool

These plants must be protected from cold drafts and they thrive in an atmosphere that is both hot and humid. It is not advisable to keep them in temperatures of less than 55°F as they are unlikely to survive. Temperatures between 59°–70°F are much more suitable.

### Watering

All varieties of pilea should be watered cautiously so that the potting mixture is damp throughout, without ever being sodden. The top half of the mixture or soil can be allowed to dry out before another watering is necessary. Pileas should never be completely immersed in water.

### Feeding

Once they are well established, pileas should be fed each time they are watered. Although small, they are greedy plants, and they may need a stronger dosage than the fertilizer manufacturers usually recommend.

### Seasonal Care

Winter Spring Summer Autumn

Trimming and pruning should be done in the spring. However, the dead leaves should be removed regularly and the growing tips should be pinched out occasionally to ensure a bushy growth. Pileas may require slightly more water during the summer as this is the period of most growth. After three or four years these plants may become straggly and messy. When they start to deteriorate, cuttings should be taken and new plants propagated.

### Soil

Peat-based mixtures are suitable for pileas, and repotting should be done in the spring or summer. As small plants, they are displayed to their best advantage in half pots rather than full-size ones.

# Plumbago auriculata

CAPE LEADWORT

Although this lovely flowering climber will happily grow outside in areas where winters are relatively mild with not too many hard frosts, it readily adapts itself to life indoors. Adaptability is really the key to this superstar, for it will thrive in all but the warmest temperatures.

Increase stock by taking 3–4-inch cuttings during spring and summer, choosing plant material that is neither too soft and fleshy, nor too hard and woody. Place the cuttings in equal parts of potting soil and perlite and provide high humidity by covering the rim of the pot with a plastic bag, or by placing the pot in a propagator. When new growth starts to appear, remove the cutting from the security of the plastic bag or propagator and allow the young plant to grow on until the roots have filled the pot. During this time keep the soil moist and do not allow the plant to stand in direct sunlight.

## Pests and Diseases

**Mealy bug** Although greenfly can be a problem on plumbago, the real villain is mealy bug. They lay their familiar wooly bundles of eggs anywhere on the plant, but seem particularly partial to old dead flower stalks and crevices in the older hard wood. The adult bug feeds by sucking sap from the plant, which will seriously weaken it, so action must be taken fast. As soon as they are large enough to see, pick them off by hand, wiping away the bundles of eggs simultaneously. Then wipe the affected parts of the plant with a cloth soaked in denatured alcohol. If the infestation has gone beyond manual control, spray with a pesticide like malathion. The biological control, *cryptolaemus* is a very effective way of keeping mealy bug under control, but will only really work if introduced before the pest is doing too much damage. Once this type of pest control has been introduced, only a safe spray can be used.

## Varieties and Purchasing

*Plumbago auriculata* (formerly *P. capensis*) Will grow easily to 10 feet or more, so it should be sold on some form of support, either a hoop or small trellis.

Both it and *P. auriculata* 'Alba', its white-flowered near relative, are on sale at good garden centers throughout the summer. Select one with plenty of fresh green growth and possibly some flowers.

**Healthy Plant**
Healthy plants are not necessarily tidy plants. If in good heart, new bright green straggly stems should be sprouting from old hard wood. The lovely powder-blue flowers appear in clusters of 20 or more at the tips of these stems during summer and autumn. If they are removed immediately after they have faded, the plant will start to bloom all over again.

## Ideal Conditions

### Light and Position

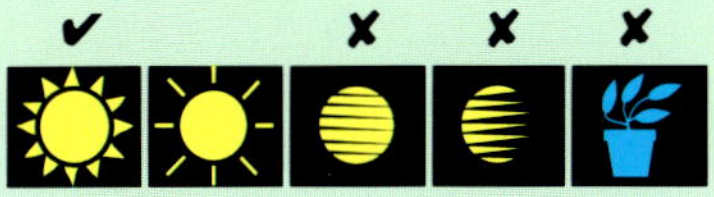

For good flowering, plumbagos must be in a position where they receive some direct sunlight every day, but are protected from midday sun, so a spot in a west- or east-facing window would be perfect. Because they are natural climbers, place them close to a wall if possible, where their developing stems will need training onto wires or a trellis.

### Temperature Range

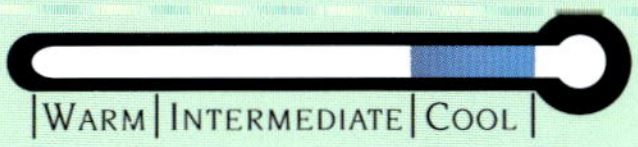


Plumbagos will tolerate temperatures close to freezing in the winter. With a minimum around 50°F, this is unlikely to happen; their growth will simply slow down, or stop, for the period of dormancy.

### Watering

Give all plumbagos plenty of water during the spring and summer. Those plants kept warmer during the winter will need moderate amounts of water, enough to moisten the soil, but allowing the top ½ inch to dry out between waterings. Those which are kept cooler need only enough water to prevent the soil from drying out completely.

### Feeding

Provide a liquid fertilizer at two-weekly intervals through the spring and summer.

### Seasonal Care

Provide plentiful amounts of water during the summer. At temperatures above 70°F, extra ventilation must be provided. Prune twice a year, first in February when last year's stems will have to be shortened by two-thirds, and second immediately after flowering when the stems will need to be cut back to about 9 inches. Plumbagos need this pruning not just to keep them in shape, but because they flower on new growth.

### Soil

Grown in pots, plumbagos need repotting once a year in the spring. Use a good soil-based mixture. If they are in their final pot size, they will need top-dressing once a year.

# Primula

The wide variety of primulas have flowers which place them among the most delicate and beautiful of all the plants used for indoor decoration. Most are grown from seed and will continue to flower for many months. P. *obconica* seems quite content to produce flowers throughout the whole year. However, it is sometimes known as the Poison Primula, because it can be a major problem for anyone with sensitive skin. It is possible for someone to become irritated by being in the same room as the plant, without actually touching it. A group of plants with different colored flowers makes a delightful display.

**Healthy Plant**

The best season for primulas is spring, and with their fresh colors and vibrant green leaves, they are appropriate symbols of the season. To make sure they are at their best, choose plants that are clean and fresh green in appearance with a few flowers showing and plenty of buds.

## Varieties and Purchasing

There are many varieties of these most delicate and beautiful plants.

*P. acaulis* The flowers of this variety appear during the winter. They have no stalks and, nestling among the leaves, look very like primroses.

*P. malacoides* This is sometimes known as the Fairy Primrose. Slender stems above clusters of pale green leaves support the star-shaped flowers which may be red, pink, or white. The plants may grow up to 18 inches tall.

*P. obconica* This is often called the Poison Primula because of its effect on people with sensitive skins, who may come out in a rash after contact with the plant. However, for those who are immune, it is a very good houseplant, being quite strong and producing flowers almost continuously throughout the year. It is less delicate in appearance than other varieties.

## Pests and Diseases

**Aphids** The soft foliage of the primula is vulnerable to all sucking insects, but aphids are the most troublesome. They may be detected by the white "skeletons" that they shed when molting. If they are not dealt with rapidly, the flowers and leaves may become distorted and sticky. Use a "safe soap" spray regularly for effective control.

**Red spider mite** It is essential to inspect the undersides of the leaves regularly, as if red spiders go unnoticed for too long, they can do great damage. They are encouraged by hot, dry conditions, so if primulas are kept in a moist, cool environment, which in any case suits them better, they are less likely to attract these pests. If red spiders do infest the plant, it must be treated with a recommended insecticide immediately, with particular attention being paid to the undersides of the leaves.

**Vine weevils** These are sometimes seen on the foliage, but it is the maggots in the soil that do most of the damage. If they do occur, the soil should be drenched with a solution of permethrin.

**Botrytis** (see illustration below). Plants may contract this disease if they are in poor cultural conditions, particularly when there is poor air circulation. It causes wet patches on the leaves, or, if the plant is potted too deeply, its entire center may be affected.

## Ideal Conditions

### Light and Position

Primulas need plenty of light but should be kept out of direct sunlight. As the plants should be kept moist, it is a good idea to plunge their pots to the rim in larger containers filled with moisture-retaining moss or peat.

### Temperature Range

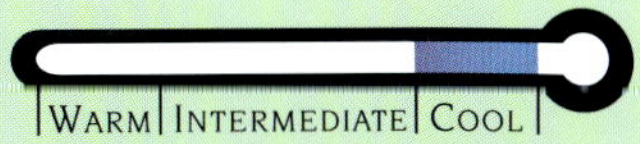


Primulas like a fairly cool environment, between 50°–59°F, especially when they are in flower. If the room temperature exceeds 59°F, the flowers are liable to fall more quickly. If the plants must be temporarily kept in a warmer environment, it is important to provide them with added humidity by standing them on trays of moistened pebbles and spraying their leaves.

### Watering

Primulas thrive on plentiful supplies of water. Water copiously, ensuring that the potting mixture is thoroughly moist. However, care must be taken to ensure that the plant is not actually standing in water.

### Feeding

From the time when the first flower stalks start to appear the plants should be fed every two weeks with a weak solution of standard fertilizer. This will extend the flowering period as long as possible.

### Seasonal Care

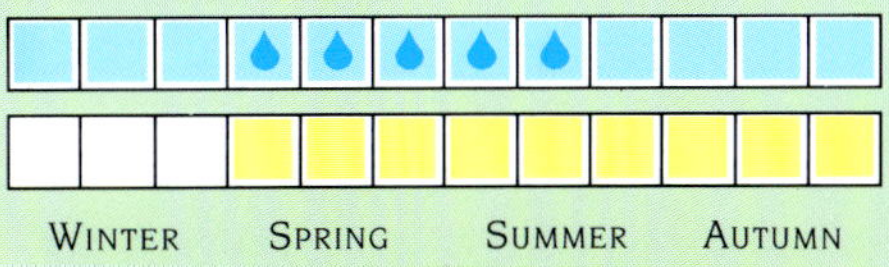


Although sodden soil is harmful, plants should be kept moist at all times. It is possible to prolong the flowering period by picking the dead flowers as soon as they fade. *P. malacoides* is an annual but *P. obconica* can be repotted to flower more freely the following year. After *P. acaulis* has flowered it can be planted in the yard.

### Soil

If on purchase the plants appear to be pot-bound, they should be repotted into larger pots immediately to give them room for development. Use a soil-based mixture and do not ram the soil into the pots too firmly.

# Rhoicissus

## Grape Ivy

The rhoicissus is among the toughest of all the dark green foliage plants, and when all else fails, it could well be the best plant to try to establish indoors. It is a climbing plant with tri-lobed, glossy green leaves. Although it does not produce any flowers, it is an invaluable plant for covering wall areas in difficult corners.

New plants are raised from 3–4-inch cuttings and inserted in peat in a temperature of around 70°F.

**Healthy Plant**
Rhoicissus is an elegant and familiar evergreen plant. It will climb or trail, even fill an awkward corner where other plants have failed to thrive. Leaf shape varies from roughly circular with deep indentations to roughly heart-shaped with shallow indentations. All leaves have toothed, slightly undulate edges and are colored bright emerald green.

### Varieties and Purchasing

Look for a plant with full, unblemished, green foliage.

*R. rhomboidea* (above) This is the original Grape Ivy and is one of the toughest houseplants. It is ideally suited to climbing if you provide a framework.

*R. rhomboidea 'Ellendanica'* (right) This variation has slightly waved indentations around the leaf margins.

## Pests and Diseases

**Mealy bug** These powdery white bugs and their young may infest congested growth in older plants. Spray the plant with malathion or soak a sponge with solution and wipe the bugs away. These bugs like a warm, dry atmosphere, so spray the plant regularly to create a humid environment.

**Root mealy bug** Similar to the leaf bugs, these attack the roots of a plant which has stayed in one pot for a long time. By sucking sap from the roots, these pests can cause stunting of top growth. Wash the soil carefully from the roots and cut away the worst affected parts, then repot in fresh mixture. If necessary, water malathion solution into the soil.

**Scorched leaf** Although rhoicissus is very tolerant of a wide range of light levels, its leaves will scorch if placed too close to glass. These leaves will develop brown papery edges before dropping off altogether.

## Ideal Conditions

### Light and Position

These plants will enjoy a bright or lightly shaded position, but cannot tolerate exposure to direct, strong sun. Provided they are not subjected to this or to cold drafts, they will do well almost anywhere.

### Temperature Range

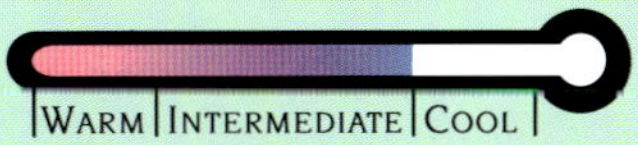


The rhoicissus copes with lower temperatures, but really prefers a range of 59°–70°F. It will benefit from light spraying in summer, when warmer conditions are prevalent.

### Watering

Water the plant well in summer and during the period of active growth, but check the condition of the soil carefully, as overwatering may damage the plant, causing the leaves to droop and even rot completely.

### Feeding

Once established, the plants require frequent feeding. Give liquid fertilizer in the water at least once a week while in active growth. Reduce or discontinue the feeding when the plant is dormant in winter.

### Seasonal Care

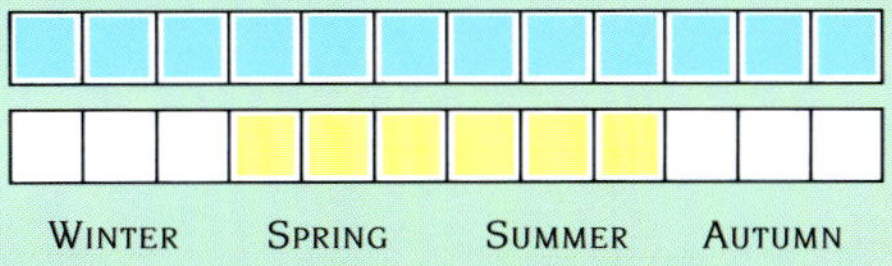


The plants require no more than the usual care, with the soil kept moist but not sodden under any conditions. Untidy growth may be trimmed back in the fall, and if young shoots at the top of the stems are pinched out regularly, a healthy, bushy growth will result. Take cuttings in spring or early summer, using growing tips furnished with a couple of full leaves.

### Soil

Annual potting is necessary, transferring the plant to a slightly larger container each time until the plant is in a 10-inch pot. Then sustain the plant with regular feeding and change just the topsoil occasionally, using a soil-based mixture.

# Saintpaulia

## AFRICAN VIOLET

Although these plants are generally difficult to manage, this does not seem to be a deterrent, as worldwide they are among the most popular of all the potted flowering houseplants. The leaves are mostly rounded, hairy, and attached to short talks that sprout from soil level, forming a neat rosette that is a background for the flowers when they appear. Flowers of many colors are now available in single and double forms, and a collection of plants growing in ideal conditions will provide a display of flowers throughout the year. Plants can be propagated from individual leaves with stalk attached. These are put into clean peat in a propagating case in a temperature of not less than 70°F.

**Healthy Plant**
The African Violet is one of the most popular flowering houseplants. It is available in a wide variety of colors and flower shapes.

### VARIETIES AND PURCHASING

The wide variety of African Violets available today vary in color and in flower shape and formation. However, a few points should be borne in mind when buying. Select a plant with firm, non-drooping leaves, and, if possible, avoid purchasing from cold premises. Plants with blemishes on the foliage and sign of root or stem rot should always be passed over. Try to choose a plant which is in bud, as this will afford more lasting pleasure than one in full flower.

*S. ionantha* This is the only variety of African Violet in cultivation. All the many examples commercially available are hybrids of *S. ionantha.*

## Pests and Diseases

The recent varieties of African Violet tend to be tougher than their predecessors, but care still needs to be taken when caring for the plants. Overwatering and wetting the leaves can cause problems.

**Root rot** Most types of root rot are aggravated by wet soil conditions which prevent oxygen from reaching the roots of the plant. Affected roots are brown and lifeless. In the early stages, treat by allowing the plant to dry out and to stay dry for several days. In an advanced state, the whole plant collapses and the leaves go limp. At this stage the plant must be destroyed.

**Botrytis** This fungus disease should also be treated with fungicide. If the attack is severe, destroy the plant.

**Mildew** This should be treated with a suitable fungicide such as propicanizole.

**Aphids** These insects may attack the plant's soft, tender leaves. Treat with pyrethrum and avoid wetting the leaves if possible. If the leaves are wet, do not place the plant in the sun.

**Cyclamen mite** Although generally uncommon, this pest can be fatal as there is no known cure. The plant should be burned so that the pest cannot spread.

## Ideal Conditions

### Light and Position

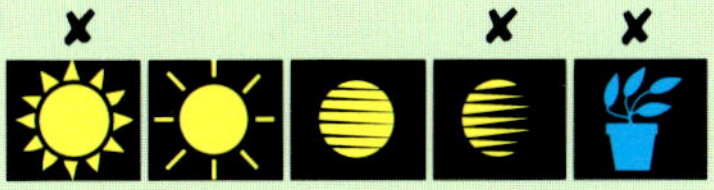

The African Violet requires good light and will tolerate direct sunlight as long as it is not magnified by the glass of a greenhouse or windowpane. It is important that this plant should be protected from all drafts.

### Temperature Range

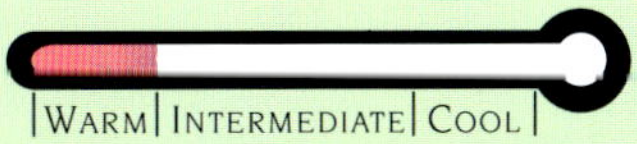


A good nursery will not sell African Violets until mild weather has arrived. They are plants which do not like being chilled and flourish in a temperature of 65°–70°F. The warmth and humidity of bathrooms and kitchens provide ideal conditions for growth.

### Watering

During the summer, spray plants occasionally with a fine mist of rainwater. Hard water causes white spots and patches on the foliage. In cold weather, water sparingly; if kept slightly dry, plants will often survive in lower temperatures.

### Feeding

It is important that the leaves of this plant should be kept as dry as possible when feeding. Add a liquid fertilizer to the soil when watering, taking care to use a weak solution regularly rather than giving an occasional large feed.

### Seasonal Care

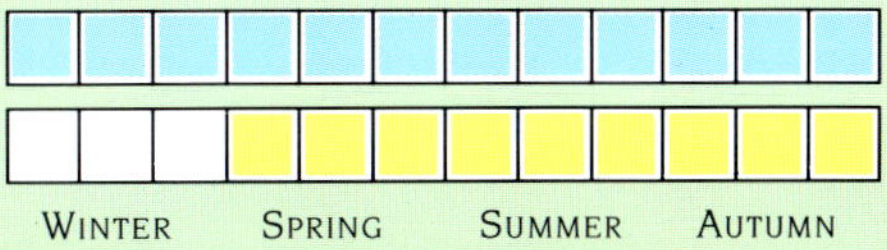


The main difference in the care of the Saintpaulia from season to season is in the amount of water required. Throughout the year, the plant should never be overwatered, but in cold weather it is even more important not to allow the soil to become too wet. Use tepid rather than cold water at all times. Remove dead flowers and leaves as soon as you notice them.

### Soil

In general, small pots are more suitable than large ones. African Violets flourish in peat-based potting mixtures.

# Schefflera

## UMBRELLA TREE OR OCTOPUS TREE

Belonging to the same family as the heptapleurum, the schefflera grows in a similar way, but is a very much more robust houseplant. In some parts of the world, it is known as *Brassaia actinophylla*; in Britain it is known as *S. actinophylla*. In tropical regions the schefflera grows to become a substantial tree, given the name Umbrella Tree because its foliage radiates like the spokes of an umbrella. These plants are strong growing, and they may, in time, achieve a height of around 15 feet.

New plants are almost invariably raised from seed which is started into growth in temperatures of around 70°F.

**Healthy Plant**
The schefflera is an excellent plant for people who are unwilling or unable to provide constant care and attention. Able to withstand most environmental conditions, in an ideal situation it will grow to a strapping height of 8 feet. When young, *S. actinophylla* can be quite unattractive, with spindly stems and oversized leaves. When full grown, however, the plant becomes a handsome specimen with rich, glossy leaves exploding outward from the top of each stem.

## Pests and Diseases

While scheffleras are prone to the pests and diseases common to all houseplants, they are also less likely to contract them. Most of these problems can be avoided by carefully spraying and wiping the leaves of the plant regularly.

**Mealy bug** This is mostly seen on older plants, but even then is not often found on the tough foliage of the schefflera. Because the bugs are easily seen, they can easily be removed or if necessary treated with malathion.

**Red spider mite** This pest tends to be found on plants growing in hot, dry environments. Light brown leaf discoloration is a sign of their presence. To cure, use a recommended insecticide which should be sprayed on the undersides of the leaves at weekly intervals.

**Aphids** These are often a problem on young leaves, but are easily treated if caught in time. A commercial insecticide will clear up the problem quite easily.

## Varieties and Purchasing

Each type of schefflera is slightly different in size and appearance, and should be purchased according to where it is to be situated. If, for example, the plant is to be the focal point of a room, then a full-sized plant is best because scheffleras can take a while to reach their full adult height. For all types, the health of the plant can be determined by the condition of its leaves. Purchase plants whose leaves are free of blemishes, firm, and supple and not drooping. The surface of the leaves should be rich and glossy with a polished appearance.

*S. actinophylla* This is the most common and largest variety available. Look for one that has well-shaped and proportioned leaves. Scheffleras today are often sold under the name *Brassaia*.

## Ideal Conditions

### Light and Position

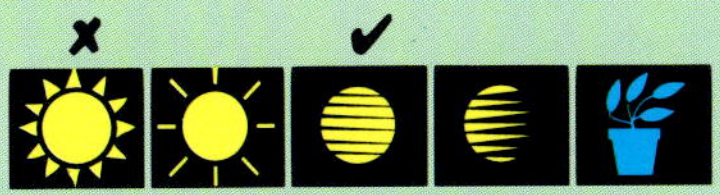

The Umbrella Tree is an accommodating plant that will tolerate many locations but prefers light shade or indirect sunlight. Young plants can be mixed in with other houseplants, but full-grown plants are best viewed when they are standing alone as a special feature.

### Temperature Range

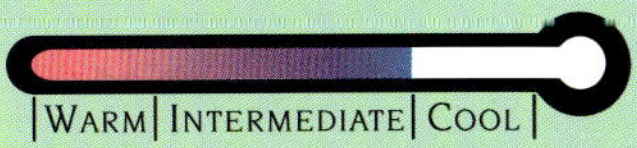


To keep the Umbrella Tree happy, reasonable warmth of around 59°–70°F is needed, 65°F being about right. These plants also like humidity, so avoid dry heat. If the room in which they are situated is dry, place the plants in pots in shallow trays filled with pebbles and water.

### Watering

The larger the plant, the more water it will require, except in winter when it becomes inactive. Keep the soil moist at all times. Good drainage is essential. A pointed stick can be used to loosen the top of the soil to assist drainage.

### Feeding

At all stages of development, a proprietary liquid fertilizer can be used with every watering. As the plant develops, two different fertilizers can be used to satisfy the plant's various needs.

### Seasonal Care

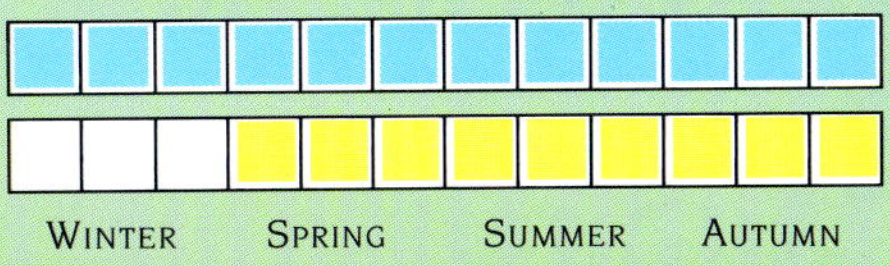


The soil of the Umbrella Tree should be kept moist at all times of the year, but only minimum watering is required during the winter months. The plants can be propagated in late winter from either seed or stem cuttings. Pot at any time except in winter when the plant is vulnerable to damage and radical changes in environment.

### Soil

In four years' time, the robust Umbrella Tree may well need a pot 10 in in diameter. Once in a large pot, the potting mixture should sustain the plant for a number of years. A good soil-based mixture is fine but add some extra grit to provide adequate drainage.

# Scindapsus

DEVIL'S IVY, POTHOS VINE, SOLOMON ISLAND'S VINE, OR GOLDEN HUNTER'S ROBE

The scindapsus is one of the most remarkable foliage plants of all. When they first appeared on the market, they were tender and difficult to care for, they are now among the most rewarding of indoor plants. Obviously, a tougher selected strain has been developed to make the radical change possible, and today the scindapsus is a decorative plant with mustard and green variegation that is tolerant of a wide range of conditions in the home. Even when placed at the farthest point from the light source, the variegation is rarely affected – a quality that is unusual in most plants with variegated foliage.

Propagation is done vegetatively by inserting pieces of firm stem with two good leaves attached. A temperature of about 70°F and a peat and sand mixture that is kept moist, but not waterlogged are required.

## Varieties and Purchasing

Scindapsus plants come in many shapes and sizes, and most outlets will have a selection. Some will be displayed as climbing, others trailing. Choose plants with firm leaves that stand out cleanly from the stem. Ignore any with curled, drooping leaves.

*S. aureus* (right). This is a green and mustard variegated plant, and probably the best buy. It may also be sold as Pothos.

*S.a.* 'Marble Queen' This plant (above) has marbled white and green foliage. It is more difficult to care for than other types.

**Healthy Plant**

There are about 20 species of scindapsus, each with a characteristic tendency to wrap itself around the nearest object. All the varieties can be grown either upright on a pole, or in a hanging basket.

**Healthy Plant**

This easy-going houseplant will thrive almost anywhere, provided it is warm. Pinch out the growing tips to promote bushy growth.

**Healthy Plant**

Although slow to start with, scindapsus make very good climbing plants given a moss pole or some alternative form of support (right).

## Pests and Diseases

Some problems scindapsus is prone to include:

**Botrytis** (see illustration, right). This causes wet, brown patches on the leaves. Remove any leaves which are infected.

**Aphids** These are found on the leaves of young plants. Control with a soapy spray.

**Mealy bug** (right) Treat the bugs with denatured alcohol.

## Ideal Conditions

### Light and Position

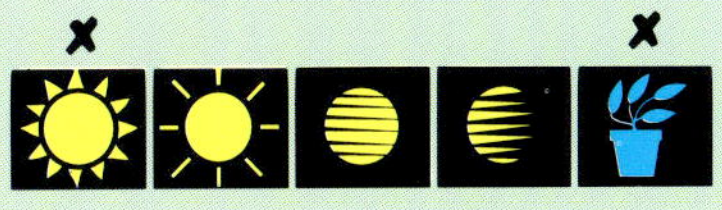

All scindapsus plants abhor strong, direct light. They also do not like shade, except for *S. aureus* which will maintain its distinctive yellow streaks if kept in low light. Bright, indirect light is ideal for most types. The plants can be grown in either a trailing or an upright fashion.

### Temperature Range

In their active period, these plants prosper in normal room temperatures between 59°–70°F, 65°F being ideal. In winter, a temperature of 59°F will give the plant a chance to rest, and they can tolerate a temperature of 50°F. If the room is dry as well as warm, stand the plants in their pots on trays of pebbles and water.

### Watering

The scindapsus does not like to be overwatered and should be allowed to dry out between waterings. During active growth water moderately. In winter, when the plant is dormant, water only enough to keep the potting mixture slightly moist.

### Feeding

Being fairly sturdy, the scindapsus does not need large amounts of fertilizer. Small, established plants should have a weak feed with each watering. Larger plants need a stronger dosage. During active growth, apply a liquid fertilizer every two weeks.

### Seasonal Care

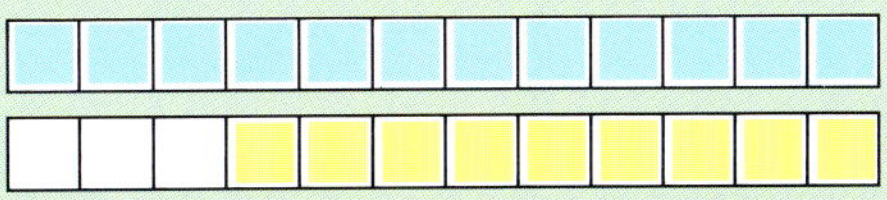

WINTER SPRING SUMMER AUTUMN

Keep the potting mixture moist throughout the year by watering every four or five days in summer and every seven to eight days in winter. Prune in early spring. If a bushier plant is desired, prune the main growth well back. Stem cuttings can be rooted in spring in either water or soil. The plants can be moved to a pot one size larger each spring. When the maximum size has been reached, replenish the topsoil.

### Soil

Avoid putting plants in pots too large for their size. When repotting, the new pots should be only 1–2in larger. Use a soil-based potting mixture. When propagating, plant cuttings in a moistened mixture of peat moss and coarse sand.

# Schlumbergera × Buckleyi

CLAW CACTUS

## VARIETIES AND PURCHASING

Although there are other varieties, *S.* × 'Buckleyi' is the one you are most likely to find.

**Healthy Plant**
The densely branching, drooping stems are made up of mid-green, fleshy segments. The flowers appear from the tip of the last segment, and a healthy plant should be abundantly covered with both flower buds and fully opened blooms.

**Healthy plant**
Look for a plant with a height and spread of about 30 cm (12 in). It is, of course, possible to buy larger plants, but they are likely to cost a great deal more.

The Claw cactus is surely one of the best plants to arrive in garden centers during winter. Their livid pink flowers brighten up any flowering display, quite different from the other plants available.

In the wild, this jungle plant lives in moist forests, living in small pockets of plant debris found in between the branches of trees. If these conditions are provided, a Claw cactus should do as it is told.

These plants are easy to propagate from cuttings during the spring and summer. Take a piece of stem with two or three jointed segments. Let the cutting dry out for a few hours before pushing it firmly into a moistened peat-based mixture. It must be pushed in deep enough to support the whole cutting upright. It should take two or three weeks to root.

Schlumbergeras can also be grown from seeds. This is not difficult, but it may take three or four years for the new plants to flower.

## Pests and Diseases

**Mealy bug** Keep an eye open for their wooly nests and for the adult bugs on leaves, leaf joints, and stems. With this plant it is a good idea to check the roots for root mealy bug as well. Carefully tip the plant out of its pot and examine the root ball. Any wooly white patches are a definite sign that infestation is underway.

To deal with those on the leaves, pick off as many adults and nests as are visible, spray all the top growth with a pressurized spray, and either paint the plant with denatured alcohol or spray with an insecticide such as malathion.

If root mealy bug is found, wash the roots clean of soil, repot in fresh dampened soil and water lightly with a solution of insecticide.

## Ideal Conditions

### Light and Position

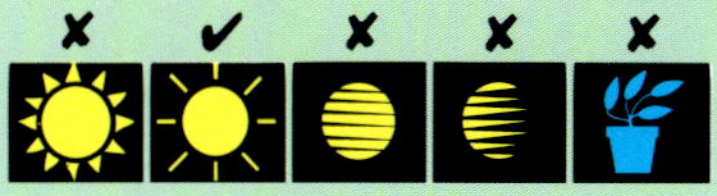

Do not subject the plants to direct sunlight during spring and summer. Weak summer sunshine will not damage them. Schlumbergeras' flowering system is triggered by shortening day length. The potentially harmful effects of artificial light on these plants can be prevented by laying sheets of black plastic over them when the house lights are on.

### Temperature Range

Schlumbergeras are best kept in cool temperatures, the recommended minimum being between 50°F and 55°F. Keep them in these temperatures while buds are forming and until the flowers are required. Then move them into warmer temperatures – 61–70°F.

### Watering

Schlumbergeras have their annual rest after flowering. At this time they need enough water to moisten the soil allowing the top ½ in to dry out before watering again. In spring when growth recommences, give more water, providing as much as is necessary to keep the soil moist at all times. Always use soft rainwater for these plants.

### Feeding

Provide liquid fertilizer once every two weeks while the buds are forming and during the flowering period.

### Seasonal Care

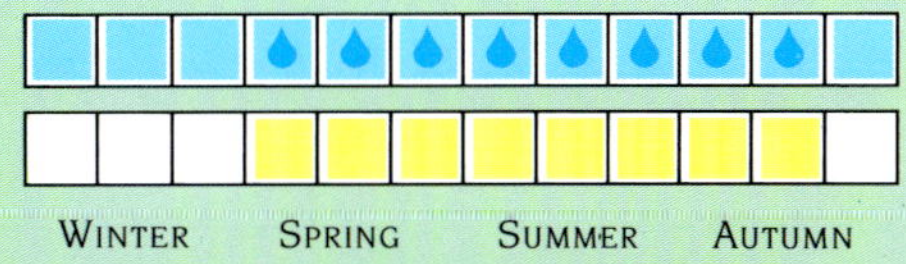


Let schlumbergeras rest after flowering. At this time give them very little water, but never let them dry out. Feed only during bud development and flowering. Keep them out of artificial light during bud formation. Remove one or two of the oldest stems after flowering.

### Soil

Although these plants need to be kept moist while flowering, they must never be allowed to become waterlogged. For this reason some washed river sand must be added to the peat-based soil when repotting them after flowering.

# Spathiphyllum

## White Sails or Peace Lily

There can be few more simple or more effective contrasts than creamy white flowers set off against dark green foliage, and this is what the exotic spathiphyllums have to offer. The common name clearly derives from the manner in which spathe flowers are held erect on stiff stalks, not unlike a sail. Although they belong to the same family as the anthuriums, the flowers of the spathiphyllum do not have the same lasting qualities when used as cut flowers. However, this is a small drawback as they will continue for many weeks if left on the plant.

Plants are propagated by the age-old method of division. This simply means that the plant is removed from its pot, and the clump of congested small plants is reduced to individual pieces or to smaller clumps which are potted individually. The pieces should be removed with as much root attached as possible and potted into 5-inch pots using a standard houseplant potting mixture.

**Healthy Plant**
*S.* 'Mauna Loa' is a pleasing, elegant plant. When choosing a plant, look for clean foliage and flowers that are in bud rather than full out. Drooping or discolored plants are unhealthy. The spathe eventually turns green. It is still attractive for a few weeks, but after that time it is a good idea to remove it.

### Varieties and Purchasing

*S. wallisii* The maximum height this variety achieves is 12 inches. The leaves, which grow in thick clusters, are about 6 inches long and 4 inches wide. The flowers, on long stalks, appear in spring and sometimes again in late summer. This variety, however, is not often found in retailers' stock. The cream or yellow-colored spadix of each flower is enclosed by the white spathe which gives rise to its common name, White Sails or Peace Lily.

*S.* 'Mauna Loa' This is a hybrid and far more popular than the other variety. It has large green leaves and majestic flowers which usually appear in spring. However, the plant does sometimes bloom at other times of the year. The flower stalks may be 15–20 inches long, and they give the flowers a very graceful appearance. The flowers have a fragrant smell, and altogether, the spathiphyllum is one of the most attractive of houseplants.

## Pests and Diseases

**Aphids** These pests tend to attack the young, maturing leaves in the center of the plant. As soon as they are noticed, steps should be taken to treat the plant, as they can cause considerable damage. Spray regularly with a "safe" soap spray to control.

**Red spider mite** If the atmosphere is too hot and dry, the spathiphyllum may be attacked by red spider mite. It is wise to spray the leaves regularly, concentrating on the undersides. If the plant does become infested, improve the growing conditions, remove and destroy infested leaves, and spray with derris.

**Mealy bug** This pest is not a frequent visitor to the spathiphyllum, but the leaves should be checked for it occasionally as it tends to be hidden between the congested leaves. If there are only a few, they can be wiped away with a pad soaked in denatured alcohol. Larger numbers can be removed by spraying with an insecticide such as malathion.

**Underfeeding** If underfed, the leaves of spathiphyllum will become patchy, yellow, and ragged. Make sure you feed these plants while they are in active growth.

## Ideal Conditions

### Light and Position

Spathiphyllums like a sunny position but direct sunlight should be avoided. They are beautifully shaped plants and so are at their best advantage when they can be viewed from all sides.

### Temperature Range

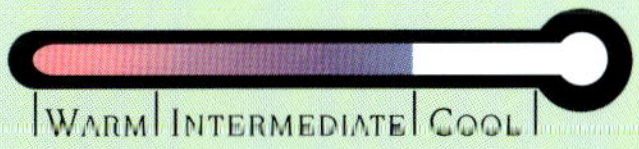


Spathiphyllums should be kept at temperatures between 59°–70°F. If they are kept at about 65°F they should grow for most of the year. They do not like drafts and they need a humid atmosphere, so keep them on trays of moist pebbles or moss.

### Watering

The spathiphyllum should be watered with moderate amounts – the potting mixture should never dry out completely. Avoid overwatering, as this could result in wilting.

### Feeding

Use a standard liquid fertilizer and administer every two weeks while the plant is growing. Older and more established plants may benefit from a slightly stronger solution than the manufacturer recommends.

### Seasonal Care

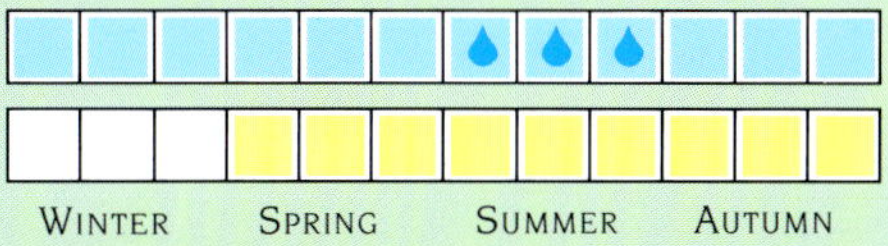


The plant grows fastest in summer and should receive greater quantities of water then. Avoid waterlogging. Decrease the amount of food in winter.

### Soil

The plants should be repotted every spring in a soil-based potting mixture. Ensure that they are properly drained by putting a few pieces of broken clay pots in the bottom of the new containers.

# Stephanotis floribunda

## MADAGASCAR JASMINE, WAX FLOWER, FLORADORA, OR MADAGASCAR CHAPLET FLOWER

These are natural climbing plants, with tough, leathery, evergreen foliage, whose main attraction is the almost over-powering fragrance of the waxy white flowers that are borne in clusters of five to nine. The individual flowers are trumpet-shaped with short stalks and are much favored by florists for bridal bouquets. New plants can be raised from cuttings of older growth taken in the spring and placed in a peaty mixture at a temperature of around 70°F. Plants may also be raised from seed that is produced from large, fruit-like seed pods which ripen in the fall to expose small seeds attached to the most beautiful, silky white "parachutes."

**Healthy Plant**
The main attraction of these climbing plants is their mass of scented white flowers.

### VARIETIES AND PURCHASING

Buy in summer, looking for healthy young plants that are fresh and green, with some flowers open and lots of buds on show. Avoid ones with yellowing foliage, or ones that have had such foliage removed. This is a sign of poor culture and root failure.

*S. floribunda* This is generally the only variety available.

### PESTS AND DISEASES

The main enemies of *S. floribunda* are bugs and insects, but do not water excessively or let the leaves become sun-scorched.

**Scale insects** Remove these with an old tooth-brush. Spray regularly with a soapy solution. If the they persist, treat with dimethoate.

**Sooty mold** This is a harmless black fungus. Wipe off with a sponge dipped in insecticide.

**Root mealy bug** Use insecticide.

### IDEAL CONDITIONS

**LIGHT AND POSITION**

Always place the plant in the lightest possible place. Full sun may scorch some of the leaves, but this is not unduly harmful. The plant's natural climbing habit makes it essential that some sort of framework be provided for the plant to cling to.

**TEMPERATURE RANGE**

WARM | INTERMEDIATE | COOL

A modest temperature of around 59°F throughout the year is fine for these plants. In winter keep them cooler at 55°F. In summer, do not let the temperature rise above 75°F.

**WATERING**

In summer, water two or three times a week and in winter, once a week. Use lime-free, tepid water whenever possible. Spray the plants once a week in summer, but avoid wetting the flowers.

**FEEDING**

Avoid giving excess food, but make sure that the plants have a weak feed with every watering while in active growth. In winter, when the plant is not flowering, feeding is not necessary.

**SEASONAL CARE**

WINTER SPRING SUMMER AUTUMN

Water stephanotis plants well during spring and summer, but avoid too wet conditions by allowing the soil to dry out between applications.

**SOIL**

Pot in the spring when the plants are getting under way for the new season. Never move plants into containers much larger than the existing pot. Use conventional potting mixture.

# Streptocarpus

## CAPE PRIMROSE

Indigenous to South Africa, the original Cape Primrose, S. 'Constant Nymph,' with its profusion of delicate blue flowers, was for many years the only streptocarpus available. Now there are many fine hybrids offering a wealth of color, and having the considerable added benefit that their leaves are smaller and very much less brittle.

New plants can be raised from seed, or particular varieties can be reproduced from leaf cuttings.

**Healthy Plant**
The stemless leaves of the Streptocarpus are coarse. The plant's pretty flowers push up from among them. It is possible to find much better specimens of hybrids than it was of the original variety.

## VARIETIES AND PURCHASING

*S.* 'Constant Nymph'
This plant has attractive blue flowers, but brittle leaves that can be damaged easily.

*S.* 'Concorde Hybrid'
This comes in a wide choice of colors.

## PESTS AND DISEASES

**Red spider mite** Can affect plants that are too dry and hot. Saturate the leaves with insecticide.

**Botrytis** This is a result of dank, airless conditions. Treat with a fungicide.

## IDEAL CONDITIONS

### LIGHT AND POSITION

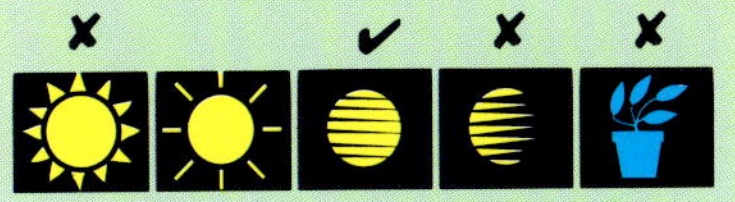

For the plant to continue to bloom throughout the spring and summer, it will need the lightest possible position, but not exposed to bright midday sun. During the winter months when not in flower, less light is tolerated.

### TEMPERATURE RANGE

Streptocarpus plants do not like heat, so an average temperature of 55°–59°F is best, while a constant of 59°F is ideal. Should the temperature drop lower, keep the soil dry because the plant will become nearly dormant. In summer, a maximum of 75°F is preferred.

### WATERING

Never let the plant stand in water or it will rot. In summer, water two or three times a week. In winter, water once a week or less. If possible, use soft, tepid water.

### FEEDING

Never feed the plant if it has just been potted, and feed sparingly during the winter. While in flower and well established, a greater number of flowers can be encouraged by using a fertilizer with a high proportion of potash.

### SEASONAL CARE

Water thoroughly when in active growth and less in winter. At all times, the soil should be allowed to dry out between waterings. When not in flower, foliage can be cleaned by holding a hand over the soil in the pot and inverting the pot into a bucket of tepid, soapy water. Keep the plant out of the sun while it is drying.

### SOIL

While in small pots, a peaty mixture is best, but when the pot reaches 5 inches in diameter, use a soil-based potting mixture. Good drainage is essential. Avoid putting plants in pots that are too large.

# Syngonium podophyllum

## Arrow Head Plant or Goose Foot Plant

Gorgeous, slightly marbled leaves of Syngonium which become visibly larger as they mature. It will creep quietly along the base of displays, forming stout, bushy masses; it will climb or it will trail. Completely versatile and beautiful, no houseplant collection should be without one.

It is well worth taking cuttings from this plant, simply take 3–4-inch pieces from the tips of stems. Make the cut just below a leaf, which must be removed before dipping the cutting in a rooting hormone. Plant two or three in a small pot containing a mixture of dampened sand and peat, then cover the rim of the pot with a plastic bag. Keep it in bright light but out of direct sunlight. Rooting should take place in three or four weeks, when fresh green growth will be seen on the cuttings. Then remove the plastic bag and provide enough water regularly to stop the soil from drying out while the plants grow on. When the roots have filled the pot, transplant into the recommended mix for adult plants.

**Healthy Plant**

The leaves should be leathery and glossy, borne on sheathed stalks. Young plants will have undivided, but deeply lobed leaves, their stems being fleshy and slender. As these plants mature, the leaves become distinctly divided into segments, and a single leaf may consist of as many as nine segments. The stems of older plants harden and thicken, sometimes growing as long as 6 feet

## Pests and Diseases

Happily, syngoniums do not seem to be troubled by pests, but keep an eye on them just the same. Check their leaves regularly, removing dying foliage, and spray them with a fine mist of rainwater to freshen them up.

**Healthy Plant**
A Syngonium is one of the few plants that is rarely troubled by pests or diseases. However, check them over regularly and mist the leaves from time to time to keep them clear.

## Varieties and Purchasing

Syngoniums are widely available throughout the year.

*S. angustatum* Worth trying to find. Its leaves change in both shape and color as they mature.

## Ideal Conditions

### Light and Position

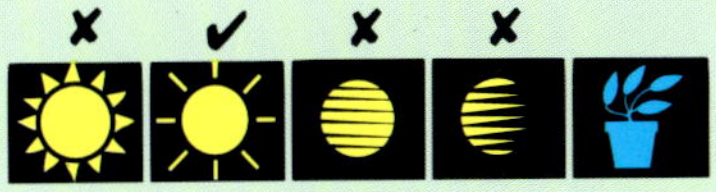

However syngoniums are displayed, they will do best in a position where they receive good light but no direct sunlight.

### Temperature Range

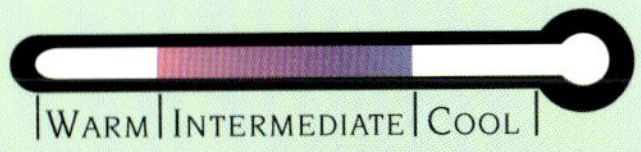


A minimum of 61°F is quite acceptable for these plants, but extra humidity is needed when the temperatures rise above 65°F. Do this by standing the plants in trays of damp horticultural aggregate.

### Watering

Make sure that the soil is thoroughly moistened when watering, but allow the top ½ inch of soil to dry out between waterings. During their short winter rest, only provide enough water to prevent the soil from drying out completely.

Syngoniums like a relatively high degree of moisture in the air around them, so mist them regularly with soft rainwater.

### Feeding

Syngoniums need a liquid feed once every two weeks throughout the year, except when they are resting.

### Seasonal Care

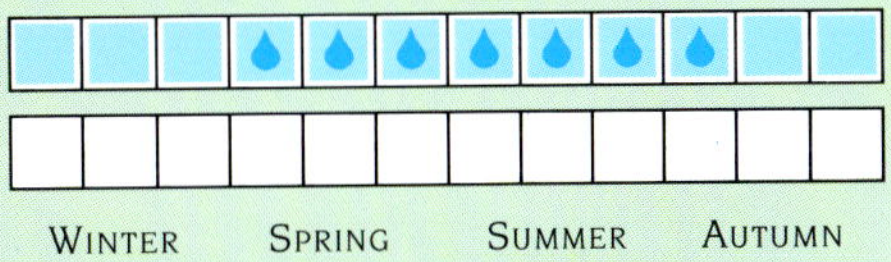


Pinch out the growing tips of trailing plants to encourage bushy growth. Provide those plants that are climbing with adequate support in the form of wires or trellis. They will only need to be anchored to this support while young; when mature they attach themselves. Remove dead leaves regularly and prune the plant to keep it within its space.

### Soil

Repot in spring using a combination of soil-based potting mixture and peat.

# Tradescantia

WANDERING SAILOR, INCH PLANT, OR SPEEDY JENNY

The numerous varieties of tradescantia are among the easiest to grow and the least expensive of all the indoor plants. They can also be very attractive if given a little bit extra care and attention.

During the summer months, cuttings about 3–4 inches in length taken from the ends of sturdy growths will root easily in any good houseplant soil mixture. Up to seven cuttings should be inserted in each small pot, and both pot and cuttings should be placed in a sealed plastic bag to reduce transpiration, so encouraging rooting.

### Tradescantia relations

Among the tradescantia, there is a small selection of slightly more difficult plants that you may find on sale. Almost all of them are grown for their decorative foliage rather than their flowers.

Most plants are propagated from cuttings, but are a little more difficult to rear than the common types, needing slightly higher temperatures in the region of 65°F. Also, if black leg rot is to be avoided on cutting stems where they enter the soil, particular attention must be paid to watering, which should be minimal until rooting has taken place. The siderasis is propagated very easily by dividing clumps into smaller sections, and the rhoeos can be propagated either from cuttings, or they may be allowed to set seed, which is not difficult to germinate in a temperature of around 65°F.

## Varieties and Purchasing

It is advisable to buy tradescantias during the spring.

*T. fluminensis* This has striped leaves with purple undersides.

*T.f.* 'Quicksilver' This variety is tougher and grows faster than *T. fluminensis.*

*T. albiflora* 'Albovittata' This form has a silvery foliage.

*T.a.* 'Tricolor' The leaves of this plant are striped white and purple.

**Healthy Plant**

Easy to grow and lots of different varieties to choose from. Select a plant with plenty of lush green growth, avoiding those with straggly stems.

## Pests and Diseases

**Aphids** These do not often attack this plant, but they may occasionally get onto soft new leaves and cause discoloration. Control them with soapy sprays.

**Red spider mite** These may be troublesome. To cure, spray with derris. Red spider will cause discoloration. Another possible cause of this is root rot from overwatering.

**Brown leaf tip** This unsightly brown leaf tip may well be the result of insect damage, but it's more likely to be due to insufficient water. These are thirsty plants, especially during warm weather.

**Hanging Plant** (right) Tradescantias make very effective displays when three or four cuttings are planted together in a hanging container.

(Below) Few plant families have such variety of leaf color, from deep greens and burgundies through to the more subtle variegated forms.

## Ideal Conditions

### Light and Position

✘ ✔ ✘ ✘ ✘

For tradescantias to retain the variegated colors of their leaves, it is essential that they are placed in plenty of light but protected from very strong sun. They are often positioned so that they can trail over shady windowsills.

### Temperature Range

Warm | Intermediate | Cool

Cool conditions are ideal for this plant, 50°–59°F, but it cannot tolerate drafts, very cold areas or continual shade. It is also advisable to keep tradescantias well away from all heating appliances. They will survive in dry surroundings, but grow better in more humid atmosphere. Chilly temperatures may cause leaf discoloration.

### Watering

✔

Tradescantias should be watered regularly, but the colors of the leaves will become dimmer if the soil is allowed to become too wet. Less water will be required during the winter period when the plants are not so active.

### Feeding

✔

These plants will respond well to feeds of weak liquid fertilizer at every watering. Obviously this will be less frequent during the winter months, but it is important that feeding does not stop completely during this time.

### Seasonal Care

Winter Spring Summer Autumn

The green shoots that occasionally appear on tradescantias should be carefully removed, as they are very vigorous and will quickly lose their variegated coloring, so marring their appearance. If the leaves become at all dry and shriveled, they should be taken off the bases of the longer stems. Less water is needed in winter when the plants are less active and more prone to root rot from overwatering.

### Soil

There is a belief that these plants thrive on little nourishment but this is not the case. Young tradescantias must be potted with great care if they are to do well. A good houseplant mixture should be used, and ideally it should be soil-based.

# Glossary

**Aerial root** A root which grows up above the level of the soil, often seen in philodendrons and the *Monstera deliciosa*, which can extract moisture from the air.

**Bloom** This term is often used to mean a flower but, more specifically, refers to a waxy or powdery coating on the leaves or fruits of certain plants. This coating is usually white or has a pale blue tinge.

**Bract** A modified leaf, shaped like a leaf or flower petal. Bracts are often highly colored, as in the Poinsettia, and may support a less showy flower.

**Bulb** A fleshy bud growing underground which stores food and protects new growth within its overlapping layers.

**Corm** The swollen base of a stem formed underground which protects new growth and stores food, and is used for propagation.

**Cutting** A piece of a plant which is used to raise a new plant, such as a leaf or stem tip, which may be potted to develop roots.

**Dormant period** A temporary period in which a plant ceases to grow at all. This often occurs during the winter months.

**Evergreen** A plant which keeps a mass of foliage throughout the year, shedding a few leaves at a time.

**Foliage plant** A plant which is grown indoors to display the beauty of its leaves. Although some bear flowers, they are usually insignificant.

**Growing shoot** A shoot which extends the growth of the plant from a stem tip.

**Half-hardy** A term for a plant which can adjust to cool conditions, but cannot survive in extremely cold temperatures or wintering outdoors.

**Hardy** A term describing a plant which can withstand prolonged exposure to cold temperatures and even frost.

**Honeydew** The sticky secretion left on plants by insects such as aphids and whitefly.

**Lateral shoot** A shoot growing sideways from a main stem at any point below the tip.

**Leggy** A term describing tall growth of a plant when the stems become spindly and bear fewer leaves, especially at the lower ends.

**Offset** A small, new plant which develops naturally from its parent and can be detached and propagated separately.

**Palmate** A term for a leaf consisting of three or more leaflets radiating from a single stalk, resembling an open hand.

**Photosynthesis** The process in a plant by which the leaves are nourished. For effective photosynthesis, plants require water, air, and adequate exposure to light.

**Pinching out** This refers to the procedure in which new growing tips are removed by pinching them between the fingertips to encourage branching and bushiness elsewhere on the plant.

**Plantlet** A small plant produced on the runners or stems of a parent plant.

**Pot-bound** The condition in which the roots of a plant are crowded inside the pot. This usually prevents healthy growth, although some plants do well if slightly pot-bound.

**Potting on** Transferring a plant to a larger container to allow continued growth of the roots.

**Pruning** Cutting back the growth of a plant selectively to encourage bushiness, a compact shape, and better flowering.

**Repotting** Transferring a plant to a new container or renewing the soil in the pot to revitalize the growth.

**Rootball** The dense mass of matted roots and the soil trapped in them which are visible when a plant is removed from its pot.

**Shards** Broken pieces of a ceramic pot, or stones and ceramic material, placed in the base of a pot to allow free drainage through the soil.

**Sharp sand** A coarse sand, free of lime, sometimes used in potting mixtures.

**Shrub** A plant with branching, woody stems which remains relatively small and compact in growth.

**Strike** The term used to describe the rooting of a stem or leaf cutting.

**Succulent** A plant with fleshy stems and leaves which are able to store moisture and can withstand a period of very dry conditions.

**Tendril** A fine, twining thread arising from the leaf or stem of a plant which clings to a frame or surface, enabling the plant to climb.

**Top-dressing** Freshening the soil in which a plant is growing by replacing the top layer, rather than repotting the whole plant.

**Transpiration** The natural process in which water evaporates through the pores in leaves.

**Variegated** A term which refers to plants with patterned, spotted, or blotchy leaves. Most common variegations are green broken by cream, white, or silver, but some plants have brighter colors on the leaves.

**Variety** A member of a plant species which differs from the others by a natural alteration such as the color of the leaves or flowers. The term is often applied to plants bred in cultivation, which strictly should be called cultivars.

**Vein** A strand of tissue in a leaf which conducts moisture and nutrients. Large veins may be known as ribs.

**Whorl** A radiating arrangement of three or more leaves around a node on a plant's stem.

# Index

# Photographic credits

Pat Brindley 133; Margery Daughtrey, Cornell University 23, 49, 111, 137*al*; Flower Council of Holland 22, 24, 26, 32, 50, 66, 100, 114*a*, 122, 126, 130, 132, 134, 152, 160, 168; International Flower Bulb Center, Holland, 53, 54; Harry Smith Horticultural Collection 48, 64, 70*r*, 102*r*, 109*al*, 110*b*, 124.

Key: *a* above, *b* below, *l* left, *r* right